SOCIOLOGY IN THE 21ST CENTURY

Edited by John Iceland, Pennsylvania State University

This series introduces students to a range of sociological issues of broad interest in the United States today and addresses topics such as race, immigration, gender, the family, education, and social inequality. Each work will have a similar structure and approach as follows:

- introduction to topic's importance in contemporary society
- overview of conceptual issues
- review of empirical research including demographic data
- cross-national comparisons
- discussion of policy debates

These course books will highlight findings from current, rigorous research and will include personal narratives to illustrate major themes in an accessible manner. The similarity in approach across the series will allow instructors to assign them as a featured or supplementary book in various courses.

1. *A Portrait of America: The Demographic Perspective,* by John Iceland

A Portrait of America

A Portrait of America

THE DEMOGRAPHIC PERSPECTIVE

John Iceland

UNIVERSITY OF CALIFORNIA PRESS

University of California Press, one of the most distinguished university presses in the United States, enriches lives around the world by advancing scholarship in the humanities, social sciences, and natural sciences. Its activities are supported by the UC Press Foundation and by philanthropic contributions from individuals and institutions. For more information, visit www.ucpress.edu.

University of California Press
Oakland, California

Library of Congress Cataloging-in-Publication Data

Iceland, John, 1970–.
  A portrait of America : the demographic perspective / John Iceland.
    pages   cm
  Includes bibliographical references and index.
  ISBN 978–0–520–27818–9 (hardback)
  ISBN 978–0–520–27819–6 (paper)
  ISBN 978–0–520–95910–1 (e-book)
  1. United States—Population.   2. Families—United States.
3. Equality—United States.   4. Immigrants—United States Social conditions.   5. Race discrimination—United States.   6. Poverty—United States.   I. Title.
  HB3505.I25   2014
  304.60973—dc23   2014010238

Manufactured in the United States of America

23 22 21 20 19 18 17 16 15 14
10 9 8 7 6 5 4 3 2 1

In keeping with a commitment to support environmentally responsible and sustainable printing practices, UC Press has printed this book on Natures Natural, a fiber that contains 30% post-consumer waste and meets the minimum requirements of ANSI/NISO Z39.48-1992 (R 1997) (*Permanence of Paper*).

To Jakob, Mia, and Jeannie

Contents

Illustrations

TABLES

Acknowledgments

I would like to thank a number of people who provided critical help for this book, often in the form of insightful reviews of draft chapters: Paul Amato, Sarah Damaske, Rick Rodgers, Jeffrey M. Timberlake, Michael J. White, and a few anonymous reviewers chosen by the University of California Press. I would like to extend a special thanks to Naomi Schneider, executive editor at the University of California Press, who has provided invaluable advice, direction, and support for my book projects. Simply put, she knows how to make them better.

I would like to give my deepest appreciation to my wife, Jean, and my children, Mia and Jakob. They are the brightest of all of the lights in my life. I would like to thank, again, my parents, Harry and Joan, whose intellectual stimulation, care, and love allowed me to make my way. Finally, I would like to thank all of my other family members, including Charles, Debbie, Matthew, Josh, Matt, John, and Edna.

Introduction

The lives of Americans have changed spectacularly from the colonial times to the present. The late eighteenth-century American woman, for example, would most likely have been of English extraction and lived in a rural community somewhere on the East Coast, such as in Massachusetts or Virginia. If she were in her mid-20s she would already be married and would eventually give birth to about seven children, though some would die in childhood. She would consider herself lucky if she lived to see her 70th birthday. She would work with her husband on a family farm, focusing mostly on tasks in and around the house. The family would live modestly but fairly well as compared with people in many other countries. Conveniences we take for granted today were still far in the future, as families relied on outhouses rather than indoor plumbing, hand washing of clothes and dishes rather than machines of convenience, candles (often homemade) rather than lightbulbs, and communication in person or by slow mail rather than tweets, texts, e-mails, telephones, or even telegrams. The final battle of the War of 1812 between the United States and Great Britain, for example, was fought two weeks after the treaty ending the war had been signed in Europe but before any of the combatants in New Orleans received word of it.

The typical American woman today is still of European extraction, though many around her are not. She lives in a metropolitan area farther south and especially west, such as in Houston, Chicago, or Phoenix. If she is still in her mid-20s she likely lives alone, with friends, or a cohabiting partner, though by the time she is in her 30s she more likely than not is married and will have two children. While she has primary responsibilities for taking care of the children, she also works for pay—perhaps to hedge her bets against future family instability and divorce. She will live long and have a good chance to live to see her 80th birthday, if not her 90th. While she might struggle to achieve a middle-class standard of living, she has more money and conveniences than her grandparents and considerably more than several generations before.

All of this is to illustrate that the United States is a country that has experienced profound changes. The gentlemen farmers who founded the nation on Enlightenment principles in the eighteenth century, such as George Washington and Thomas Jefferson, gave way to the nation builders and industrialists of the nineteenth and early twentieth centuries, including Andrew Jackson, Cornelius Vanderbilt, and Henry Ford. The past one hundred years have been equally tumultuous, as our country witnessed two world wars, a deep depression, and yet also the consolidation of the welfare state and tremendous growth in living standards. Even if we narrow the window to the last fifty years, by any measure the change in American society has been astounding. Consider this—in the United States between 1960 and 2010

- The population increased from 179 million to 309 million.[1]
- The percentage of births to unmarried women soared from 5 percent to 41 percent.[2]
- The number of immigrants who entered annually increased from about 270,000 to over 1 million. The percentage of immigrants who were from Europe declined from 75 percent to 12 percent.[3]
- The percentage of the population who had finished high school rose dramatically from 41 percent to 87 percent.[4]
- Median family income rose from $36,000 to $60,000 (in 2010 dollars), though accompanying declines in poverty were more moderate, from 22 to 15 percent. Notably, the African American poverty rate, while still

remaining well above that of whites, fell by half, from 55 percent to 27 percent.[5]

- After no progress from 1960 to 1980, the earnings of full-time working women as a percentage of men's began to rise from 60 in 1980 to 77 in 2010.[6]

- Life expectancy increased from 70 to 79. Disappointingly, both the level and increase in life expectancy lagged behind the average among other high-income countries.[7]

Some notable social divisions in the United States have softened over the past fifty years. Race and gender gaps, for example, have narrowed. The women's and civil rights movements pushed open many doors that were previously closed to women and minority group members. Women today, while heavily underrepresented among the ranks of corporate CEOs, are more likely to be in high-management positions than they used to be. They are likewise the top breadwinner in the family much more often than in the past. In terms of racial progress, blatant acts of discrimination have declined, the black middle class has grown, and African Americans are in many positions of political power.

Nevertheless, there is tremendous diversity and considerable inequality in American communities. The "typical" women described at the beginning of the chapter—while accurately representing the modal experience of women—do not shed as much light on the considerable variation in life trajectories. Today, children of college-educated, married professionals tend to have access to excellent health care, safe neighborhoods, and good schools and will in all likelihood attend college, get married, and have reasonably well-paying jobs as adults. In contrast, children of less-educated, unmarried parents are more likely to attend failing schools and live in unsafe neighborhoods, are in turn less likely to attend college, have children within marriage, and achieve financial stability, and are more likely to suffer from poor health as adults.

Among the most important trends observed over the last several decades is that, despite the narrowing of racial and gender gaps over time, the relative impact of socioeconomic status has increased. This has had profound implications for the life chances of Americans born into different economic circumstances. These changes are a direct result of (1) our economic system, which has increased both standards of living and income inequality over the course of many decades, and (2) cultural changes that emphasize the primacy of individualism and self-actualization. Rising living standards provide people with the means to make choices. Poor people living in poor countries often don't have the luxury of choosing what kind of person they want to be or what life they want to live; their focus tends to be on how to get by from day to day. The growth of individualism then provides a larger "tool kit" of socially permissible choices in an affluent society. In the 1950s, for example, out-of-wedlock births were relatively uncommon and stigmatized—a sign of shame; today, not so much. Finally, growing inequality means that different people have a different range of choices at their disposal. This explains why in recent years we have seen:

- growing diversity in family formation patterns, permitted by changing norms but strongly correlated with socioeconomic differentials, as some are able to fulfill their marital and family goals more easily than others.
- declining racial and gender inequality. Discrimination based on these ascribed characteristics has become socially more unacceptable (though not absent), because it runs contrary to the widely shared values of freedom, equality of opportunity, and individualism. Notably, economic changes have served to reduce gender inequality, as men have been harder hit by deindustrialization and globalization than women, but have increased racial inequality, as minorities have been hurt more by these economic changes than whites.
- continuing immigration, as immigrants are drawn by economic opportunities and high standards of living in the United States. Declines in racial/ethnic bias have facilitated the integration of immigrants in U.S. society, even if integration remains uneven.
- regional variation in economic change and migration leading to declines in the Rust Belt and growth in the Sun Belt. Racial and ethnic residential segregation remains an important feature of the metropolitan landscape, though such segregation has gradually declined. Residential segregation by socioeconomic status, however, has increased.
- declining (though still significant) racial and ethnic disparities in health and mortality accompanied by increasing disparities by socioeconomic status.

As a result, the rich and poor often live worlds apart. Those in the top 1 percent of the income distribution in the United States include:

> doctors and actuaries, executives and entrepreneurs, the self-made and the silver spoon set. They are clustered not just in New York and Los Angeles, but also in Denver and Dallas. The range of wealth in the 1 percent is vast— from households that bring in $380,000 a year, according to census data, up to billionaires like Warren E. Buffett and Bill Gates. . . . Most 1 percenters were born with socioeconomic advantages, which helps explain why the 1 percent is more likely than other Americans to have jobs, according to census data. They work longer hours, being three times more likely than the 99 percent to work more than 50 hours a week, and are more likely to be self-employed. Married 1 percenters are just as likely as other couples to have two incomes, but men are the big breadwinners, earning 75 percent of the money, compared with 64 percent of the income in other households.[8]

As with the rich, those in poverty also have varied experiences, ranging from young single mothers coping with multiple responsibilities to couples hit hard by tough economic times. Here is just one of these stories:

> Until a few months ago, Brandi Wells lived paycheck to paycheck. She was poor, but she got by. Now, the 22-year-old lives "penny to penny." Wells started working as a waitress at 17 and continued when she got pregnant last year. She worked until the day she delivered 10-month-old son Logan, she says, and came back a week later. But finding child care was a challenge, and about three months ago, after one too many missed shifts, she was fired. In no time, she was homeless. The subsidized apartment in Kingwood, W.Va., that had cost her only $36 a month came with a catch: She had to have a job. Without one—and with no way to pay her utilities—she was evicted. Logan went to live with his grandmother in another town while Wells stayed with a friend for three weeks in a filthy house with no running water. . . .
> Wells filed for assistance from the state human resource department and got three free nights at a low-budget motel and $50 for gas to hunt for a new job. It didn't last long. "The way it is now, you can't hardly find a job," she says. "I've applied here, there, everywhere." Eventually, Wells and her fiance, Thomas McDaniel, found a two-bedroom apartment. After a few weeks, its walls and floors remain bare. The only furniture is in the living room—an old green sofa, a foam twin mattress, a play pen stuffed with toys. Rent is $400 a month, and Wells is hoping that since McDaniel has just landed a job at Subway, they'll be able to afford it.[9]

The purpose of this book is to describe our nation's changing population and in the process understand some of its most pressing contemporary challenges, ranging from poverty and economic inequality to racial tensions and health disparities, primarily through a *demographic lens* that captures population-level changes. Specifically, in the chapters ahead I discuss America's historical demographic growth; the American family today; gender inequality; trends in the economic well-being of Americans; immigration and diversity; racial and ethnic inequality; internal migration and residential segregation; and finally health and mortality.

The discussion of these is informed by several sources, including an examination of household survey data (such as the U.S. Current Population Survey and the decennial census), as well as syntheses of existing published material, both quantitative and qualitative. I also discuss current issues and controversies around each theme to highlight their role in everyday debates taking place in Congress, the media, and American living rooms. All of the chapters include some historical background as well as a discussion of how patterns and trends in the United States compare with those in other peer countries.

AMERICA'S DEMOGRAPHIC GROWTH

To understand America's changing population today we need to know something about its historical roots. Fertility, mortality, and migration together explain the size and composition of the U.S. population. The United States, like many countries in western Europe, experienced a demographic transition in the nineteenth and early twentieth centuries. It went from a country with high birth and death rates to one of low birth and death rates. However, U.S. population growth before and during this transition exceeded those of its peers, mainly because of exceptionally high fertility rates through the early nineteenth century and later on because of high levels of immigration from an increasingly diverse group of countries. The demographic transition reflected social processes such as urbanization, growing levels of education and affluence, and growing gender equality—all of which increased the cost of raising children and thus reduced fertility. The decline in mortality was initially a function of effective public health measures and individual health practices (such as water filtration systems and the practice of washing hands) and later on was due to medical advances, such as the development of penicillin and vaccines.

Two long-term processes characterize internal migration: westward expansion, especially in the early days of the republic, and urbanization. After about 1950, following relentless westward expansion through the nineteenth and early twentieth centuries, we also saw the rise of the Sun Belt, which included migration from the Northeast and Midwest to southern states such as Texas, Florida, and New Mexico. While only 5 percent of the U.S. population lived in urban areas in 1790, by 1900 this had risen to nearly half, and today over four-fifths of Americans live in urban areas. The population also has become increasingly suburbanized. Whereas initially most residents in the suburbs were middle-class and affluent whites, suburbs today have become much more diverse, both ethnically and socioeconomically. Immigration has driven the increase in racial and ethnic diversity in communities across the country in recent decades.

THE AMERICAN FAMILY

As in most other Western countries, American fertility levels declined over the twentieth century, though with a notable spike during what is known as the baby boom, from about 1946 to 1964. Today, the total fertility rate is just under 2, meaning that women are having on average two children— a figure that is higher than in most of Europe.[10] Family arrangements have become more diverse over the past several decades, with a growing number of children being raised by a single parent or within blended families. Differences in family structure that are associated with the education of parents are particularly pronounced and growing: about 92 percent of women with a bachelor's degree or more are married when they give birth, compared with 43 percent of women with a high school diploma or less.[11] However, more than half of nonmarital births occur within cohabiting relationships.[12] Many of these changes in the family have occurred in wealthy countries around the world.

The causes of these changes in family living arrangements and their effects on the well-being of parents and children have been widely debated. Research indicates that causes of these changes are rooted in both changing cultural norms concerning out-of-wedlock childbearing and economic changes that have served to increase the earning power of women (providing them with greater economic independence) and decrease the employment prospects, and hence "marriageability," of men.[13] Those living in single-parent families are more likely to be poor, because single parents face the challenge of supporting a family on one income and taking care of children and managing a household typically with less support than two parents can provide. For these reasons, children of such families tend to fare not as well as their peers who live with both parents.[14]

GENDER INEQUALITY

In 1963 Betty Friedan's *The Feminine Mystique* was published; many believe it played an important role in sparking the "second-wave" feminism movement that decade. The book describes how dissatisfied many highly educated stay-at-home mothers were with their lives, despite their affluence. They were following the cultural expectation of quitting their paid jobs and tending to the house and family after having children. Among those women who worked, occupations were highly segregated by gender, with women concentrated in "pink-collar" occupations, such as teaching and secretarial work. These jobs typically paid less than others requiring a similar level of education where men were concentrated. Women have often been paid less for the same kind of work too.[15]

Much has changed since then. More women are in the labor market, including women with children. For example, the labor force participation rates of mothers rose from 47 percent in 1975 to 71 percent in 2008.[16] Women's median annual earnings as a percentage of men's for full-time, year-round workers rose, albeit more slowly than many expected, from 61 percent to 77 percent from 1960 to 2010.[17] Thus, while women have made progress, they still tend to earn less than men. There is continued debate about the underlying reasons for this persisting inequality. Is it discrimination? Is it gender socialization that encourages women to make more family-oriented choices? Regardless, it is clear that gender norms continue to evolve. Men's earnings and attachment to the labor market have been declining, especially among those with less education.[18] Women now constitute half the workforce. They are more likely to attend college and receive advanced degrees.[19] These trends strongly suggest that women's relative economic position will rise in the coming years.

ECONOMIC WELL-BEING

More Americans are attending college than ever before. Educational attainment has a very strong influence on a person's employment and earnings, and it has grown stronger over time. For example, in both 1979 and 2007 about 90 percent of men with at least some college were in the labor force, but during that span of years labor force participation rates among those without a high school diploma fell from 79 percent to 73 percent.[20] Likewise, weekly wages among less-skilled men declined by 31 percent between 1979 and 2010, during a time when weekly earnings grew by 20 percent among men with a bachelor's degree or higher. These general trends are also present among women, though not as pronounced.[21]

What accounts for these trends? Several things do, including the increasing demand for high-skill workers due to technological changes, globalization, and international trade, the decline in unionism, and changes in government policies that favor the rich at the expense of the poor.[22] As a result, a much higher proportion of jobs is most suitably filled by college graduates than before. The Great Recession of 2007–9 and its aftermath have not changed this dynamic. Some of the sectors that were hit the hardest contained many blue-collar (male) workers, such as construction and manufacturing.

After poverty reached a low of 11 percent in 1973, progress against it has stalled. Growing inequality has served to hamper efforts to reduce poverty, as has the general turn away from policies that redistribute income. The 2007–9 recession, which caused a spike in unemployment to 10 percent, likewise caused an increase in poverty to 15 percent in 2010. While unemployment has since declined from its peak, the decline has been slow, and unemployment remains well above the very low levels of the late 1990s. Poverty is especially high among blacks and Hispanics, those with a high school degree or less, and single-parent families. While future gains in employment will likely serve to reduce poverty, the nature of our economy and the political climate will do little to reduce income inequality in the near term.

IMMIGRATION AND GROWING DIVERSITY

The United States has long been a country of immigrants. Consecutive waves of immigration from a variety of countries (northern and western Europe until the mid- to late 1800s, then southern and eastern Europe through the early twentieth century) changed the character of the country. Since the 1960s, immigration from Latin America and Asia has surged. Over the past couple of decades there has been a relatively small but growing stream of immigrants from Africa as well. The post-1960s wave of immigration has fundamentally changed the racial and ethnic composition of the United States and will continue to do so for the foreseeable future.

This has stimulated debates on a number of topics, such as the effect of immigration on the economy and the assimilability of immigrants in U.S. society. These debates echo similar debates of the early twentieth century, when many natives were alarmed by the changing stock of immigrants, as those from southern and eastern Europe were often thought to be unassimilable.

Research indicates that by and large, in the past and today, immigrants are integrating into American society. Over time they learn English, and the second generation tends to experience educational advantages over their parents and live in more integrated settings.[23] Immigrants also have a net long-term positive effect on the U.S. economy and society, though in the short term not everyone benefits to the same degree. Some local areas and particular populations are negatively affected by immigration, as are some native low-skill workers, and there may never be unanimity on whether cultural changes wrought by immigration are "good" or "bad."[24]

RACIAL AND ETHNIC INEQUALITY

Through much of the twentieth century, the most prominent racial divide in the United States was the stark black-white color line, manifested in "American apartheid"—or the subjugation of blacks through violence and both institutional and individual discriminatory behavior.[25] However, the rapid growth in immigration from Latin America and Asia since the 1960s has changed the ethnic mix in the United States. The civil rights movement also helped abolish legal forms of racial and ethnic discrimination, and whites are less likely to express blatantly racist attitudes than they did in past decades.[26]

Some have thus wondered about the trajectory of the American color line. Is there a white-nonwhite divide, where whites continue to be uniquely advantaged as they have been through much of U.S. history? Is there a black-nonblack divide, where blacks are uniquely disadvantaged while other groups are experiencing significant upward mobility? Or are color lines softening altogether: is the United States postracial? The evidence suggests that color lines have softened, but racial inequality remains prevalent. Blacks and Hispanics continue to have lower levels of educational attainment and income and higher levels of poverty than whites. Asians are faring well socioeconomically with high levels of educational attainment and household income. The processes affecting black and Hispanic disadvantage differ, with discrimination and the legacy of poverty playing a larger role among blacks. Among Hispanics, low initial levels of educational attainment among immigrants and the undocumented status of many serve to produce relatively low labor force outcomes.[27]

MIGRATION AND RESIDENTIAL SEGREGATION

The dominant pattern of migration in the United States until the early twentieth century was one of westward migration and settlement. The twentieth century was characterized by more complicated patterns. First, there was the "Great Migration" of southern blacks to the North from about 1910 until 1970.[28] African Americans left the South for many reasons, including the good manufacturing jobs in northern factories and the desire to leave behind the subjugation imposed by Jim Crow apartheid in the South.[29] By the late 1960s, however, the Great Migration had slowed, and by the mid-1970s not only was it over, but black population flows had begun to swing back to the South.[30] During this period, deindustrialization—characterized by declines in U.S. manufacturing employment in several industries such as steel and automobiles—was well under way, and northern cities lost both jobs and population (of all races) to other regions of the country. The last few decades of the twentieth century thus saw the rise of the Sun Belt—or fair-weather states in the South (e.g., Florida, North Carolina) and West (Arizona, Nevada).

Within metropolitan areas we also saw continued suburbanization, including, in more recent decades, the suburbanization of various immigrant and racial and ethnic groups. The percentage of the U.S. population living in the suburbs rose from 31 percent to 51 percent from 1960 to 2010.[31] The 2000s, however, saw a slowdown in suburbanization and, from 2010 to 2011, even a slight decline—for the first time in over ninety years—as many cities thrived and the suburban housing market remained slack.[32] Within metropolitan areas, we have seen the continued decline in black-white residential segregation over the last forty years, meaning that blacks and whites are considerably more likely to share neighborhoods than they were before. Nevertheless, blacks remain fairly highly segregated, especially in older metropolitan areas in the Northeast and Midwest. Hispanics and Asians tend to live in more diverse neighborhoods than blacks and whites, and their segregation levels have, by some measures, remained fairly stable; though, because of their growing population size, they are more likely to live with coethnics than they were earlier. Overall, race and ethnicity play a smaller role in shaping residential patterns than they did in the past.[33]

HEALTH AND MORTALITY

Like most countries across the globe, the United States has experienced a mortality transition, in which the primary causes of death are no longer infectious diseases but rather chronic and degenerative ones that typically accompany old age. Life expectancy at birth was only about 47 years in 1900 in the United States, rising to 79 by 2010.[34] Countries with low life expectancies typically have relatively high infant mortality. And indeed, the largest age-specific declines in death rates from 1935 to 2010 occurred among infants and children. Since at least the last half of the twentieth century the leading causes of death in the United States have been heart disease and cancer.[35] Racial and ethnic health disparities in mortality and morbidity are striking but have gradually declined. Instead, socioeconomic disparities in health outcomes have increased. These disparities are driven by a number of factors, including differential access to health care services and lifestyle choices.

Now that the baby boom generation is retiring, the United States has an aging population that is straining its principal (and popular) social insurance programs: Social Security and Medicare. This is putting considerable pressure on government budgets. The United States has an inefficient health care system that places little incentive on reining in costs. Moreover, health outcomes are, on average, worse in the United States than in many other rich countries. This is driven by disparities in people's access to health care, individual health behaviors, and the physical and social environment.

PLAN OF THE BOOK

In chapter 1, I provide a historical overview of population growth and change in the United States. I review how patterns of fertility, mortality, and immigration have shaped the country from colonial times to the twentieth century. The following seven chapters then examine the themes introduced above: the American family; gender inequality; economic well-being; immigration and growing diversity; racial and ethnic inequality; internal migration and residential segregation; and health and mortality. Each chapter begins with an introduction to the importance of the topic and a short historical overview. This is followed by a review of contemporary patterns and trends and a discussion of current issues and controversies, including international comparisons. The final chapter provides a few concluding thoughts.

1 American Demographic Growth

The American colonies, while still sparsely populated through much of the 1700s, were nevertheless recognized as having tremendous potential for demographic growth, wealth, and power. In his 1776 book, *An Inquiry into the Nature and Causes of the Wealth of Nations*, Scottish philosopher and economist Adam Smith noted:

> But though North America is not yet so rich as England, it is much more thriving, and advancing with much greater rapidity to the greater acquisition of riches. The most decisive mark of the prosperity of any country is the increase in the number of its inhabitants. . . . Nor in the present times is this increase principally owing to the continued importation of new inhabitants, but to the great multiplication of the species. . . . Labor is there so well rewarded that a numerous family of children, rather than being a burthen, is a source of opulence and prosperity to the parents. . . . Notwithstanding the great increase occasioned by such early marriages, there is a continual complaint of the scarcity of hands in North America.[1]

The territorial and demographic growth of the United States has historically also been accompanied by considerable individual social and economic mobility. American culture is infused with a deep egalitarian spirit and admiration of self-made men and women. This is represented by the creed of "American exceptionalism"—first described by Alexis de Tocqueville in the 1830s. In this view, there is a unique American ideology based on liberty, egalitarianism, individualism, populism, and laissez-faire that has fostered mobility.[2]

American exceptionalism, as the term was originally conceived, meant not necessarily that the country was better than others but mainly that it was different. Seymour Martin Lipset, a well-known political scientist and sociologist, argued in a 1996 book on the topic that this rugged individualism marked a strong departure from the tradition-bound order of the Old European World. "Americans remain much more individualistic, meritocratic-oriented, and anti-statist than peoples everywhere."[3] In his view these attributes have promoted entrepreneurship and economic growth. This is perhaps best represented in the recent past by the ascendancy of Silicon Valley. Steve Jobs was an iconoclastic figure in this respect—he saw himself as a rebel against authority and urged people to "Think Different." Many argue that this emphasis on individualism and innovation helps explain why the United States today has the world's largest economy and one of the highest GDPs per capita.

Lipset also argued, however, that this emphasis on individualism, and by extension nonconformity, has a downside if completely unchecked by social mores that promote the good of the community. An ethos centered on individualism means that inequality is more widely accepted in the United States than in other countries. This helps explain why U.S. poverty rates are higher and average life expectancies are lower than those in other rich countries, not to mention America's large prison population, litigiousness, and low levels of voter participation.[4]

Before delving into the contemporary state of social and economic affairs in the United States, this chapter first reviews America's demographic history—its ascent from a group of sparsely settled colonies on the eastern seaboard of the continent to one of the world's superpowers today. I focus on the roles that changing patterns of fertility, mortality, and immigration played in this growth and some of America's commonalities with and differences from other Western countries. Having a grasp of this "exceptional" history—and its demographic origins—is necessary for understanding our changing population today.

AMERICA'S DEMOGRAPHIC TRANSITION

The first U.S. census was taken 1790—not long after the founding of the nation. At the time, the population of the thirteen original states and the territories that would become Vermont, Kentucky, Tennessee, and Maine came to just 3.9 million people. Over the next seven decades the United States grew at a clip of over 30 percent per decade, such that by 1860, on the eve of the Civil War, there were 31.4 million people in the country. The population then more than doubled by 1900 (to 76.2 million), added another 100 million by 1960 (to 179.3 million), and by the 2010 census there were 308.7 million people living in the United States, making it the world's third largest country after China and India. Assuming a constant rate of immigration, the United States will have nearly 400 million people by 2050 (see figure 1).

American population growth has outpaced that of most other peer countries. Figure 2 compares American population growth with that of many large countries in Europe over the nearly two-hundred-year period from 1820 to 2012. All countries grew, with even the slowest-growing country of those shown—France—doubling its population. American growth, however, was much more dramatic: it grew by over 3,000 percent. The world's total population also grew rapidly over the period, from 1.04 billion to 7.06 billion, but this increase (578 percent) was still well below that of the United States. The largest countries today—China (1.35 billion) and India (1.26 billion)—were already relatively large in 1820 (381 million and 209 million, respectively), so their growth rates were also smaller than the U.S. one.[5]

The size and composition of a country's population are determined by the interplay of three forces: fertility, mortality, and migration. Rates of all three have changed considerably through the course of American history. Many of the changes in the United States reflect those that have occurred in all developed countries, and they collectively represent its *demographic transition*. According to demographic transition theory, societies typically experience a change from a regime of high fertility and high mortality to one of low fertility and low mortality. During the pretransition stage, population growth is slow because of the balance between high fertility and mortality. Couples typically have many children to ensure that at least some of them will survive to adulthood. The first stage of the demographic

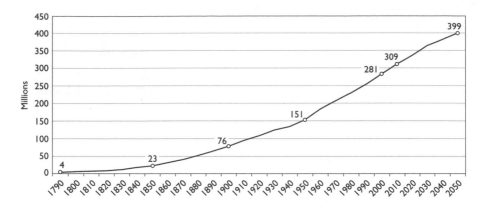

Figure 1. Population of the United States, 1790–2050. Sources: Data from 1800 to 2010 are from U.S. Census Bureau 2012e, table 1; 2020–50 projections are from U.S. Census Bureau 2009, table 1.

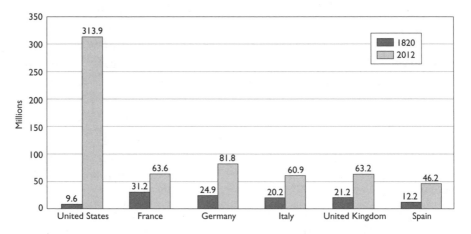

Figure 2. Population of the United States and selected European countries, 1820 and 2012 (in millions). Sources: U.S. population in 1820 is from U.S. Census Bureau 2012e, table 1; remaining 1820 population figures are from Maddison 2001, table B-10; all 2012 population figures are from Population Reference Bureau 2012.

transition involves a decline in mortality. The decline is caused by advances in public health and medicine. As mortality declines, a population's growth rate increases. In the next stage, fertility begins to fall; this occurs after the decline in mortality, because social customs, traditions, and habits centered on having many children are often slow to change.[6]

Eventually, according to demographic transition theory, low mortality is matched by low fertility, and population growth once again stabilizes. All developed countries, and indeed most countries around globe, now have relatively low levels of mortality and fertility. Fertility rates, however, are still quite high (though declining), mainly in a number of African countries today.[7]

These days many developed countries have what is termed *below replacement* fertility—fertility rates that are so low that if they do not increase, the country (in the absence of immigration) will eventually face a decline in its population. For populations to remain stable, women have to have on average just over two children (essentially to replace the mother and father and to allow for some infant mortality). Fertility rates in Europe and East Asia are currently well below replacement level, as their total fertility rates (TFRs, which refer to the average number of children per woman over her lifetime) are close to 1.5. Mortality is quite low in these countries, women (and couples) are choosing to have small families, and often they invest heavily in the children they do have. Fertility in the United States today is also low, but high relative to fertility in many of these other countries; in 2012 the U.S. TFR was 1.9.[8] The U.S. population will likely continue to grow at a significant pace for many years to come because of persistent immigration as well. I now offer a more detailed look at historical patterns of mortality, fertility, and migration in the United States.

U.S. Mortality

In 1789 life expectancy at birth was only about 35 years in the United States. Mortality remained fairly stable and perhaps even increased in the first few decades of the nineteenth century as a result of greater urbanization, exposure to diseases, and poorer nutrition than at the beginning of the century.[9] Not until 1870 did mortality begin to decline significantly. Life expectancy in turn began to increase rapidly—to about 49 years in 1900 and 64 years in 1940.[10] Since then, life expectancy has continued to inch up, reaching 79 in 2010.[11] One in five Americans born in 1900 died before reaching the age of 18. In contrast, only one in five Americans born in 2000 will die by the time they reach 75, according to recent estimates.[12]

Advances in life expectancies in the late nineteenth century through the early twentieth were most affected by declines in infant and child mortality, though mortality declined across the entire age spectrum. Declines in mortality among children were achieved mainly by progress in controlling the spread of infectious diseases. In contrast, increases in life expectancy in recent decades have been driven more by extending life among the elderly, especially those who are very old.[13]

Table 1 shows the leading causes of death in the United States in 1860, 1900, and 2012. In 1860, the leading causes of death were overwhelmingly infectious diseases such as tuberculosis and cholera (ranked first and third) and illnesses that infants and young children are particularly susceptible to, such as diarrhea (ranked second). By 1900, many of the same causes were still conspicuous, but we see a couple of prominent diseases that tend to occur later in life creep onto the list, including heart disease (ranked fourth) and cancer (ninth). By 2010, the list is dominated by causes of death that typically occur later in life, with heart disease and cancer topping the list—about 47 percent of all deaths were attributed to these two causes alone in that year.

Declines in mortality in the nineteenth century were achieved by public health measures, including garbage and waste removal, the building of community water and sewage systems, the isolation and quarantining of infected individuals, and health behavior campaigns that advocated changes in individual and institutional hygienic practices, such as hand and food washing and the boiling of milk.[14] These practices helped reduce mortality in many relatively rich countries, such as England, Sweden, and France, at approximately the same time within about a 20-year period in the late 1800s.[15]

Cholera, for example, killed tens of millions of people across the globe in the nineteenth century and about 150,000 Americans in one pandemic alone from 1827 to 1835.[16] Conventional wisdom of the time had it that cholera was caused by "miasma"—a form of "bad air"; this was the time before the germ theory of disease had been developed. Eventually, the cause of cholera and other infectious diseases became better understood. The physician John Snow, for example, tracked down the source of the 1854 cholera outbreak in London by talking to local residents of the Soho neighborhood. He found a cluster of cholera cases right around a

Table 1 Leading Causes of Death in the United States, 1860, 1900, and 2010

Rank	Cause of Death	Percentage of Total Deaths
	1860	
1	Tuberculosis	19.8
2	Diarrhea and enteritis	15.0
3	Cholera	6.4
4	Pneumonia, influenza, bronchitis	6.1
5	Infantile convulsions	5.9
6	Stroke	2.7
7	Diphtheria and croup	2.7
8	Dysentery	2.7
9	Scarlet fever	2.5
10	Nephritis	2.4
	1900	
1	Pneumonia, influenza, bronchitis	14.4
2	Tuberculosis	11.3
3	Diarrhea and enteritis	8.1
4	Heart disease	8.0
5	Nephritis	4.7
6	Accidents	4.5
7	Stroke	4.2
8	Diseases of early infancy	4.2
9	Cancer	3.7
10	Diphtheria	2.3
	2010	
1	Heart disease	24.1
2	Cancer	23.3
3	Chronic lower respiratory diseases	5.6
4	Stroke (cerebrovascular diseases)	5.2
5	Accidents (unintentional injuries)	4.8
6	Alzheimer's disease	3.4
7	Diabetes	2.8
8	Nephritis, nephrotic syndrome, and nephrosis	2.0
9	Influenza and pneumonia	2.0
10	Intentional self-harm (suicide)	1.5

SOURCES: The 1860 and 1900 data from Gill, Glazer, and Thernstrom 1992, table 2–3; 2010 data from Centers for Disease Control and Prevention 2012a.

public water pump on Broad Street. People later discovered that the water pump had been dug only three feet from an old sewage pit that had leaked fecal bacteria.[17] Knowledge about the sources of disease eventually led to effective public action. The first water filtration was introduced in the United States in 1872 (in Poughkeepsie, New York), though the largest cities did not build filtration plants until the early 1900s.[18] Chlorine treatment of water also became the norm during this period, and the pasteurization of milk and other dairy products became standard practice everywhere. The last decades of the nineteenth century also saw the development of a number of vaccines for rabies, typhoid, cholera, diphtheria, and the plague.[19]

While public health measures and sanitation practices were the most important triggers of the decline in mortality through the early twentieth century, nutritional improvements also allowed people to avoid contracting disease and better withstand it once it was contracted.[20] Even with the decline in mortality from infectious diseases, such illnesses were still prominent causes of death through the middle of the twentieth century. During 1918 through 1920, for example, somewhere between 50 and 130 million people died during a global flu pandemic, including about 500,000 to 675,000 in the United States. The high death toll was caused by both a very high infection rate and the severity of the symptoms.[21]

The continued decline in infectious diseases in the middle decades of the twentieth century was driven by the growing importance of medical care in the form of the widespread diffusion of medicines, including sulfa drugs and penicillin. These drugs were used extensively in treating pneumonia but were used for other diseases as well. Pneumonia and flu deaths declined at an annual rate of 3.9 percent per year between 1940 and 1960, faster than the 2.4 percent annual decline over the forty years previous.[22] This eventually led to the more recent mortality regime in which chronic and degenerative diseases mentioned above are the leading causes of death rather than infectious ones.

While the decline in mortality and the lengthening of life expectancy played some role in the growth in the U.S. population over the past two hundred years, other factors were also clearly at work. After all, most European countries depicted in figure 2 experienced the same kind of mortality transition and increasing life expectancy that the United States did over a similar period of time but did not grow as quickly as the United States. Does fertility, then, explain exceptional U.S. growth rates?

U.S. Fertility

The United States initially had very high fertility rates. In 1800, the total fertility rate was 7.0, indicating that women were having, on average, about seven children in their lifetime. This figure might have been even higher in the preceding decades, though the data for this period are sparse.[23] Writing in 1798, Thomas Malthus believed that the growth rate of the American colonies was "probably without parallel in history."[24] Benjamin Franklin also weighed in on rapid U.S. population growth fueled by high fertility:

> Land being thus plenty in America, and so cheap as that a laboring man that understands husbandry can, in a short time, save money enough to purchase a piece of new land sufficient for a plantation, wheron he may subsist a family; such are not afraid to marry. . . . Hence marriages in America are more general, and more generally early, than in Europe. And if it is reckoned there that there is but one marriage per annum among 100 persons, perhaps we may here reckon two; and if in Europe they have but four births to a Marriage (many of their marriages being late), we may here reckon eight, of which if one half grow up, and our Marriages are made, reckoning one with another twenty years of age, our people must at lest be doubled every twenty years.[25]

U.S. fertility was thus very high by the standards of the European countries from which much of the U.S. population had emigrated. England and France, for example, had total fertility rates closer to 5.[26] As also recognized by Franklin, U.S. fertility rates were also much higher than the country's death rates, such that the population was on pace to double every 20 to 25 years from natural increase alone.[27] It has thus been estimated that about three-quarters of the growth in the U.S. population from the founding of the nation until the Civil War was due to natural increase (an excess of births over deaths), with the remaining quarter due to immigration.[28] While there is some debate on the exact timing of the beginning of the fertility decline in the United States, it is clear that fertility rates fell substantially in the nineteenth century to 3.6 in 1900.[29] By the late 1800s

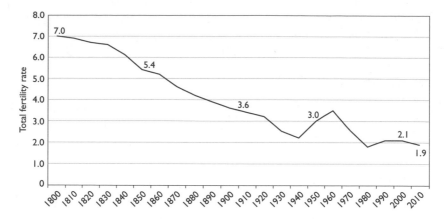

Figure 3. The total fertility rate in the United States, 1800–2010. Sources: 1800–1980 data from Gill, Glazer, and Thernstrom 1992, table 3–2; 1990–2010 data from Martin et al. 2012, table 4.

the U.S. fertility rate matched those of western European countries, where fertility declines were only just beginning.[30] U.S. fertility continued its descent to the near replacement level of 2.2 in 1940 (see figure 3).

The post–World War II period saw a remarkable spike in fertility, popularly known as the baby boom, which peaked with a TFR of 3.8 in 1957—a level not seen in the United States since the late 1890s. Thereafter, fertility resumed its decline, though it has been nearly stable in the vicinity of 1.8 to 2.1 since 1980.[31] It is important to note that these TFRs represent averages, and variability has always occurred among the experiences of women and couples. For example, while women were having on average 3.6 children in 1900, about 20 percent of them had 7 or more children and another 20 percent had 1 or none at all.[32]

The U.S. pattern of fertility decline does not altogether conform to demographic transition theory. Specifically, fertility began falling in the 1800s even before the onset of widespread mortality declines. In nearly all major western European nations (except France), birthrates remained stable for most of the nineteenth century and began declining only after significant mortality declines.[33] Some speculate that fertility fell before mortality in the United States because fertility was so high in the first place and mortality was moderate—yielding very high rates of natural increase. Thus, the early decline in American fertility may mainly reflect the country's distinctive starting conditions involving very high fertility rates.[34]

Many other social changes also accompanied fertility declines and thus may have played a role in reducing it. First, the United States transformed from a rural and agricultural society to a more urban and industrial one. In 1800 more than 90 percent of the population lived in rural areas, and 80 percent were engaged in agriculture. By 1900, the proportion of the population living in rural areas had declined to 60 percent, and there were corresponding declines in agricultural work.[35] Land became scarcer as the century progressed.[36] Families in rural areas were more likely to want to have many children to lend a hand on the family farm; in contrast, children were more expensive to raise in urban areas, where food had to be bought rather than produced.[37]

Second, technological change and rising incomes may have served to reduce fertility. Technological progress spurred greater demand for an educated workforce. This led more families to invest in their children's schooling and education and thus increased the cost of raising children.[38] Technological change also increased household incomes and the range of consumer goods available, which may have offered new alternatives for spending family income in ways other than rearing children and created new possibilities for upward social mobility.[39] Third, the changing role of women in society made it increasingly possible and desirable for women to work outside the home. There was a growth in the number of white-collar (nonmanual labor) jobs, which were seen as more suitable for women. Over time gender equality increased, which made careers outside the home more socially permissible.[40] A combination of all of these factors resulted in a new cultural norm of having a relatively small family.[41]

The baby boom, which began in 1946, peaked in 1957, and lasted until about 1964, represents an aberration in the long-term downward trend in fertility. Fertility spiked for a number of reasons, including the end of the Great Depression and World War II and the booming postwar economy. The baby boom also occurred, to a smaller degree, in a number of other Western countries.[42] The Depression and the war had served to depress fertility. Thus, when men came home from the war with ample opportunities to make a family wage (facilitated in the United States by the GI Bill) and many women left the labor market, couples who may have deferred having children decided that the time was right for them. This was also a time of suburbanization, which translated into larger homes and more space for metropolitan families. Improved nutrition, medical advances that reduced infertility, and cultural practices that led Americans to marry younger and have children sooner also played a role.[43] The baby boom, however, was followed by a "baby bust," which lasted until the mid- to late 1970s. During this period fertility dropped precipitously (from 3.8 in 1957 to 1.7 in 1976), likely reflecting changing gender norms (e.g., more women in the labor market) and the increased availability of contraception and abortion, which allowed women and couples to regulate their fertility more effectively.[44]

Overall, high fertility in the United States, especially from its founding to the last decades of the nineteenth century, played an important role in the country's rapid growth during that time. However, there was an additional reason for America's demographic rise: immigration.

U.S. Immigration

The first migrants to North America traveled in small bands from the Siberian plains across the Bering Straits into Alaska from about 30,000 to 40,000 years ago. Many moved south and eventually spread throughout the Americas. In more modern times, starting with the settlement at Jamestown, Virginia, in 1607, roughly four waves of immigration to the United States have occurred. The first wave lasted until about 1820.[45] From 1607 to the adoption of the Constitution in 1789, close to a million people came to the United States—about 600,000 from Europe and 300,000 African slaves.[46] A solid majority of the total U.S. population at the time of the first U.S. census, in 1790, was from England (60 percent), but many settlers also came from Scotland, Germany, the Netherlands, and France. These European immigrants came to the colonies for a variety of religious, economic, and political reasons, such as economic opportunity or the desire for freedom from religious persecution in their home country.[47] Thus, even at this time the United States was very ethnically and religiously diverse, especially compared with the societies from which the immigrants came. As indicated above, the large number of involuntary black migrants who were victims of the slave trade also contributed to the growth of the U.S. population. These slaves were overwhelmingly concentrated in southern states: slaves constituted a full third of the population of the states south of Delaware.[48] The arrival of the European settlers also had the effect of drastically reducing the Native American population through warfare and especially the spread of unfamiliar diseases to which they had no immunity.[49]

The second wave of immigration spanned the period between 1820 and 1860. This wave included farmers, laborers, and artisans displaced by the Industrial Revolution in Europe. The primary countries of origin during this wave included Germany, England, and Ireland. Unlike in the first wave, Roman Catholics predominated in the second. This caused great apprehension among certain segments of the native U.S. population. Anti-Catholic sentiment occasionally turned violent, such as in the destruction of Catholic churches in the 1850s in places including Sidney, Ohio, and Dorchester, Massachusetts. Politically, the anti-immigration forces came together to form the American Party (also known as the Know-Nothing Party) of the 1840s and early 1850s, which called for the stiffening of naturalization laws. These efforts were generally unsuccessful.[50]

The third wave of immigration occurred roughly between 1880 and 1914. During this period, over 20 million southern and eastern Europeans arrived, as well as several hundred thousand Chinese, Japanese, and other Asians. By 1910, about 15 percent of the U.S. population was foreign born. In 1882, 87 percent of immigrants were from northern and western Europe and 13 percent from southern and eastern Europe, but by 1907 only 19 percent arrived from northern and western Europe and 81 percent came from the southern and eastern portions of the continent.[51] This wave of immigrants was again met with considerable alarm by nativists, but this time their efforts were more successful than previous attempts to restrict immigration. First, the Immigration Act of 1882 prohibited immigration from China. This act, rooted in racial prejudice, was passed in response to complaints from workers in California who opposed "unfair competition" from Chinese immigrants.[52] Immigration from Japan was also later restricted in 1907.

Antipathy toward immigrants extended to those from southern and eastern Europe, who were often considered to be genetically inferior and unassimilable. A 1907 U.S. House of Representatives commission study concluded that immigrants from these regions had more "inborn socially inadequate qualities than northwestern Europeans."[53] This eventually led to broad quantitative restrictions on immigration passed by Congress in the form of the Immigration Act of 1921, followed by the more stringent Immigration Act of 1924. These acts, along with two world wars and a depression, led to a lull in immigration from 1915 to the end of World War II.

After World War II immigration policy generally became less restrictive. Many government officials and commentators felt that for the United States to be perceived as a beacon of freedom and democracy—in contrast to its Cold War rival, the Soviet Union—it needed to revise its overtly discriminatory policies.[54] An increasing proportion of the public came around to the idea that racial oppression was antithetical to the Enlightenment principles on which the country was founded. They felt that such oppression was hypocrisy, to put it plainly, and a blot on the nation's character and international reputation. Immigration began creeping upward during this period (from the late 1940s to the early 1960s), with a rising tide of Mexican immigrants admitted via the Bracero Program—a temporary worker program designed to fill labor shortages in agriculture.

The fourth wave of immigration has occurred from 1965 to the present. In 1965 Congress passed the amendments to the Immigration and Nationality Act (also known as the Hart-Celler Act), which fundamentally revised immigration policy. This act eliminated the discriminatory national quota system, which favored northern and western Europeans, and opened up immigration to areas outside Europe and the Americas. This opening of immigration policy resulted in a spike in immigration, especially from Asia.

Figure 4 illustrates these long-term trends in immigration. The sharp peak in the number of legal immigrants in the late 1980s and early 1990s mainly reflects the passage of the Immigration Reform and Control Act (IRCA) in 1986, which had provisions that allowed previously undocumented immigrants already in the United States to receive legal status. The real peak of immigration occurred before World War I (the peak year was 1907, with the arrival of 1,285,349 legal immigrants), and then the country experienced a rapid decline after the restrictive policies in the 1920s. The all-time low was registered in 1933, when only 23,068 immi-

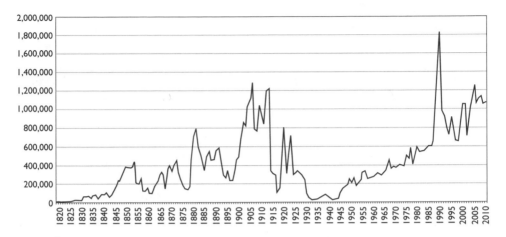

Figure 4. Legal immigrants to the United States, 1820–2011. Source: U.S. Department of Homeland Security 2012, table 2.

grants arrived and when the U.S. unemployment rate hit a high of 25 percent during the Great Depression. The figure also indicates that the growing number of immigrants after World War II eventually matched the numbers from the early twentieth century. Through most of the 2000s, over 1 million legal immigrants have arrived annually.

However, because the overall population of the United States has continued to grow, the proportion of its foreign-born population today does not quite match that segment's historical highs (see figure 5). In both 1890 and 1910 nearly 15 percent of the U.S. population was foreign born. This reached a low of only 4.7 percent in 1970—a time when many of the immigrants from the previous wave were dying and the post-1965 growth in immigration was just gaining steam. The baby boomers essentially came of age during a time when the percentage of the U.S. population that was foreign born was at an all-time historical low. By 2010, however, nearly 13 percent of the U.S. population was foreign born.

As indicated earlier, through most of the nineteenth century a majority of immigrants came from northern and western Europe, with the three largest sending countries being Germany, Ireland, and the United Kingdom. The late 1800s saw a large increase in the proportion of immigrants coming from southern and eastern Europe; between 1900 and 1909,

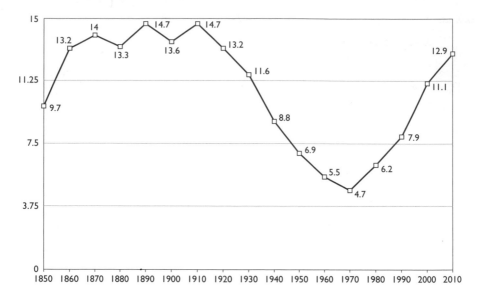

Figure 5. Percentage of the U.S. population foreign born, 1850–2010. Sources: 1850–1980 data from Daniels 2002, tables 6.4 and 16.2; 1980–2010 data from Migration Policy Institute 2012b.

42 percent of immigrants came from Russia and Italy alone. Immigration from Mexico slowly accelerated after World War II, and the rapid increase in the percentage of immigrants from Asia began in the 1960s. The 2000s have also seen an appreciable number of immigrants from Africa (7 percent of all immigrants).[55] As a consequence, the proportion of all legal immigrants in the United States who were from Europe was only 13 percent from 2000 to 2009, down from 86 percent in the 1900–1920 period. The share of all immigrants from Asia grew from 4 percent to 34 percent and from Latin America from 10 percent to 41 percent over the same time period.[56] Immigration from Asia has accelerated in recent years and in fact has surpassed the number of Hispanic immigrants since 2009.[57]

Internal Migration

High levels of immigration were accompanied by high levels of internal migration through U.S. history. Two long-term processes characterize this

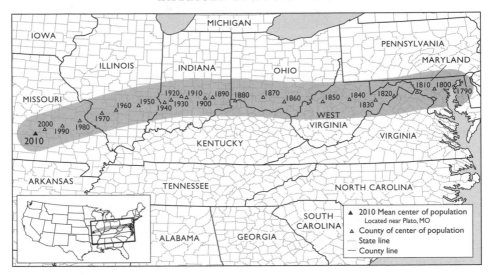

Figure 6. Mean centers of population for the United States, 1790–2010. Source: U.S. Census Bureau 2011b.

internal movement: the westward expansion of the population and its movement from rural areas to urban ones. With regard to westward expansion, at the time of the first census in 1790 only 13 percent of the total population lived in territories west of the thirteen original states, which of course were situated on the eastern seaboard of the United States, where the first European colonists had settled. By 1860, however, a full 55 percent of the population was living west of these states. The framers of the Constitution had made it easy for new territories to gain statehood, and by the eve of the Civil War in 1860 there were thirty-four states in the Union.[58] Americans were also considered more mobile than their European counterparts. As remarked by an English observer, Americans "acquire no attachment to Place. . . . Wandering about Seems engrafted in their Nature; and it is a weakness incident to it, that they should forever imagine that the Lands further off, are still better than those on which they have already Settled."[59]

The westward movement of the population is illustrated in figure 6. It shows how in 1790, the center of the population was east of Baltimore, Maryland. By 1860 it was in southern Ohio, by 1950 it was in Illinois, and

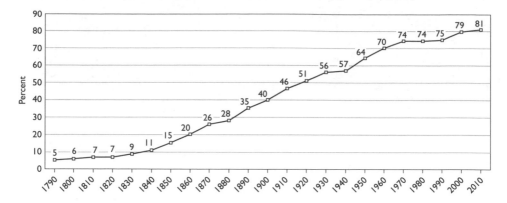

Figure 7. Percentage of the U.S. population living in urban areas, 1790–2010. Note: A change occurred in the definition of "urban" in 1950. Sources: 1790–1990 data from U.S. Census Bureau 1993; 2000 and 2010 data from U.S. Census Bureau 2010d.

by the time of the 2010 census the center of the U.S. population was in Missouri, well southwest of St. Louis. The map also shows the more recent southern movement of the population since about 1950. This represents the rise of the Sun Belt, or the southern migration of the U.S. population away from the Northeast and Midwest to the South and West, to states such as Texas, California, Nevada, New Mexico, and Florida.[60] Also illustrating this pattern of mobility, over a quarter (27 percent) of the native-born population lived outside their state of birth in 2010; this is in line with historical patterns, in which 22 to 31 percent of the population lived outside their state of birth at different points in time.[61]

The second pattern of internal migration was the movement of people from rural areas to urban centers. In 1790 only six towns in the United States had more than 8,000 people, with New York City the largest with 33,000 people and Philadelphia the second largest with 29,000 people. Only 3 percent of the U.S. population lived in these six towns at the time.[62] However, cities grew at a faster rate than rural areas in subsequent decades as they became centers of bustling trade. The proportion of the U.S. population living in all urban areas grew from just 5 percent in 1790 to a 26 percent in 1870, 51 percent in 1920, 75 percent in 1990, and 81 percent in the latest 2010 decennial census (see figure 7). The rapid growth of

cities in the late 1800s and through the 1900s was fueled by industrialization, for example, the steel factories in Pittsburgh, the textile industry in
New York, meatpacking plants in Chicago, and the explosive growth of the
automobile industry in Detroit.[63]

Industrialization and urbanization are reflected in the growth rates of
individual cities. In 1860, New York had 814,000 inhabitants, followed by
Philadelphia with 566,000. Just forty years later, in 1900, New York City
had grown to 3.4 million people, Chicago had 1.7 million, and Philadelphia
1.3 million.[64] Immigrants swelled the populations of these cities. New
York itself was a major port of entry at the turn of the twentieth century
and was largely divided into ethnic neighborhoods. Jacob Riis, in his
classic book on poverty, *How the Other Half Lives,* describes the often-
desperate conditions in which poor immigrants lived, crowded as they
were in dense, poorly constructed tenement housing. As Riis writes,

> A map of the city, colored to designate nationalities, would show more stripes
> than on the skin of a zebra, and more colors than any rainbow. The city on
> such a map would fall into two great halves, green for the Irish prevailing in
> the West Side tenement districts, and blue for the Germans on the East Side.
> But intermingled with these ground colors would be an odd variety of tints
> that would give the whole the appearance of an extraordinary quilt. From
> down in the Sixth Ward ... the red of the Italian would be seen forcing its
> way northward along the line of Mulberry Street to the quarter of the French
> purple on Bleecker Street and South Fifth Avenue. ... the Russian and Polish
> Jew, having overrun the district between Rivington and Division Streets, east
> of the Bowery, to the point of suffocation, is filling the tenements of the old
> Seventh Ward to the river front, and disputing with the Italian every foot of
> available space in the back alleys of Mulberry Street. The two races [Italians
> and Jews], differing hopelessly in much, have this in common: they carry
> their slums with them wherever they go, if allowed to do it.[65]

But in tandem with the growth of these poor, racially distinct immigrant
neighborhoods were the architectural marvels representative of the growing wealth and standards of living of the city: the modern skyscraper. New
York and Chicago initially dueled to be the home of the tallest of these new
buildings in the 1880s. New York took the lead for many years beginning in
the 1890s and saw a sustained period of skyscraper construction between
the 1910s and early 1930s, culminating with the erection of the Empire

State Building, which was the world's tallest from 1931 until 1972.[66] These cities continued to grow and thrive even with the relative lull in immigration in the middle decades of the twentieth century. They also saw a rapid growth in their black populations, fueled by a large-scale migration of blacks from the Jim Crow South to the North in search for jobs in bustling factories, in what became known as the Great Migration. By 2010, the largest three metropolitan areas in the U.S. 2010 census were New York (18.9 million people), Los Angeles (12.8 million), and Chicago (9.5 million).[67]

As an aside, it should be noted that the world's tallest buildings today are in countries elsewhere in the world. These include the Burj Khalifa in the United Arab Emirates, the Makkah Royal Clock Tower Hotel in Saudi Arabia, Teipai 101 in Taipei, and the Shanghai World Financial Center in Shanghai. The One World Trade Center in New York City, completed in 2013, is in the top ten and is the tallest building in the United States.[68] The eclipse of American cities as the homes of the tallest buildings coincides with the urbanization and development of large industrial cities across the globe. As of 2011, the five largest urban agglomerations (cities and their surrounding commuting areas), as defined by the United Nations, included Tokyo, Japan (37.2 million); Delhi, India (22.7 million); Mexico City, Mexico (20.4 million); New York, U.S. (20.4 million according to the U.N. definition); and Shanghai, China (20.2 million). Close on their heels and rounding out the top ten are Sao Paulo, Brazil (19.9 million); Mumbai, India (19.7 million); Beijing, China (15.6 million); Dhaka, Bangladesh (15.4 million); and Kolkata, India (14.4 million).[69] It is no surprise that a number of the largest cities in the world are in China and India—the two most populous countries, which are also experiencing rapid economic development.

Back to the development of U.S. cities: during the twentieth century we also saw a considerable redistribution of populations *within* urban centers. While only a quarter of the population of U.S. metropolitan areas resided in suburbs in 1910, by 1960 about half did, and by 2010 this figure was up to 61 percent.[70] This suburbanization in the twentieth century was a result of several developments, including the rise of the automobile, which allowed residents to live farther from their central city jobs than they used to, the movement of jobs themselves to suburban locations, and the desire of many families to "escape the noise, dirt, crowding, and crime that city dwellers must tolerate."[71]

Public policy also fostered suburbanization, such as through the provision of generous credit terms to home buyers, especially in the suburbs, after World War II and the Interstate Highway Act of 1955, which facilitated suburban commuting.[72] While affluent and middle-class whites initially propelled suburbanization, and whites remain overrepresented in the suburbs today, minority suburbanization rates have increased rapidly in recent decades, and many immigrants today move directly to suburban ethnic communities rather than to traditional central city enclaves.[73]

CONCLUSION

The United States has experienced profound social and demographic changes over the decades. Several demographic processes described in this chapter characterize the period from colonial settlement to today. The United States, like western European countries, experienced a demographic transition in the nineteenth and early twentieth centuries. This involved a change in a regime of high birthrates and high death rates to one of low birthrates and low death rates. However, U.S. population growth rates exceeded those of its peer countries. U.S. birth rates in colonial times through the early nineteenth century were particularly high, and its death rates comparatively moderate, yielding a very high rate of natural population growth. At its peak the U.S. population was doubling every 20 to 25 years from natural increase alone (i.e., not counting immigration). The 1800s saw a substantial decline in the U.S. fertility rate that continued through the middle decades of the twentieth century. These declines occurred by the end of the nineteenth century in other Western and developed countries and reflected social processes such as urbanization, growing levels of education and affluence, and growing gender equality—all of which tend to increase the cost of raising children. After a baby boom in the 1950s, fertility in the United States declined to what is now close to replacement levels—just under 2.0 children on average per woman.

As in a number of other western European countries, U.S. mortality remained moderately high before declining substantially in the last decades of the nineteenth century. This decline in mortality continues today. The initial reason for the decline was a better understanding of the transmission of infectious diseases, which led to effective public health measures and individual health practices, and later on, medical advances drove declines. The net result was a decline in infectious diseases, such as cholera, as the primary cause of death and the rise of chronic and degenerative diseases such as heart disease and cancer.

Immigration historically played a significant role not only in the country's growth but also in its composition. Through colonial times a majority of settlers came from England, though a substantial number of immigrants came from other countries such as France and Germany. Many slaves—involuntary immigrants—were also brought from Africa. During the early to mid-1800s a growing number of Catholic immigrants came to the United States, raising nativist concerns. These concerns were also later evident in response to the growing tide of immigrants from southern and eastern Europe (and China and Japan on the West Coast) in the last decades of the nineteenth century. This led to restrictions of immigration from the 1880s to the 1920s, and indeed the middle decades of the twentieth century saw a plunge in the number of immigrants coming to the United States. The latest wave of immigration occurred after changes in immigration laws in 1965 that overturned prejudicial immigration policies favoring immigration from northern and western Europe. Today, immigration flows are quite diverse, with significant numbers of immigrants coming from Latin America, Asia, and Africa.

Two long-term processes characterize internal migration: westward expansion, especially in the early days of the republic, and urbanization. The nineteenth century saw the continual addition of states as pioneers extended the frontier westward. The twentieth century saw additional population growth in western states, but after about 1950 we also see the rise of the Sun Belt, which included migration from the Northeast and Midwest to southern states.

Regarding the second process, urbanization, whereas only 5 percent of the U.S. population lived in urban areas in 1790, by 1900 this had risen to nearly 50 percent, and today over 80 percent of Americans live in urban areas. In addition, the population within metropolitan areas has become increasingly suburbanized. Whereas initially most residents in the suburbs were middle-class and affluent whites, suburbs today have become much more diverse, both ethnically and socioeconomically.

Fertility, mortality, and migration together thus explain the size and composition of the U.S. population. The growth of the country has in many ways been exceptional, driven initially by extraordinarily high fertility rates and continually by immigrants drawn to its affluence. The United States does not stand alone as a country of immigrants (Australia and Canada, for example, have been shaped by immigration as well), but it is one of relatively few with a long history of being a destination of immigrants from very diverse origins. This diversity has helped shape American political, cultural, and social institutions and helped propel the nation's continued economic growth.

2 The American Family

Changes in the American family over the last half century have been astonishing. The idealized view of the American family consisting of a married mom and dad with two children has nearly gone by the wayside, and we have instead seen a large increase in the number of single-parent families and people living alone or with housemates. Jason DeParle, a journalist who has written extensively about household living arrangements and poverty, described one woman's path to single parenthood: Jessica Schairer, a mother of three, grew up in a traditional small town outside Ann Arbor, Michigan.

> Her father drove a beer truck, her mother served as church trustee and her grandparents lived next door. She knew no one rich, no one poor and no one raising children outside of marriage. "It was just the way it was," she said.
>
> William Penn University, eight hours away in Iowa, offered a taste of independence and a spot on the basketball team. Her first thought when she got pregnant was "My mother's going to kill me." Abortion crossed her mind, but her boyfriend, an African-American student from Arkansas, said they should start a family. They agreed that marriage should wait until they could afford a big reception and a long gown. . . .
>
> Ms. Schairer has trouble explaining, even to herself, why she stayed so long with a man who she said earned little, berated her often and did no parenting.

They lived with family (his and hers) and worked off and on while she hoped things would change. "I wanted him to love me," she said. She was 25 when the breakup made it official: she was raising three children on her own.[1]

Jessica represents one of the growing number of women in the United States who are raising children either on their own or in untraditional household arrangements. But just how much have American marriage and childbearing patterns actually changed? What factors explain these changes? What are some of the consequences of these changes? This chapter addresses these questions and examines the broad diversity in life course transitions that Americans experience today, including cohabitation, marriage, and childbearing.

THE TRADITIONAL FAMILY

Traditional notions of the family have evolved over time. What we now consider the 1950s traditional family of the male breadwinner working outside the home and the stay-at-home mother taking care of the kids in fact differed from traditional families of the colonial era and much of the nineteenth century. In pre-urban, preindustrial times, a husband and wife often worked together on a farm. As Richard Gill and his coauthors describe the colonial-era family: "Although the husband was considered the head of the family and although there was a sexual division of labor in terms of kinds of work, the sharp division between provider-husband and homemaker-wife did not exist."[2] Family members all contributed to economically productive tasks in and around the home. This included children, who, after the age of six or seven, were expected to do their fair share. That men and women both worked in and around the home is not to say that this was a period of gender equality; families were still strongly patriarchal, and women lacked many rights.[3]

Industrialization and urbanization were key catalysts in spurring changes in the economic functioning of families. Industrialization led to the growth in employment in places more physically removed from the home. Among families with children, the husband was more likely to be employed in a wage-paying job. Since he was more removed from the home, the wife took on the tasks involved in what is often called home production: caring for the children and maintaining the home. Single women often worked outside the home in occupations including domestic service, teaching, and as secretaries, but once they married the strong expectation was that the woman would leave the labor force—if the family could afford it—and take care of the home and children.[4]

CHANGES IN HOUSEHOLD LIVING ARRANGEMENTS IN RECENT DECADES

There have been several trends in family living arrangements in recent decades. These include a rising age at marriage, a decline in fertility, an increase in divorce, cohabitation, same-sex unions, and nonmarital childbearing. These patterns are collectively termed the *second demographic transition* (the first demographic transition consisted of the decline in fertility and mortality, described in chapter 1). One result of these trends is that only 49 percent of all households contained a married couple in 2012, down from 78 percent in 1950.[5] The underlying causes of all of these trends have been much discussed and debated, as have their consequences. These issues are the focus of the rest of this chapter.

Age at First Marriage and Fertility

Figure 8 shows trends in age at first marriage, by gender, from 1890 to 2011. The first half of the twentieth century saw small declines in the median age at marriage for both men and women. In 1950, the median age was just 23 for men and 20 for women. The decline has been attributed to the growth of well-paid wage labor employment for men that accompanied industrialization. This provided men with a sufficient income to support a family, even at a relatively young age.[6] Not by chance, the years with the youngest ages at first marriage (1950 and 1960) coincided with the baby boom. Early marriage is typically associated with greater fertility, because childbearing in these circumstances tends to begin at younger ages. Since 1960 the median age at first marriage has been rising. By 2010, the median age had risen to nearly 29 for men and 27 for women. In addi-

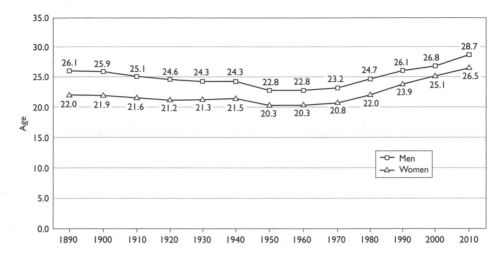

Figure 8. Median age at first marriage, by gender, 1890–2011. Source: U.S. Census Bureau 2011g.

tion to marrying later, since about 1990 an increasing proportion of men and women have not married at all by the age of 45.[7]

Chapter 1 described the long-term decline in U.S. fertility rates from a time when American women were having, on average, 7.0 children in 1800 to just under 2.0 children today. A growing proportion of women today are also having no children. Whereas among women born in the 1930s, about 10 percent had no children by the time they reached their early forties, among those born in the 1960s this proportion was up to 19 percent.[8] Similarly, while 35 percent of women in the earlier cohort had four or more children, the same could be said for only about 10 percent of the more recent cohort of women. Overall, fertility levels have been fairly stable at near-replacement levels (where women have on average about 2.0 children) since about 1980, though with a small dip since the late 2000s.

Divorce

Divorce rates were historically low in the United States, with well under one in ten marriages ending in divorce in 1870. This percentage crept up over the twentieth century and then rose rapidly in the 1960s and 1970s

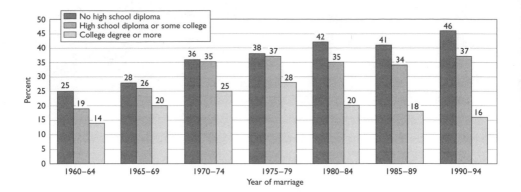

Figure 9. Percentage of women experiencing separation or divorce within ten years of a first marriage, by educational level. Source: Martin 2006, 552. Copyright by S. P. Martin.

before declining modestly since. Whereas about one in four marriages that began in the 1950s ended in divorce, close to half of those that occurred in the 1970s are predicted to end in divorce. Somewhere between 40 and 50 percent of more recent marriages are expected to end in divorce, given current patterns.[9] The probability that a marriage will end in divorce varies considerably by education and ethnicity. Divorce rates have continued to increase for women with no high school diploma but have actually declined for college-educated women since the late 1970s. Among marriages that began in the early 1990s, 46 percent of those involving women with no high school diploma ended in divorce ten years later compared with only 16 percent of marriages among women with a college degree (see figure 9).[10] Divorce rates are also higher among blacks than whites.[11] Much of the difference in divorce rates by educational attainment can be attributed to the early age of marriage among less educated men and women (people who marry young are more likely to divorce), plus the diverging economic prospects of Americans of different educational levels.[12] The latter issue is discussed at greater length below.

Cohabitation

Cohabitation before marriage is now normative. Of all first marriages between 1965 and 1974, only 11 percent were preceded by cohabitation.

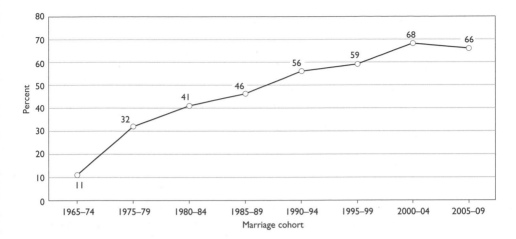

Figure 10. Trends in the percentage of women (19–44) who cohabited prior to first marriage. Source: Manning 2013, 2.

During 2005–9, this was up to two-thirds of all first marriages (see figure 10). Cohabitation has risen for all racial and ethnic groups. As of 2009–10, 62 percent of white women ages 19 to 44 have cohabited, compared with 60 percent of black women and 59 percent of Hispanic women. However, there are important differences by educational attainment. About 74 percent of women with less than a high school education have cohabited, compared with 50 percent of women with four years of college or more, who are more likely than other women to proceed directly to marriage rather than to cohabit first.[13]

Cohabiting relationships tend to be less stable than marriages. According to 2002 data, about 50 percent of children born to cohabiting parents experience a breakup of the household by the age of 9, compared with about 20 percent of children born to married parents.[14]

Qualitative research has indicated that many young adults "slide" into cohabitation rather than carefully plan for it. Sociologists Wendy Manning and Pamela Smock report the following conversation with a respondent when he was asked how he started living with his partner: "It began with, first, I had an apartment and she lived with her parents. And it began with her just spending more and more time, staying overnight, um, basically just out of the, you-know, just gradually becoming a fixture and uh, there was never any discussion of the matter. When my roommate moved out and I didn't have a roommate, it just sort—well, it had become permanent even before that, probably, but just wasn't said."[15] Similarly, another respondent describes how he finally realized that he was in a cohabiting relationship: "She stayed at my house more and more from spending the night once to not going home to her parents' house for a week at a time and then you know further, um, so there was no official starting date. I did take note when the frilly fufu soaps showed up in my bathroom that she'd probably moved in at that point."[16]

In an era in which life course transitions are not as clear-cut as in the past, cohabitation has become a lower-risk option than marriage for many people to see if living together works for them or not. Likewise, the commitment to partners tends to be more provisional in cohabiting relationships than in marriage. However, with the increase in cohabitation, the distinction between cohabitation and marriage could erode in the future, much as it has in a few European countries where cohabitation is close to becoming an outright substitute for formal marriage.[17]

Same-Sex Unions

Same-sex unions have also become a lot more common in recent years. Estimates of the size of this population are complicated by challenges in gathering accurate data, but a careful Census Bureau analysis suggests that in 2010 there were an estimated 650,000 same-sex couple households in the United States, up from 360,000 in 2000 (an 80 percent increase). Of the 650,000 couples in 2010, a few over 130,000 consisted of married spouses, while the rest were unmarried partners living together.[18] Just over half of same-sex couples consisted of women living together.[19] Among same-sex couple households, about 1 in 6 (16 percent) included children, with female couples more likely to have children (22 percent) than male couples (10 percent).[20] The number of same-sex unions, including those with children, will likely continue to increase with the growth in public acceptance of same-sex relationships and gay marriage.

Figure 11. Percentage of births to unmarried women, by race and Hispanic origin, 1940–2009. Sources: Ventura and Bachrach 2000; Martin et al. 2011.

Nonmarital Childbearing

Having children outside marriage is no longer uncommon. Whereas in 1940 only 2 percent of births were to unmarried women, by 2009 this figure had risen to 41 percent (see figure 11). Moreover, more than half of births to young women (those under 30 years old) occur outside marriage. These percentages have been growing for all racial and ethnic groups. The proportion of all white births to unmarried women increased sharply over the past two decades, from 20 percent in 1990 to 36 percent in 2009. Among black women, increases occurred earlier; from 1970 to 1990 the proportion of black births to unmarried women jumped from 38 to 67 percent, before gradually continuing to drift upward to 72 percent in 2009. In 2009, over half of Hispanic births (53 percent) were to unmarried women. Only among Asians is the corresponding figure much lower— 17 percent in 2009.[21]

However, complicating the picture of trends in nonmarital childbearing is that much of the rise in recent years has occurred among cohabiting couples. In fact, more than half of nonmarital births occur within cohabiting relationships, compared with 29 percent in the early 1990s.[22] Thus,

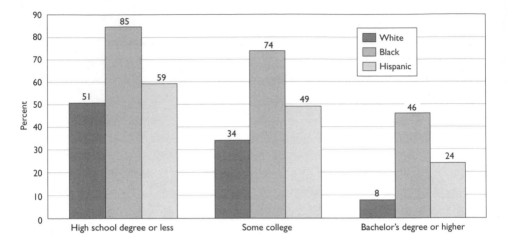

Figure 12. Percentage of births to unmarried women (ages 20–29 years), by race/ethnicity and level of education, 2009. Source: Child Trends 2012.

the actual percentage of families headed by single women living alone (without a coresident partner) has not changed much since about 1995. As of 2010, 26 percent of all families, 21 percent of white families, 29 percent of Hispanic families, and 55 percent of African American families were headed by a single woman living with no other parent present in the household.[23] As mentioned earlier, however, the unions of cohabiting couples are more than twice as likely as marriages to dissolve, even though in many ways they resemble married families.[24]

Notably, differentials in nonmarital births by educational status are about as prominent as those by race and ethnicity and have become more pronounced over time. Over half (51 percent) of all births to white women without a high school degree occur outside marriage; in contrast, the figure for white women with a bachelor's degree or more is only 8 percent (see figure 12). The percentage of births among African American women with a bachelor's or more that occur outside marriage is fairly high (46 percent) but nevertheless much lower than among African American women with a high school diploma or less (85 percent).[25] The percentage for Hispanics is in between those of whites and African Americans.

International Comparisons

The dramatic changes in family living arrangements over the past few decades have not been confined to the United States alone. Many wealthy countries around the world have experienced a second demographic transition, including delays in marriage and childbearing and increases in cohabitation, divorce, nonmarital childbearing, and women's employment.[26]

Total fertility rates, for example, are below replacement level (which is 2.1 births per woman) in almost all OECD countries, their average being 1.7. (The Organisation for Economic Co-operation and Development consists of a group of mainly wealthy countries.) Women are having children later in life, and more are having no children at all. Fewer people are getting married, divorce rates are up, and more children are born outside marriage than in the past. Cohabitation is often seen as an acceptable alternative to marriage in much of the developed world. Table 2 illustrates these patterns by showing the distribution of children living in different kinds of families in OECD countries. Topping the list of countries with the highest percentage of families with two married parents is Greece (92 percent of children live with two married parents); at the bottom is Sweden, where about half (51 percent) live with two married parents. The United States, at 68 percent, is a little lower than the average across the 27 OECD countries (73 percent).[27]

Notably, the table also shows while only half of children in Sweden live in married-couple households, just 18 percent actually live in a household with only one parent. (The OECD average is 15 percent.) Most of the rest live in cohabiting households (31 percent); indeed, Sweden has the highest percentage of children living with cohabitors. The United States has the highest percentage of children living in households with only one parent (26 percent) and a fairly modest percentage living in cohabiting couple households. It should be noted that the table somewhat understates the percentage of U.S. children living in cohabiting households.[28] Recent analyses with better data indicate that about 6 percent of U.S. children live with cohabiting parents rather than the 3 percent indicated in the table.[29] Even with the correction, however, the United States still has a lower percentage of children living with cohabiting parents and a higher percentage living with a single parent than OECD averages.

Table 2   Distribution of Children, by Household Type, in Selected OECD
Countries, 2007

	Percentage of children living with			
	2 MARRIED PARENTS	2 COHABITING PARENTS	1 PARENT	0 PARENTS
Greece	92	1	5	1
Slovak Republic	85	4	11	1
Italy	84	5	10	1
Spain	84	8	7	1
Luxembourg	83	7	10	0
Poland	79	9	11	1
Germany	78	6	15	1
Czech Republic	76	8	15	1
Austria	76	7	14	2
Netherlands	76	13	11	0
Portugal	76	10	12	3
Hungary	74	10	15	1
OECD 27 average	73	11	15	1
Slovenia	69	20	10	1
Finland	69	16	14	1
Ireland	68	6	24	2
United States	68	3	26	4
Belgium	68	14	16	3
Canada	67	11	22	0
Denmark	66	15	18	2
France	65	21	14	1
United Kingdom	65	13	22	1
Estonia	53	24	22	2
Sweden	51	31	18	1

SOURCE: OECD 2011a, table 1.1.

While these changes in family formation patterns initially began in western Europe, Canada, Australia, and the United States, such changes have begun to spread to central and eastern Europe and several developed countries in Asia, including Japan, South Korea, Taiwan, Hong Kong, and Singapore. All five of these Asian countries, for example, have very low total fertility rates, in the 1 to 1.3 range. The age at first marriage has increased in most East Asian countries, as has the percentage of never-married women. The percentage of men and women who have cohabited has also increased in countries such as Taiwan and Japan. For example, in just the six-year period between 1998 and 2004, the percentage of women aged 20 to 49 reporting a cohabitation experience increased from 11 to 20 percent in Taiwan. Japanese women born during 1975–79 were more than twice as likely to have reported that they had ever cohabited (21 percent) than women born during 1954–59 (10 percent), according to a survey taken in 2004.[30]

WHY HAVE FAMILY LIVING ARRANGEMENTS CHANGED?

Here I focus on the forces that have shaped family living arrangements in the United States, though many of these conditions also exist in other developed countries that have experienced the second demographic transition. Two general arguments have been offered to explain the growth in untraditional families over the past several decades: cultural versus economic perspectives. Below I review both of these explanations, but it should be noted that economic and cultural shifts have occurred hand in hand, and it is thus difficult to draw a definitive distinction between the effects of each.

Culture refers to shared values, expectations, and modes of behavior. Culture is learned in childhood and transmitted through families and communities, and it includes habits of thought and action. Marriage culture in the United States traditionally had two bases: (1) marriage is a given—everyone is expected to marry, and it is the proper thing to do; and (2) marriage is forever. Clearly marital norms have shifted, and today less stigma is attached to being unmarried or divorced than in the past.[31]

Conservative commentators in particular point with alarm to cultural changes that have promoted family dissolution. Some emphasize that misguided government policies aimed at helping the poor have provided work disincentives and encouraged dependency on benefits. According to this view, these policies have also lowered the incentive for marriage and led to all sorts of other wayward behaviors, such as single parenthood and illegitimacy, criminal activity, and drug and alcohol abuse. These patterns are most evident in poor, inner-city African American neighborhoods.[32]

Charles Murray, in his book *Coming Apart: The State of White America, 1960–2010,* focuses on recent family formation patterns among whites. He argues that cultural norms in America have sharply diverged since the early 1960s. Specifically, today we have a group consisting of affluent, highly educated whites who overwhelmingly decide to get married before having children and who live in residential enclaves surrounded by like-minded people. They value marriage, hard work, honesty, and religiosity, and this allows them to enjoy secure and affluent lives. Their choices are also a function of their higher cognitive abilities, which allow them to plan ahead and envision the consequences of their actions.

The second group is the less-educated lower class, which has experienced an erosion of family and community life and for which having children outside marriage has become the norm. Murray attributes the declining fortunes of the lower class to the corresponding decline in the traditional values just named. This population finds itself at or near the bottom of the economic ladder because, according to Murray, its members, on average, have less cognitive ability—and are thus less well equipped to resist the lure of the sexual revolution and doctrines of self-actualization. They live in different neighborhoods from those of the elite and therefore lack appropriate role models. They thus succumb to higher rates of family dissolution, nonmarital births, work avoidance, and criminality. Murray sharply criticizes liberal elites because they do not do enough to publicly defend and affirm the traditional values to which they personally subscribe, and this has both served to exacerbate growing class divisions in society and will lead inexorably to America's decline unless this unhealthy dynamic is reversed.

Murray's thesis has drawn two criticisms. One, focusing on *cultural* values, is that while there has obviously been some shift in normative practices, the institution of marriage is still held in high esteem and most people strive to attain it. In other words, a wholesale cultural turn against marriage has not occurred, even among those with less education. Sociologist Andrew Cherlin holds that in contemporary American society we can describe marriage culture as consisting of the following four elements: (1) marriage is the best way to live one's family life; (2) a marriage should be a permanent, loving relationship; (3) a marriage should be a sexually exclusive partnership; and (4) divorce should be a last resort. Cherlin draws upon survey data (e.g., 76 percent of Americans agreed with the statement that "marriage is a lifetime relationship that should never be ended except under extreme circumstance") and detailed interviews to form conclusions about the continued importance of marriage in society. For example, one low-income unmarried respondent said, "If I get married, I wanna be with this person for the rest of my life. I don't wanna just get married and then our relationship goes wrong, and then I have to go and get a *divorce!*"[33]

A second criticism of Murray's analysis is that it does not focus enough on the role of *economic* factors in driving the growth in nonmarital births. The economist Gary Becker (writing before Murray) has argued that marriage is in large part an economic arrangement, and that its chief benefit arises from the interdependence of men and women. In colonial times, as previously stated, husbands and wives often worked together on family farms. During the heyday of industrialization men were the primary breadwinners in the labor market, and women were in charge of home production. As women's labor market prospects increased over time, the economic incentive to get married declined.[34] As is reflected in the increase in divorce rates in the post–World War II period, women today are also less likely than in the past to be trapped in bad marriages.[35]

Moreover, not only are women's economic prospects increasing, but also those of less-educated men have declined in the United States. Deindustrialization, globalization, and the decline in unionization have led to lower employment levels and wages for men with less than a college degree, many of whom were previously employed in relatively well-paying blue-collar occupations. This in turn has led to a decline in the number of "marriageable" men and further reduced women's incentive to marry.[36] The recent divergence in trends in divorce by education described earlier likely results from people with lower incomes and high economic insecurity experiencing more stress, which increases their likelihood of divorce.[37]

In elucidating the view that economic factors have driven changes in family formation patterns—and as a direct response to Murray—columnist Nicholas Kristof writes:

> Eighty percent of the people in my high school cohort dropped out or didn't pursue college because it used to be possible to earn a solid living at the steel mill, the glove factory or sawmill. That's what their parents had done. But the glove factory closed, working-class jobs collapsed and unskilled laborers found themselves competing with immigrants. . . . So let's get real. A crisis is developing in the white working class, a byproduct of growing income inequality in America. The pathologies are achingly real. But the solution isn't finger-wagging, or averting our eyes—but [economic] opportunity.[38]

A fair reckoning of these two arguments—one economic and the other cultural—is that both help explain recent trends. Sociologists Pamela Smock and Fiona Rose Greenland argue that unmarried couples with children articulate at least three perceived obstacles to marriage: concerns about financial stability, relationship quality, and fear of divorce, with financial concerns often the most paramount.[39] Men and women value marriage and aspire to it but believe, because of fears of divorce, that marriage should occur after financial stability is achieved. Low-income women, because of their expectations of low earnings, have less to lose by having children early and outside marriage, and they also place a very high value on children as adding meaning to their lives.[40] Good mothering is seen not as something that requires tremendous resources but as something that involves being there for the children (an approach to parenting that differs from that of the middle class).[41]

Finally, Smock and Greenland also note that cohabitation offers a marriage-like relationship with many of the same advantages of marriage, such as companionship, shared expenses, sexual access, childbearing, and childrearing. With cohabitation available as an increasingly normative option, the incentive to get married has declined. This helps explain rapid increases in cohabitation in recent years.

A news story on rising nonmarital births in the United States offers the following anecdote, which is consistent with the view that both economic conditions and culture shape family formation patterns:

Over the past generation, Lorain [a city in Ohio] lost most of two steel mills, a shipyard and a Ford factory, diminishing the supply of jobs that let blue-collar workers raise middle-class families. More women went to work, making marriage less of a financial necessity for them. Living together became routine, and single motherhood lost the stigma that once sent couples rushing to the altar. Women here often describe marriage as a sign of having arrived rather than a way to get there.

Meanwhile, children happen. Amber Strader, 27, was in an on-and-off relationship with a clerk at Sears a few years ago when she found herself pregnant. A former nursing student who now tends bar, Ms. Strader said her boyfriend was so dependent that she had to buy his cigarettes. Marrying him never entered her mind. "It was like living with another kid," she said.

When a second child, with a new boyfriend, followed three years later—her birth control failed, she said—her boyfriend, a part-time house painter, was reluctant to wed. Ms. Strader likes the idea of marriage; she keeps her parents' wedding photo on her kitchen wall and says her boyfriend is a good father. But for now marriage is beyond her reach. "I'd like to do it, but I just don't see it happening right now," she said. "Most of my friends say it's just a piece of paper, and it doesn't work out anyway."[42]

In short, many studies indicate that there has been a cultural shift in American's views of marriage and especially of nonmarital childbearing. While single parenthood is generally not something people aim for—most would like to be in committed, fulfilling unions—it is nevertheless generally socially accepted when it occurs. There is greater emphasis today on individualism and self-actualization than on community and conformity. Nevertheless, the decline in marriage and increase in nonmarital childbearing are also rooted in economic changes that have served to decrease the employment and earnings of men with less than a college degree at the same time that those of women have increased. The traditional economic foundations of marriage have eroded.

Ron Lesthaeghe, who has written at length about the "second demographic transition" in Western and a growing number of non-Western countries, argues that structural factors, including economic conditions, and cultural changes are interconnected and have likewise effected changes in families across a broad array of wealthy nations. Increases in female education have led to greater economic opportunities for women. Similarly, he argues, "the rise of individual autonomy and freedom of

choice has legitimized the adoption of non-traditional living arrangements in a very short time. . . . Furthermore, one should also realize that
mass media are producing a 'world culture' in which individual autonomy
and self-actualization have a very prominent, if not dominant place, and
that these provide both motivations and justifications for the onset of the
[second demographic transition]."[43]

Thus, not just the American family is changing; so are families in a
large number of nations, particularly wealthy countries, where individuals
now feel less constrained by traditional cultural practices. People's choices
about their living arrangements, however, have important implications
for the well-being of not only the individuals themselves but also their
families and communities.

CONSEQUENCES OF CHANGES IN FAMILY LIVING ARRANGEMENTS

Changes in household living arrangements in the United States (and other
countries) have been met with hand-wringing by many public commentators. The "breakdown" of the American family has been implicated as a
cause of rising child poverty, increasing household inequality, and lower
educational outcomes among children born in single-parent families.
Many bemoan cultural shifts in nonmarital childbearing, feeling that
these are indicative of moral decay and foreshadow the country's fall from
its lofty position as the global economic superpower. Before I analyze
some of these arguments and review evidence that supports the notion
that single-parent families are indeed more economically vulnerable than
other families, it is first worth noting some of the positive aspects of
changes in household living arrangements.

Perhaps most important, to the extent that people enjoy having a
broader array of socially acceptable choices available to them, the crum-
bling of the more restrictive norms of past generations is a good thing.
These norms were particularly restrictive of the choices available to
women, who were for the most part expected to focus on getting married,
bearing children, and taking care of the home. The barriers for entering
high-level professional positions (scientists, lawyers, corporate managers)

were very high, and the related stereotypes of women's intelligence and emotional stability were degrading. As Cherlin notes, "The increase in personal choice has brought important benefits. It has broadened the opportunity for wives to realize their full potential in paid employment as well as in the home. It has made marriage more egalitarian, with husbands and wives sharing more responsibility for home and wage earning. . . . Gone are the days when husbands could beat their wives with little fear of prosecution, demand sex at any time, or decide to sell their wives' property. Most people view all of these changes positively."[44]

Cherlin also notes that men's options have broadened as the stigma attached to men caring for their children full time has declined. For example, a *New York Times* story on the growing numbers of stay-at-home dads recounts the following:

> There was little discussion of male ego when David Worford, a former Web editor in Fort Collins, Colo., and his wife, Cherie, an obstetrician and gynecologist, agreed that he would stay home with their young sons a few years ago. "Most of my income was going directly to child care," he said. "Throw on that I was handling most of the domestic workload anyway because of the hours Cherie was working. It just made sense to make the move both economically and for family life. It was great to have a constant at home."[45]

In the same story, another stay at home dad related the following observation about rapidly changing social norms: "'Just a few years ago, I was usually the lone dad on the playground during the day,' Mr. Somerfeld, 39, said on a recent sunny Wednesday morning, while hanging out with eight other dads at the Heckscher Playground in Central Park. 'The moms and nannies gawked at me like I was an exhibit at the zoo. Now, I'm the new normal.'"[46]

In addition to changes in the household division of labor among couples, exiting highly unsatisfying marriages or not entering one at all is also generally more acceptable for both men and women. Young people have the option, and are indeed often encouraged, to explore their wants and needs before settling down. Cohabitation allows one to try on different relationships in a less threatening and permanent way than usually implied by marriage. More people are living alone than at any time in the recent past in the United States and a number of other countries. The proportion of households with a single person has increased from 9 percent in 1950 to 27 percent in 2010. In Scandinavia, between 40 and 45 percent of households contain a single person.[47] Of these changes, conservative-leaning commentator David Brooks notes, "At some point over the past generation, people around the world entered what you might call the age of possibility. They became intolerant of any arrangement that might close off their personal options. The transformation has been liberating, and it's leading to some pretty astounding changes. For example, for centuries, most human societies forcefully guided people into two-parent families. Today that sort of family is increasingly seen as just one option among many."[48]

However, greater choice does not always bring greater happiness or fulfillment. More choice can mean greater uncertainty and anxiety. Brooks, after introducing the notion of the age of possibility, goes on to argue against its potentially positive aspects: "My view is that the age of possibility is based on a misconception. People are not better off when they are given maximum personal freedom to do what they want. They're better off when they are enshrouded in commitments that transcend personal choice—commitments to family, God, craft and country."[49]

Analysts have also noted that the movement in and out of relationships among adults can be particularly disruptive for their children. Children who experience a series of changes in their parents' partnerships are more likely to act out, be delinquent, or become pregnant at a young age.[50] Divorce has the potential to produce considerable turmoil in people's lives. However, it should be noted that divorce can benefit some individuals (particularly if they are exiting an abusive relationship) or can lead to only temporary declines in well-being. How people respond often depends on the presence of various protective factors, such as having the educational and financial resources and the active skills to cope, as well as support from family and friends.[51] Overall, however, evidence indicates that children growing up in a stable two-parent family are less likely to experience a wide range of cognitive, emotional, and social problems both as children and later on as adults than other children. This finding can be explained by the tendency for children in these stable two-parent families to have a higher standard of living, receive more effective parenting, be emotionally closer to both parents, and experience fewer stressful events.[52]

Changes wrought by the second demographic transition have been linked with broader patterns of poverty and inequality. Some changes, such as the delay in childbearing and the increase in maternal employment, have likely served to increase the economic security among women and children. Other trends, however, including divorce and nonmarital childbearing, have served to depress women's well-being. Sociologist Sara McLanahan has argued that these developments have led to diverging trajectories for women. And because women with the most opportunities and resources to begin with tend to follow the more beneficial trajectory and women with the fewest opportunities and resources follow the more harmful one, these trends as a whole have reinforced and exacerbated economic inequality in the United States. She notes:

> Children who were born to mothers from the most-advantaged backgrounds are making substantial gains in resources. Relative to their counterparts 40 years ago, their mothers are more mature and more likely to be working at well-paying jobs. These children were born into stable unions and are spending more time with their fathers. In contrast, children born to mothers from the most disadvantaged backgrounds are making smaller gains and, in some instances, even losing parental resources. Their mothers are working at low-paying jobs. Their parents' relationships are unstable, and for many, support from their biological fathers is minimal.[53]

Similarly, McLanahan also finds diverging trajectories for women in other wealthy countries. Specifically, she finds that single motherhood (where there is no marriage or cohabitation) is most common among mothers with the least education in countries like Sweden, Norway, Germany, and Italy. In all countries she studied, fathers in the top educational category were also spending more time with their children than the least educated fathers.[54]

Many researchers have drawn a specific link between single parenthood and poverty in particular. W. E. B. DuBois's 1899 study of the African American community in Philadelphia documented high levels of family disorganization and instability in black families, and he linked this to the legacy of slavery, in which families were sometimes split up and its members sold at will. DuBois's groundbreaking study was followed over the years by a number of others that described the contribution of family instability to black poverty.[55] For example, Daniel Patrick Moynihan's 1965 report *The Negro Family: The Case for National Action* set off an explosive debate on the issue. Critics of the report charged that it put too much blame on ghetto culture for family instability rather than on structural conditions, such as deeply entrenched racism, discrimination, and the lack of economic opportunities for blacks in the wake of deindustrialization in many cities in the Northeast and Midwest. More recently, the link between single parenthood and disadvantage among white families has been highlighted by Charles Murray, who, as discussed above, also emphasized the role of culture in producing these changes.[56]

The culture-structure argument aside, these commentators all rightly note that single-parent families are considerably more likely to be poor than other families. In 2011 the poverty rate among married-couple families with children in the United States was 8.8 percent, compared with 40.9 percent among female-headed families with children.[57] Poverty is high among female-headed families for several reasons. Single parents often face the challenge of supporting a family on one income, as well as running a household alone and finding and paying for child care while they work. Lower average levels of education among women who head such families also significantly contribute to their lower earnings. Furthermore, women tend to earn less than men, and mothers tend to accumulate less work experience than others in the workplace. Finally, single mothers often receive only marginal child support from their children's absent fathers, because fathers sometimes don't make enough money to provide much child support.[58]

Cross-national comparisons likewise suggest that single-parent families are more vulnerable to poverty than others, though their poverty rates varied greatly across countries in the mid-2000s. If a relative poverty line equaling 50 percent of the national median income is used, the poverty rate for children in single-mother families across twenty countries in Europe and Latin America as well as Australia, Canada, and the United States ranged from a low of 8.2 percent in Denmark to a high of 50.5 percent in the United States. The United States is known for having high levels of poverty more generally in comparison to other wealthy countries because of its weaker safety net.[59] In nearly all countries poverty rates in single-mother families were considerably higher than among two-parent families. Poverty rates in single-parent families in Anglophone countries

(Australia, Canada, Ireland, the United Kingdom, and the United States) averaged 41 percent, compared with 10 percent in two-parent families. Even in low-poverty Nordic countries (Denmark, Finland, Norway, and Sweden), poverty rates among single-mother families averaged 11 percent, compared with 3 percent among two-parent families.[60] These countries with low poverty rates rely significantly on generous government programs such as universal child allowances, food assistance, and guaranteed child support for single parents to keep their poverty rates low.[61]

CONCLUSION

The first demographic transition, described in chapter 1—declining mortality and fertility—has been followed by momentous changes in family living arrangements of the second demographic transition. These changes include delays in marriage and childbearing, increases in cohabitation, divorce, and nonmarital childbearing in many wealthy countries. These trends have been driven by both cultural and economic changes. Culturally, the emphasis on individualism and self-actualization has been ever growing, making people less likely to want to conform to traditional familial roles. Economically, greater gender equality in the labor market, mainly fueled by the increasing labor force participation of women, has made women less dependent on men, thus reducing the economic incentive to marry. Meanwhile, the economic fortunes of less-educated men in the United States have fallen in recent decades, in large part as a result of deindustrialization and globalization. This has reduced the number of "marriageable" men and further dampened the incentive for women to marry. While people generally still value the institution of marriage and aspire to it, many low-income Americans feel it is out of reach, because marriage should happen only after a certain level of financial stability has been achieved.

These trends have consequences for the well-being of individuals and their communities. On the one hand, the greater diversity in family living arrangements and the growing emphasis on individualism mean that people have a greater range of socially acceptable choices available to them than in the past. Women in particular are no longer confined to the very circumscribed gender roles that once anchored them to the home. Likewise, men who choose to spend more time in the home raising their children do not face the level of scorn that they might have in the past. On the other hand, this degree of choice has a dark side, especially when it involves the disruption of families and instability for young children and adolescents. Children living with single parents fare worse by a number of measures (e.g., educational attainment, delinquency) than children living in stable two-parent households. Growing economic inequality today contributes to, and is in turn exacerbated by, changing family living arrangements, such as less-educated men and women being less likely to marry and stay married than highly educated men and women, which serves to reinforce their disadvantaged socioeconomic position. Single parents are also considerably more likely to be poor, given that they often have to rely on only one income and often struggle to obtain affordable child care for their children. Poverty rates among single parents are particularly high in the United States, where government benefits tend to be less generous than in many other wealthy countries.

Americans therefore generally view these changes in family living arrangements with some ambivalence. Many conservative commentators are alarmed by these trends and seek to reinforce traditional values. For the most part, however, people cherish this liberty and their own pursuit of self-actualization. This move toward greater individualism is increasingly characteristic of most modern, wealthy countries, and so the growing diversity of family living arrangements is unlikely to reverse any time soon.

3 Gender Inequality

The last fifty years have been marked by profound changes in people's views on gender norms and patterns of gender inequality. The women's rights movement and accompanying social changes have significantly reduced women's disadvantage in the labor force and other arenas. The changes have been so deep that some commentators have questioned whether current trends portend a reversal in patterns of gender inequality, leaving men at a distinct disadvantage. Hanna Rosin argues: "For much of history, the mark of an enviable woman has been her ability to secure a superior match, through her beauty, cleverness, or artful deception. After civil rights, that expectation mellowed into something called 'homogamy,' meaning women marrying men of equal money and education. But that happy place of equilibrium seems to be fading as well. Instead, women have started doing something demographers thought they would never see: they are marrying down, not just in the United States but all over the world."[1]

The reason women are marrying down, according to Rosin, is that they are now often outearning their male peers and thus need to settle for spouses with lower salaries. However, others are not so sure that the evidence supporting the ascendancy of women and the decline of male power in society is that compelling. As Stephanie Coontz, a scholar of the family and gender, has argued: "How is it, then, that men still control the most important industries, especially technology, occupy most of the positions on the lists of the richest Americans, and continue to make more money than women who have similar skills and education? And why do women make up only 17 percent of Congress?"[2]

This chapter takes a look at the role of gender today from a sociological point of view. Sociology is the study of how social structure affects our everyday life. Some of these structures are so ingrained in us that we take them for granted. We often assume that things are the way they are simply because they are "natural." However, anthropologists have long noted that what is natural and commonplace in one society seems unnatural and positively puzzling in another. Gender is one such social construction that we often take for granted. As sociologist Judith Lorber has written:

> Gender is so pervasive that in our society we assume it is bred into our genes. Most people find it hard to believe that gender is constantly created and re-created out of human interaction, out of social life, and is the texture and order of that social life.... For the individual, gender construction starts with assignment to a sex category on the basis of what the genitalia look like at birth. Then babies are dressed or adorned in a way that displays the category because parents don't want to be constantly asked whether their baby is a girl or a boy.... Once a child's gender is evident, others treat those in one gender differently from those in the other, and the children respond to the different treatment by feeling different and behaving differently.[3]

Much of what we do is gendered. Boys and girls in school typically have same-sex friends and often role-play games following social norms. Toy stores reinforce this; they are full of toys that are distinctly for boys (action figures) and others that are clearly targeted at girls (dolls and accessories). Gender stereotypes are also perpetuated in the media, as male characters are more likely to act aggressively and be leaders, and females are more likely to be cast in the role of caregivers.[4] Parenting is gendered, with mothers usually playing the leading role in child raising. Housework is gendered, such as with "outdoor" work assigned to men (lawn mowing) and indoor work to women (cooking). Jobs and careers are gendered— construction jobs are still overwhelmingly filled by men, and receptionists are still much more likely to be women. Caregiving for sick family members is gendered, with women more typically caring for aged parents.

However, gender norms, at least in Western countries, are generally more fluid these days than they used to be. A generation ago, a husband taking care of the children while his wife worked would have been a striking oddity and perhaps an object of derision. Today, women can be soldiers, and men can be nurses. Many would argue that women can be smart and tough, and men can be expressive and emotional and still fall within the socially acceptable bounds of femininity and masculinity. The increasing emphasis on individualism and self-actualization discussed in chapter 2 has released people from the tyranny of very tightly bound gender norms. This has led to a withering of gender inequality in the United States and other wealthy, modern countries around the world.

Or has it? How much have gender norms and gender inequality in American society really changed? Are men and women now just about on equal footing? These are the central questions guiding the rest of this chapter. What follows is a review of the evidence on gender inequality in education, labor force attachment and occupations, and earnings. I explore patterns and trends in gender inequality in other countries as well. I evaluate arguments about the rise of women and the decline of men and discuss emerging patterns of gender inequality in American society today.

TRADITIONAL DIVISION OF LABOR IN THE HOUSEHOLD

Conventional wisdom used to hold that differences between men and women, including the division of labor between the two, were rooted in biological differences. For example, researchers writing in the 1960s documented how among some primates the male is dominant and aggressive, extrapolating that humans are much the same. However, others have shown that significant variation occurs in primate social systems, in which females of many species are "fiercely competitive, resourceful and independent, sexually assertive and promiscuous and, in some cases, more prone than males to wanderlust at puberty."[5]

While it would be wrong to say that there are no meaningful biological differences between men and women that can affect their behavior, biological predispositions are strongly affected by social influences and the culture in which individuals are embedded. The goal here is not to definitively determine to what extent biology affects the behavior of boys and girls and men and women, but rather to discuss the role of social constructions of gender in shaping normative behavior and in particular how such norms have changed over time.

Societies today vary considerably in their level of *patriarchy*, or the systematic dominance of males over females. In several countries in the Middle East and South Asia, women who have committed adultery or have had premarital sex are in some cases killed by their father, brothers, or husbands as a way to protect the family's honor.[6] The practice of purdah in many such societies, or the concealing of women from men, is viewed by many as an institutional method of subordinating women and signals their subjugation (though individual women sometimes choose to wear some kind of covering, such as a *hijab*, for varying personal, cultural, or political reasons).[7] Gender inequality is not confined to developing countries. In the United States into the 1960s and Japan into the 1970s (just to provide two examples), a woman could be legally fired from a job if she married or had children.[8] Thus, there is considerable variation in gender norms across countries that is not necessarily contingent on their level of development or wealth. The overall status of women in Thailand is fairly high; in most professions, in universities, and in the corporate sector, the occupational attainment of Thai women is higher than in most Western industrial nations, including the United States.[9]

Historically, patterns of gender inequality have been linked to changes in the family. As we've seen, in preindustrial America, men and women worked alongside each other in the home and around it, often specializing in particular activities. The husband was generally seen as the ultimate arbiter and decision maker. With industrialization and urbanization, men increasingly worked away from the home, and the home itself became the province of women, which created different economic spheres for the two. Many advocated for men to be paid a "family wage" that could support not only the husband but the wife and children as well. Henry Ford, for example, promoted paying a family wage to workers in his factories in the early 1900s in part as a way of keeping more women in the home with children.[10] Men's authority as head of the household was reinforced by the money they were responsible for earning to support the family. A significant amount of productive work in which women were engaged (e.g., taking care of the home, childrearing, caring for the sick and elderly, volunteer work) was at least implicitly not valued as highly as men's paid work.

It should be noted, however, that while this traditional family arrangement—the husband earning a family wage and the wife taking care of the home and children—was the cultural ideal, in lower-income families women still continued to work to help make ends meet. Single-parent families were not entirely anomalous either. For example, 9 percent of children lived in such families (mainly with a widowed mother) in 1900.[11] In the 1950s, before the women's rights movement, only about half of all families with children were in the traditional breadwinner/homemaker family model.[12]

Women's labor force participation increased through the twentieth century for several reasons. For one, as family sizes generally declined, less time and energy were needed to care for children and maintain a household. Technological changes, including the invention of time-saving household appliances such as vacuum cleaners, washing machines, refrigerators, dishwashers, and microwaves, all reduced the time needed for housekeeping and the need for a full-time homemaker. The availability of new consumer products and rising living standards may have also made earning money through paid labor more attractive to families.[13]

Changes in the economy, such as the increase in the number of white-collar versus blue-collar jobs, especially with the service sector generating more of the former, provided greater opportunity for women in the paid labor market. Similarly, the rise of women's earnings and the stagnation of men's earnings, especially in the second half of the twentieth century, provided greater impetus for women to work. Increasing divorce rates likewise led many women to gain job experience to prepare for the possibility of marital dissolution. In the social and cultural realm, changing ideas about gender norms made work for women more socially acceptable, including for mothers of young children. The feminist movement emphasized the importance of women having the ability to pursue independence and self-actualization on an equal footing with men, both in and outside the home.[14] The Civil Rights Act of 1964, along with other anti-discriminatory measures and affirmative action, expanded the opportunities open

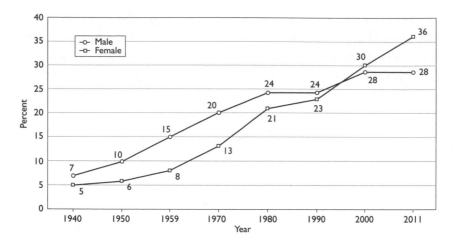

Figure 13. Percentage of 25- to 29-year-olds who completed four years of college or more, by gender, 1940–2011. Source: U.S. Census Bureau 2012f.

to women.[15] As a result, women today are better educated and are more likely to work, have higher-status jobs, and receive more in terms of wages than before.

EDUCATIONAL ATTAINMENT

An increasing number of Americans pursue a college degree. However, there are important differences in educational trends by gender. Figure 13 shows the percentage of 25- to 29-year-old men and women who have completed four or more years of college over the 1940 to 2011 period. Men were consistently more likely to be college graduates than women from 1940 to about 1990, when the two lines intersect. For example, in 1940, about 7 percent of young men had completed four or more years of college, compared with 5 percent of women. If anything, the male educational advantage grew larger, such that in 1959 the percentage of men (15 percent) who had completed four or more years of college was nearly double that of women (8 percent). By 1990, however, 24 percent of men and 23 percent of women had four or more years of college, after which women consistently achieved higher levels of educational attainment. In 2011, 36

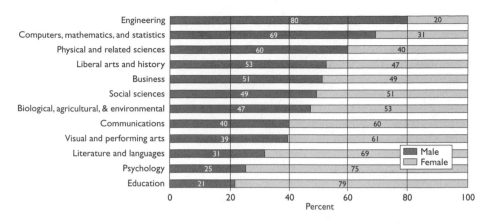

Figure 14. Gender distribution by field of study among 25- to 39-year-olds holding bachelor's degrees, 2009. Source: Siebens and Ryan 2012, table 2.

percent of young women, compared with just 28 percent of men, had finished four or more years of college.[16]

While more women are completing college than men, there are striking differences in the major fields of study chosen by gender (see figure 14). Among 25- to 39-year-olds surveyed in 2009, about 80 percent of engineering majors and 69 percent of majors in computers, mathematics, and statistics were men. In contrast, women were overwhelming concentrated in education (79 percent of education majors were women), psychology (75 percent), and literature and languages (69 percent). Although these differences are notable, the imbalances were even greater among respondents who were 65 years old and over (most of whom presumably finished their bachelor's degrees decades ago). Among this group, 97 percent of engineering majors were men, as were 83 percent of those majoring in physical and related sciences.[17] The choice of majors has implications for the types of jobs men and women have and hence gender differentials in earnings. For example, median annual earnings in 2011 for those with degrees in computers, mathematics, and statistics was $80,180, and for those in the physical sciences it was $80,037; in contrast, median earnings among those in education and psychology, both majors in which women are more highly represented, were $50,902 and $55,509, respectively.[18] Many argue that the "choice" of majors should not necessarily be

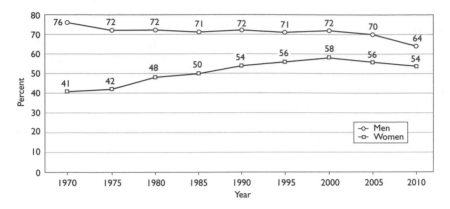

Figure 15. Percentage of the population age 16 years and older who are employed, by gender, 1970–2010. Source: U.S. Bureau of Labor Statistics 2011c, table 2.

viewed simply as an act of free will; choices are strongly influenced by others' expectations of what is socially acceptable for women and men and also by popular perceptions of their capabilities.[19]

Nevertheless, the increase in women's education has also translated into greater labor market participation. Whereas only 41 percent of women age 16 years and older were employed in 1970, by 2000 that figure had risen to 58 percent, before dipping somewhat to 54 percent in 2010 (see figure 15). Among women with children at home (which includes mainly women who are working age), the proportion who were in the labor force increased from just 47 percent in 1975 to 71 percent in 2007.[20] In contrast to the general upward trend in employment among women, the overall percentage of men age 16 and older who were employed declined slightly, from 76 percent in 1970 to 72 percent in 2000, before falling precipitously to 64 percent in 2010 in the wake of the 2007–9 Great Recession.[21] Thus, the gender employment gap has narrowed significantly in recent decades.

OCCUPATIONAL SEGREGATION

The gender employment gap has narrowed, but to what extent do men and women still have different kinds of jobs? Through most of the twentieth

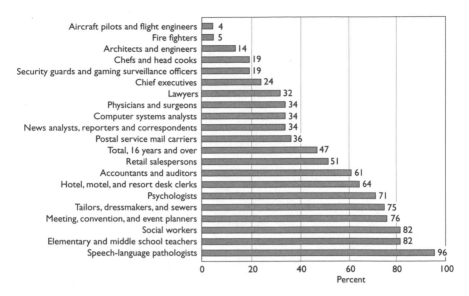

Figure 16. Women as a percentage of the total number employed in selected occupations, 2011. Source: U.S. Bureau of Labor Statistics 2012c.

century men and women were concentrated in very different occupations. At times, men actively resisted the entry of women into highly paid "male" jobs, and informal job networks reinforced the gender divide in the workplace. Differences in educational majors also contributed to occupational segregation, many of which persist today. Figure 16 shows that women constitute an overwhelming percentage (over 80 percent) of schoolteachers, social workers, and speech-language pathologists. They are also very highly represented among meeting and event planners and psychologists. At the other extreme, only 4 to 5 percent of firefighters and aircraft pilots and flight engineers are women, as are just 14 percent of architects and engineers. About three-quarters of chief executives are men. Thus, many of the jobs women occupy require a relatively high level of education (a BA or more) but are not known for paying all that well (such as social workers and teachers) for that level of education.

The extent to which men and women are clustered in different occupations has declined over time, though the pace of this decline has slowed in recent years. Figure 17 illustrates the slow of the downward trend using a

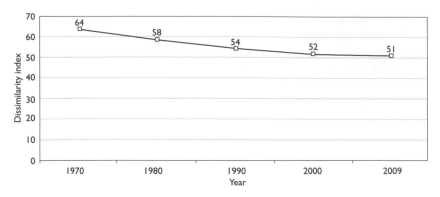

Figure 17. Occupational segregation, by gender, 1970–2009. Source: Blau, Brummund, and Yung-Hsu Liu 2012, table 3.

summary indicator called the segregation (or dissimilarity) index. This measures the proportion of women or men who would have to change occupations for the occupational distribution of the genders to be the same. The index stood at 64 in 1970, before declining to 54 in 1990. By 2009 it had inched down to 51. The decline was driven much more by women entering what had been male-dominated occupations—mainly white-collar and service jobs—than by men moving into predominantly female ones. More specifically, women have been increasingly likely over time to be employed as management, business, financial, and other professionals, including as lawyers, physicians, and veterinarians.[22] As a result, professional occupations have become less segregated over time, whereas working-class jobs have retained their higher levels of occupational segregation. White middle-class women have benefited most from these changes.[23]

It is not clear if, in the future, men will move into predominantly female occupations, particularly since such jobs continue to pay less than jobs in male-dominated occupations with similar educational requirements (though men in women's occupations typically are paid better than women).[24] Future changes in the labor market may help determine whether men will enter traditionally female occupations. For example, the extent to which manufacturing and other blue-collar jobs continue to disappear may determine if men will increasingly look for jobs in other sectors. Also of critical importance is the extent to which different choices become culturally less gendered, thus permitting both women and men to consider a broader range of opportunities with little social penalty and greater family and spousal support.[25]

EARNINGS INEQUALITY

As we've seen, gender inequality extends to differences in earnings. Figure 18 shows the change in the female-to-male ratio of earnings since 1960. It relies upon a common indicator of the gender wage gap—women's median annual earnings as a percentage of men's among full-time, year-round workers. While the ratio of earnings did not budge (remaining at close to 60 percent) over the 1960 to 1980 period, it finally began to increase thereafter. By 2011 women earned 77 percent of what men earned.[26] It is important to note that some of the narrowing of the wage gap was a function of the decline or stagnation in men's wages rather than just the increase in women's earnings.[27] Some of the earnings gap is explained by occupational segregation and the tendency for women's work, such as care work, to be devalued.[28] However, women tend to earn less than men even within the same occupational categories. For example, among elementary and middle school teachers, waiters, and chief executives, women earn, respectively, 91 percent, 77 percent, and 69 percent of what men earn, even when only full-time workers are considered.[29]

So why does the gap persist? In contrast to the gap caused by the blatant and broad-based gender discrimination that occurred in the past, the gap today is probably best explained by gender socialization and women's resulting weaker attachment to the labor market, as well as continued discrimination faced by mothers in particular. A greater percentage of women than men still tend to leave the labor force for childbirth, child care, and elder care. As of 2009, about a quarter of married-couple households with children still had a stay-at-home mother (down from 44 percent in 1969), though fewer than 10 percent of mothers stay at home until their oldest child hits the age of twelve.[30] Stay-at-home dads have until recently been viewed as oddities, and this arrangement is still relatively rare. Exiting the labor force or even working part-time, especially if it is for an extended period of time, leads to a lower accumulation of human

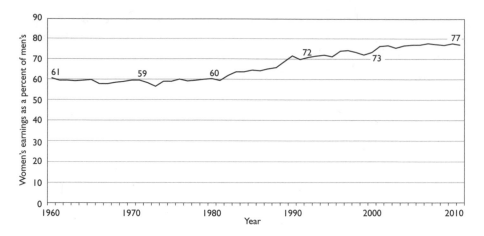

Figure 18. Women's median annual earnings as a percentage of men's earnings for full-time, year-round workers, 1960–2011. Source: U.S. Census Bureau 2012m.

capital (job-related skills) and hence lower pay, which affects women disproportionately. Similarly, working mothers tend to value workplaces that have "family-friendly" policies; many of these offer less pay, if perhaps better fringe benefits. One study estimated that once many of these factors (such as accumulated human capital and differences in occupations) are taken into account, the gender wage gap is reduced to between 4.8 and 7.1 percent, rather than about 20 percent.[31]

The wage penalty among low-income mothers in particular is not attributable to lost human capital alone; it is also strongly suggestive of continued discrimination and other barriers to work.[32] Some argue that women still have to strike a delicate balance between femininity and assertiveness in male-dominated environments. Women, for example, have had a notoriously difficult time making inroads into high-paying jobs on Wall Street.[33] Informal job networks and mentoring opportunities may still favor men, and women may be stereotyped as having a low commitment to work and be put on a "mommy track" that keeps them from moving into higher management positions as quickly as men.[34]

Sheryl Sandberg, who has served as the chief operating officer of Facebook, has attributed the gender gap in part to chauvinism and corporate obstacles and in part to socialization early in life that results in women not pursuing economic opportunities as aggressively as men. "We internalize the negative messages we get throughout our lives, the messages that say it's wrong to be outspoken, aggressive, more powerful than men. We lower our own expectations of what we can achieve. We continue to do the majority of the housework and child care. We compromise our career goals to make room for partners and children who may not even exist yet."[35] Others stress that in addition to women choosing to leave the workplace, they also feel pushed out by inflexible workplace environments that are inhospitable to working moms that seek some balance between work and home.[36]

It is important to note that the gender wage gap is smaller among younger workers. For example, one study found that women 16 to 34 years old make somewhere between 91 and 95 percent of what men make, even without taking into account the wide array of factors (e.g., differences in occupations) described above. In contrast, women above 35 years old earn between 75 and 80 percent of similarly aged men.[37] A growing number of women are remaining employed steadily throughout their young adulthood, and this contributes to wage parity. Some of the movement toward gender equality has thus been the result of a gradual process of "cohort replacement," in which younger women are taking on new roles and earning more in the labor market than their mothers. In recent years women have been more likely than in the past to find good jobs, with opportunities for advancement, and to experience social support from their spouses and significant others for their continued employment.[38]

The role of socialization and gendered behavior is also reflected in the differing amounts of housework men and women do. In 2009–10, married women ages 25 to 64 reported doing on average 18 hours of housework per week. This is considerably higher than the 10 hours reported by married men in the same age range (see figure 19). Notably, the gap in housework has narrowed over time, though it has changed little since the 1990s. In 1965, married women reported doing 34 hours of housework, compared with only 5 hours among men. The narrowing of the gap is partly accounted for by an increase in housework reported by men and, more important, a sharp decline in housework being done by women. This decline reflects mainly the increase in the number of hours women have come to spend in the paid labor force. Interestingly, both men and women

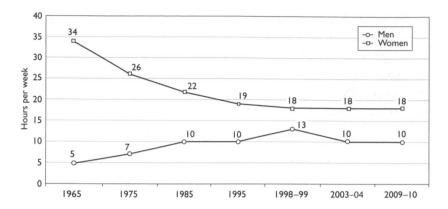

Figure 19. Trends in average weekly housework hours, by gender, among married women and men of ages 25 to 64, 1965–2010. Source: Bianchi et al. 2012, table 1.

spent more time caring for their children in 2009–10 than in 1975, indicating that childrearing has become more time intensive than it was a generation ago, especially among middle-class families who have adopted the "concerted cultivation" model of raising children.[39] More specifically, the time spent caring for children rose from 7 hours to 14 hours among women and from 2 to 7 hours among men over the 1975–2010 period. Because men are more likely to be in the paid labor force than women, overall work hours (those spent both inside and outside the home) of men and women are quite similar.[40]

INTERNATIONAL COMPARISONS

How do patterns of gender inequality in the United States compare with those in other countries? Figures 20 and 21 show female employment rates and gender earnings gaps across mainly wealthy countries of the OECD. Figure 20 shows that employment rates of women of ages 25 to 64 in the United States (72 percent) is very close to the OECD average (71 percent). There is considerable variability across countries, with the highest employment rate in Iceland (86 percent) and the lowest rate in Turkey (28 percent). In terms of gender gaps in earnings, figure 21 shows that the

United States fares a little worse than average, with a 20 percent gender gap among full-time workers, compared with the OECD average of 16 percent. Again, we see significant variation, with the gap as high as 39 percent in Korea and 28 percent in Japan to a low of 4 percent in Hungary and 8 percent in New Zealand.

The World Economic Forum created the Global Gender Gap Index a number of years ago to track the magnitude and scope of gender disparities across a larger number of countries and indicators. Specifically, it measures gender gaps in economic, political, educational, and health dimensions in 135 countries. It takes into account measures such as the ratio of women to men in earned income, the ratio of women to men with high levels of education, the ratio of women's to men's life expectancy, and the ratio of women to men in parliamentary positions, to name a few indicators. In 2012, Iceland ranked first among the 135 countries, indicating that it had the smallest gender gap. The Scandinavian countries of Finland, Norway, and Sweden (which have a reputation for being particularly egalitarian across many social and economic dimensions) occupied the second through fourth ranks. The United States ranked 22nd overall, slightly behind countries such as the United Kingdom and Canada and ahead of others such as Australia and Spain.[41]

The United States fared quite well on some specific indicators, such as women's estimated earned income (ranked 4th, in large part reflecting high overall standards of living in the United States) and numbers of legislators, senior officials, and managers (10th); rather moderate on others, such as female representation among professional and technical workers (30th), female labor force participation (43rd), and wage equality (61st); and poor on yet others, including women represented in Parliament/ Congress (78th) and number of years with a female head of state (the United States ranks last with dozens of other countries that have never had a female head of state).[42] The United States therefore has a moderate record on gender inequality overall when compared with other countries.

Honing in on one comparative aspect of gender inequality— employment—some scholars hold that in most Western countries the norm is that both women and men work. Married men with children in particular display nearly universally high employment rates. What varies more across these countries is the extent to which *women with children*

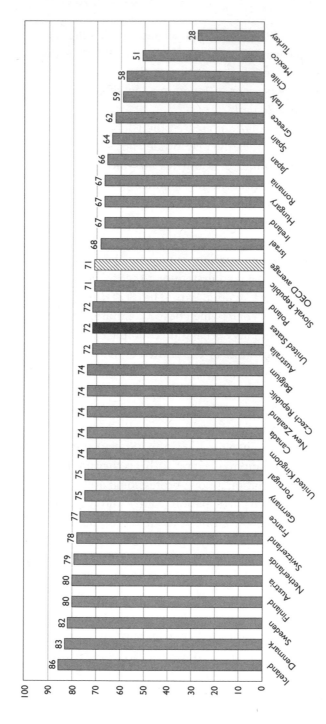

Figure 20. Percentage of women of ages 25 to 54 who are employed in selected OECD countries, 2009. Source: OECD 2012, table LMF1.2.

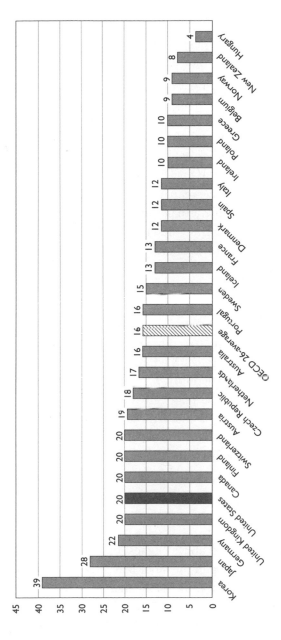

Figure 21. Percentage of difference in the median earnings of men and women among full-time employees in selected OECD countries, 2009. Source: OECD 2012, table LMF1.5.

work; this pattern is indicative of the extent to which raising children remains a gendered activity and the availability of resources that support work among parents with children. In some European countries, including Italy and Spain, a large percentage of women do not work at all; in others, such as Sweden, few mothers do not work, but a high percentage work part-time. The United States falls somewhere between these two models, as a significant percentage of mothers in the United States do not work, but a fairly high proportion work full-time.[43]

Researchers find that countries' governmental work-family policies play a role in shaping women's work patterns. Some policies seem to boost work among mothers, such as those that facilitate access to child care by subsidizing it. Parental leave policies can have a mixed effect on female employment: short- and moderate-length parental leaves can help parents remain attached to the labor force immediately after the birth of their children, whereas very long parental leaves may be used to ease women out of the labor market or perhaps to reinforce "mommy tracks." The United States is one of the very few countries in the world that does not provide paid time off for new parents. Current policy in the United States (as specified in the Family and Medical Leave Act of 1993) is that all public agencies and private companies with 50 or more employees must provide 12 weeks of unpaid leave to parents. In contrast, in the United Kingdom, for example, all female employees are entitled to 52 weeks of maternity leave, 39 weeks of which are paid. The relatively ungenerous policy in the United States may serve to strain parents and keep them attached to the labor market, but the difficulty that many parents continue to have in finding affordable child care is likely serving to depress parental employment.[44]

EMERGING TRENDS REVISITED: MEN IN DECLINE?

Many of the trends outlined above suggest that we will continue to see a narrowing of the gender gap in the labor market. In fact, some education, employment, and earnings trends among men in particular are alarming. For example, over the 1969 to 2009 period, the proportion of men of ages 25 to 64 who were not working increased by 11.8 percentage points (from approximately 6 percent to 18 percent), and most of this change is not a function of men staying at home and taking care of kids. Among high school dropouts, the increase in those not employed was 23 percentage points (from 11 to 34 percent).[45] In contrast to the trend among women, only college-educated men have seen their earnings rise over the past three decades. Among male high school dropouts, median weekly earnings plummeted by 38 percent.

Women now make up half the workforce. They also earn 58 percent of all bachelor's degrees awarded in the United States, as well as 59 percent of master's degrees and about half of the doctoral degrees. Women are likewise awarded about half of law and medical degrees. The general educational advantage among women occurs among all racial and ethnic groups but is largest among blacks, among whom, for example, women earn 66 percent of all bachelor's degrees awarded.[46] Whereas in 1987, 24 percent of wives of all ethnicities earned more than their husbands, by 2011 this figure had risen to 38 percent.[47] These trends strongly suggest that women's relative economic position will rise in the coming years.

Those who believe that the day is near when women will surpass men offer different arguments to explain this startling reversal. Columnist David Brooks argues, "To succeed today [given the kinds of jobs that are available], you have to be able to sit still and focus attention in school at an early age. You have to be emotionally sensitive and aware of context. You have to communicate smoothly. For genetic and cultural reasons, many men stink at these tasks."[48] Brooks also gives credence to Hanna Rosin's related theory on these trends, which emphasizes that women are facing changes in the labor markets with more adaptability, largely because of their historically disadvantaged position within it, while men are clinging to the old order. As she puts it:

> While millions of manufacturing jobs have been lost over the last decade, jobs in health, education and services have been added in about the same numbers. The job categories projected to grow over the next decade include nursing, home health care and child care. Of the 15 categories projected to grow the fastest by 2016—among them sales, teaching, accounting, custodial services and customer service—12 are dominated by women. These are not necessarily the most desirable or highest-paying jobs. But they do provide a reliable source of employment and a ladder up to the middle class.
>
> In Alexander City [Alabama], while the men were struggling, women either continued on with their work or found new jobs as teachers, secretaries

or nurses or in the service industry. . . . More important than the particular jobs available, which are always in flux, is a person's willingness to adapt to a changing economy. These days that usually requires going to college or getting some job retraining, which women are generally more willing to do. Two-thirds of the students at the local community college are women, which is fairly typical of the gender breakdown in community colleges throughout the country.[49]

Rosin tells the stories of several couples, including Charles and Sara Beth, now in their fifties, living in Alabama where many construction and manufacturing jobs have disappeared over the years. Charles had worked in a textile plant as a manager making a considerable salary before employment at the company withered; he left at one point to try to start his own business, though without much success. Meanwhile, Sara Beth, who started as a nurse, ended up becoming an executive at a large medical center. In Rosin's interview with Charles, he remarks on his wife's achievements: "I know what you're asking. How does it feel to go from being the major breadwinner to the secondary breadwinner? It used to bug me, but now I've gotten used to it"—in part because he wasn't the only person in town in that situation.[50]

Not everyone is so optimistic that gender equality is on the immediate horizon. After all, many of the jobs in growing, traditionally female sectors, such as care work, do not pay all that well.[51] In response to a number of books and articles that have predicted the rise of women and decline of men, Stephanie Coontz has argued:

> These books and the cultural anxiety they represent reflect, but exaggerate, a transformation in the distribution of power over the past half-century. Fifty years ago, every male American was entitled to what the sociologist R. W. Connell called a "patriarchal dividend"—a lifelong affirmative-action program for men. The size of that dividend varied according to race and class, but all men could count on women's being excluded from the most desirable jobs and promotions in their line of work, so the average male high school graduate earned more than the average female college graduate working the same hours. At home, the patriarchal dividend gave husbands the right to decide where the family would live and to make unilateral financial decisions. Male privilege even trumped female consent to sex, so marital rape was not a crime. The curtailment of such male entitlements and the expansion of women's legal and economic rights have transformed American life, but they have hardly produced a matriarchy.[52]

Coontz goes on to point out that women's wages have grown faster than men's, but mainly because discrimination had held them down for so long. What she argues, and my review of the evidence also indicates, is that we are seeing a convergence in economic fortunes and not necessarily the ascendancy of women. Young women are probably in no worse shape when entering the labor market than young men; one study, for example, showed that median full-time income for young, single, childless women is 107 percent of their male counterparts in the largest metropolitan areas.[53] However, once we take into account educational and other differences between men and women, men remain at an advantage within and across most occupations. Gender norms about who should care for children and the elderly still influence behavior and serve to weaken women's labor force attachment over the course of their lives. As researchers Joan C. Williams and Nancy Segal put it, "We all know about the glass ceiling. But many women never get near it; they are stopped long before by the maternal wall." Thus, while the wages of young women without children are close to young men's, the wages of mothers are roughly 60 percent of those of fathers, in part because some have observed a fatherhood "bump" in wages—fathers have higher earnings than seemingly similar men without children.[54] Women have many more choices than they used to, but cultural expectations still tend to funnel women into caregiving much more often than men. How much this will continue remains to be seen.

Some recent research suggests that fathers now report higher levels of work-family conflict than mothers do. Men still work more hours a week than women do, and with changing norms many feel that they should or would like to spend more time with their children. As Joan Williams, a researcher of these issues, put it, "Men face as many struggles when it comes to using flexible work policies—if not more—because child care, fairly or unfairly, is still seen as a feminine role."[55]

CONCLUSION

American society has traditionally been patriarchal. In the past this has manifested in a number of ways, such as unequal educational opportunities for women, lower rates of female participation in the paid labor force, and lower earnings for women than men. Men have historically excluded women from many kinds of jobs and limited women's social roles more generally. Labor market discrimination is a manifestation of unequal power. First, discrimination occurs when men are paid more than women for the same work. Second, discrimination contributes to occupational gender segregation, when men and women are highly concentrated in different types of jobs. The result is that women's work is typically accorded both lower status and lower earnings than occupations with high concentrations of men.[56] Inequality in the labor market may also result from common social practices or discrimination prior to a person's entrance into the labor market, such as in the education system or in the family. For example, girls have traditionally been socialized into family-oriented roles, while boys and young men have been expected to build careers that pay enough to support a family.[57]

Gender norms have changed, however. The women's rights movement, which took flight in the 1960s, pressed for more equal treatment in the workplace, such as in the form of equal pay for equal work, and for the easing of gender norms that limited women's opportunities in society at large. Until that time, women were rarely in positions of power—be it in private business or in politics—nor were they represented among a wide range of professionals, such as lawyers, judges, doctors, professors, and scientists. For a while, progress in reducing inequalities seemed slow. However, by the 1970s and 1980s there were clear indications that women's educational attainment was rising, women were entering new occupations, and the gender earning gap was beginning to narrow.

By some measures, progress has slowed in recent years. There have been relatively small changes in occupational segregation by gender, and there is a persistent earnings gap, even among full-time workers. By other measures, however, women continue to do very well, as they now handily surpass men in educational attainment. Job growth is greatest in jobs in which women are currently concentrated. However, women are still much more likely to be caregivers to both children and sick family members and aged parents. This has resulted in women's weaker attachment to the labor force, which in turn has translated into lower lifetime earnings. The extent to which gender norms continue to become more egalitarian in the coming years will likely determine the future level of gender inequality in the labor market.

4 Economic Well-Being

The growth of the U.S. economy over the long haul has been exceptional. This growth has been accompanied by rising living standards—meaning that children could generally expect to earn more, in real terms, than their parents. Increasing standards of living have also been accompanied by the widespread dissemination of wondrous household appliances and consumer products, including—over just the last hundred years or so—automobiles, radios, televisions, dishwashers, microwave ovens, personal computers, smart phones, and tablets. The health of the population has also improved, and life expectancies have grown longer. Far fewer people in the United States die of disease or abject poverty today than a century ago.

This general pattern of economic growth has been accompanied by considerable volatility. Recurring booms and busts are a central feature of capitalism and, therefore, of the American economy. The Great Depression of the 1930s represented perhaps the most serious downturn: lasting about ten years, and with unemployment reaching as high as 25 percent, it produced considerable hardship and poverty across the country. Many people's faith in the laissez-faire economic system was shaken, leading a substantial majority of Americans to support Franklin Delano Roosevelt's vigorous attempts, in the form of his New Deal programs, to moderate the system's excesses. These efforts yielded the creation of regulatory structures like the Securities and Exchange Commission and the introduction of many crucial elements of the social safety net still in existence today, such as Social Security, welfare, and federally funded unemployment insurance. Nevertheless, the sustained sluggishness of the economy led some at the time to believe that the country had reached the end of economic growth and rising living standards. Commenting on the popular mood in the depths of the Depression, historian David Kennedy writes:

> But the worm of doubt about the New Deal's effectiveness and even its ultimate purposes also began to gnaw at others, including liberals. As 1935 opened, some ten million persons, more than 20 percent of the work force, still remained jobless. The country seemed to flounder, without a workable remedy to the afflictions from which it had been suffering now for half a decade. . . . In a summary report to Hopkins [a Roosevelt adviser] on New Year's Day 1935, Hickok [an American journalist] rehearsed her worries about a "stranded generation": men over forty with halfgrown families, people who might never get their jobs back.[1]

The Great Recession of 2007–9, while not nearly as severe as the Great Depression (unemployment reached a high of 10 percent during the recession), was nevertheless the gravest economic downturn over the nearly seventy intervening years. It was longer than previous recessions, the unemployment rate rose more sharply, and the pace of recovery was slower than after most previous ones.[2] Relatively high and persistent unemployment, stagnant wages, and growing income inequality again led many to question whether broadly shared economic prosperity was a thing of the past. For example, one news story from 2013, which echoes the picture seventy-five years earlier, reported:

> Five years after the start of the Great Recession, the toll is terrifyingly clear: Millions of middle-class jobs have been lost in developed countries the world over. And the situation is even worse than it appears. Most of the jobs will never return, and millions more are likely to vanish as well, say experts who study the labor market. . . . They're being obliterated by technology. Year after year, the software that runs computers and an array of other machines and devices becomes more sophisticated and powerful and capable of doing more efficiently tasks that humans have always done. For decades, science fiction warned of a future when we would be architects of our

own obsolescence, replaced by our machines; an Associated Press analysis finds that the future has arrived.[3]

Has our prophesied decline finally arrived? How entrenched is slow growth and rising inequality and poverty? What explains current trends in inequality? Is inequality even necessarily a bad thing for our economy? These are the questions I address in this chapter. I begin with a brief historical review of economic trends in the United States. I then track recent changes in economic growth, income inequality, and poverty and discuss the forces that help explain these patterns. I compare U.S. trends with those in other wealthy countries and end with a discussion of the overall effect of inequality on individuals and society.

RISING LIVING STANDARDS

The U.S. economy has generally grown briskly over time. Economic growth and rising living standards are a function of forces that boost productivity: mainly continued human and capital investment and technological improvements. Agricultural production, for example, is far more efficient today than it used to be as a result of plant breeding, pesticides, fertilizers, and modern farm equipment. Manufacturing is likewise becoming increasingly efficient. As one newspaper article describing changes in high-tech industries pointed out: "At the Philips Electronics factory on the coast of China, hundreds of workers use their hands and specialized tools to assemble electric shavers. That is the old way. At a sister factory here in the Dutch countryside, 128 robot arms do the same work with yoga-like flexibility. Video cameras guide them through feats well beyond the capability of the most dexterous human. . . . And they do it all without a coffee break—three shifts a day, 365 days a year."[4]

Greater economic productivity generally leads to higher standards of living because it lets workers produce more for the same amount of work. This means greater profit for owners and typically higher wages for workers. Figure 22 shows the pattern of per capita economic growth from 1790 to 2011 using a common indicator, the gross domestic product (GDP). GDP measures the market value of all goods and services produced in a

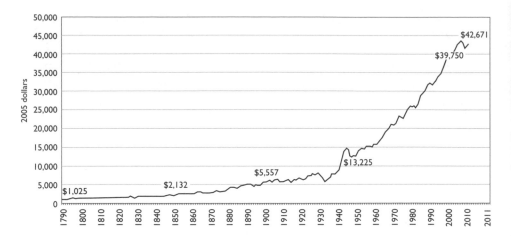

Figure 22. Real GDP per capita, 1790–2011 (in 2005 dollars). Source: Johnston and Williamson 2012.

country in a given period of time. Real GDP per capita rose from $1,025 in 1790 to $5,557 in 1900 to $42,671 in 2011 (in constant 2005 dollars). We see dips in GDP per capita during the Great Depression, the more recent Great Recession, and in other periodic economic downturns. Nevertheless, the overall upward slope is striking.

Increases in GDP per capita show up in other concrete ways as well. Whereas just over 10 percent of the population had toilets in their homes (i.e., indoor plumbing in general) in 1890, by 1970 inside toilets were pretty much universal. In 1900 virtually no one owned a car; by 1920, 25 percent of households had a car, by 1930 this figure was up to 50 percent, and today over 90 percent of American households own a car. Because of growing incomes, Americans today do not need to devote as great a proportion of their income to purchasing basic necessities such as food and instead now devote considerably more to recreational activities.[5] Growing standards of living are associated with improvements in health as well. The average life expectancy at birth in the United States rose from about 35 years in 1789, to 49 years in 1900, 64 years in 1940, and 79 years in 2010.[6] The U.S. population has likewise become more educated. Whereas in 1940 just one-quarter of the population of ages 25 and over had earned a high school diploma, and only 5 percent had four or more years of

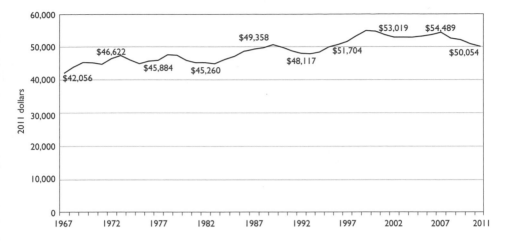

Figure 23. Median household income, 1967–2011 (in 2011 dollars). Source: U.S. Census Bureau 2012k.

college, by 2012, 88 percent of the population had completed high school, and 31 percent had four or more years of college.[7] Educational gains have in turn helped fuel economic productivity and growth.

Reflecting these trends, figure 23 shows the increase in household income over the past forty-five years. Median household income rose from $42,056 in 1967 to $49,358 in 1987, before reaching its peak of $54,932 in 1999. Median household income fell in the 2001 recession, much as it did in other recessions. However, unlike after past recessions, the economic recovery in the years after 2001 did little to boost the median household income. There was a further sharp drop in household incomes after the 2007–9 recession, and again incomes have yet to recover. Unfortunately, the 2000s stand out as the only decade during the period when household incomes did not rise. Increasing health care costs are putting a further dint to households' purchasing power, and the amount businesses spend on health care may be putting downward pressure on wages.[8]

Trends in poverty tell a fairly similar story: while poverty declined rapidly in the 1960s and into the early 1970s, it has mainly fluctuated with the business cycle since. The 2000s stand out as a decade with little respite from increasing poverty (see figure 24).[9] There is some disconnect between the trends shown in figure 22 (GDP per capita) and figures 23 and 24

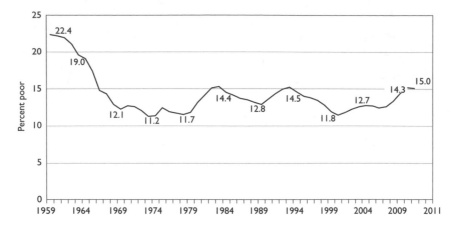

Figure 24. Poverty rates, 1959–2011. Source: DeNavas-Walt, Proctor, and Smith 2012, table B2.

(income and poverty): while all measures show a dip during recessions, the upward climb in GDP per capita, especially during the 2000s, occurred even while median household incomes were stagnant or declining and poverty for the most part increased. Thus, income and poverty have been less responsive to economic growth than in previous decades. One of the main culprits of this disconnect is the growing level of income inequality.[10]

GROWING INCOME INEQUALITY

Even though per capita GDP has risen over time, some Americans have benefited more from economic growth than others. Figure 25 shows the trend in family income by where families stood in the income distribution. Between 1947 and the late 1970s, families along all points of the income distribution experienced increases in income. For example, between 1947 and 1979, the income of families at the 20th percentile of the income distribution increased from $13,952 to $28,471 (in 2011 dollars). Thereafter, income at this percentile stagnated, such that by 2011 it stood at just $27,218. The increase in income is most striking for the top 5 percent of earners. Family income at the 95th percentile was $71,098 in 1947, before

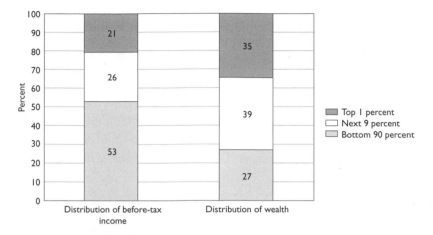

Figure 27. Distribution of income and wealth, 2007. Source: Stone, Trisi, and Sherman 2012, 12; original data from Wolff 2010.

people's net worth rose steeply between 2007 and 2010, as did the racial and ethnic disparity in wealth.[14]

There are a number of plausible explanations for why inequality has increased over the past few decades.[15] The most prominent include the increasing demand for high-skill workers due to technological changes; globalization and international trade; the decline in unionization; the rising salaries for people who are considered "superstars"; and changes in government policies that have favored the affluent. Regarding the first of these, some have argued that technological advancements since the 1970s have led to "skill-biased technological change" (SBTC), which calls upon workers to be increasingly familiar with computers or high-tech equipment and machinery. The increased demand for more-skilled workers drove up wages for people with higher levels of education during a time when demand for less-skilled workers, such as those employed in blue-collar manufacturing jobs, fell.[16]

Strong evidence for this perspective comes from the effects that education has on changing patterns of employment and wages. Labor force participation rates of college-educated men have held steady, while those of men with a high school diploma have declined. Women of all educational levels have experienced increases in work over the past three decades,

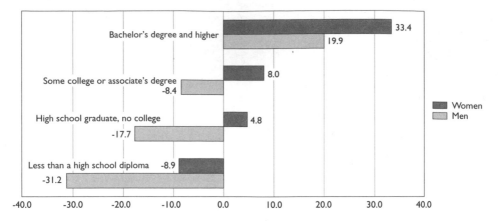

Figure 28. Percentage of change in median usual weekly earnings, by educational attainment and gender, between 1979 and 2010. Source: U.S. Bureau of Labor Statistics, 2011a, chart 3.

though increases were highest among the most educated women.[17] Meanwhile, while weekly wages among less-skilled men declined by 31 percent between 1979 and 2010, such earnings grew by 20 percent among men with a bachelor's degree or higher (see figure 28). Among women, high school dropouts also saw a decline in wages (9 percent), while those with a college education experienced a large increase (33 percent).[18] The importance of receiving a college degree has occurred during a time when the price of a college education has also increased significantly, making it more difficult for low-income students to attend college. Some argue that colleges could be doing more to meet increased consumer demand and expand the number of slots available to prospective students.[19]

Globalization and international trade may have contributed to growing wage inequality, as U.S. workers increasingly compete with workers around the world. Highly skilled U.S. workers often have a comparative advantage in the global economy because of the high quality of postsecondary education in the United States and because many multinational corporations are headquartered there. Conversely, less-skilled American workers are at a disadvantage given the lower production costs and wages in other parts of the globe. This has, at least in part, contributed to continued deindustrialization in the United States, which began in the second half of the twentieth century, when many manufacturing jobs were outsourced to lower-wage countries such as China and Mexico.[20]

One good example of this phenomenon is Apple computers, which employed 43,000 people in the United States and 20,000 overseas in 2012—a small fraction of the over 400,000 workers General Motors employed in the United States in the 1950s. An additional 700,000 people work for Apple's contractors, engineering, building, and assembling various Apple products such as iPhones and iPads, and nearly all of these jobs are staffed by foreign companies in Asia, Europe, and elsewhere overseas.[21] Apple has considerable company in this trend. Between 2001 and 2012, General Electric lost 37,000 American jobs and added 25,000 overseas (though some of the job losses are due to the sale of NBC to Comcast); likewise, Xerox, Boeing, and American Express also increased their overseas workforce during these years, in jobs ranging from manufacturing to call service centers.[22]

Outsourcing is not confined to large corporations either. As one news story reported:

> Philip Chigos and Mary Domenico are busy building a children's pajama business. They are refining patterns, picking fabrics and turning the basement of their two-bedroom apartment into an office. Then there is the critical step of finding the right seamstresses in China. Instead of looking for garment workers in this city, they plan to have their wares manufactured by low-cost workers overseas. In doing so, they've become micro-outsourcers, adopting a tactic of major American corporations, which are increasingly sending production work abroad. A growing number of mom-and-pop operations, outsourcing experts say, are braving a host of potential complications and turning to places like Sri Lanka, China, Mexico and Eastern Europe to make clothes, jewelry, trinkets and even software programs. "We'd love it to say 'made in the U.S.A.' and use American textiles and production," Mr. Chigos said of his product. But, he said, the cost of that would be 4 to 10 times what was planned. "We didn't want to sell our pajamas for $120."[23]

In addition to globalization, the decline of unions has also contributed to growing inequality in the United States over the past few decades. The proportion of the workforce that is unionized has been falling since the 1950s, and this decline accelerated after the mid-1970s.[24] Only 12 percent of workers were in unions in 2011, down from 29 percent in 1975.[25] Nonunionized workers typically are paid lower wages and have less job security.[26] There has been much debate on whether immigration has contributed to inequality, but studies on the whole suggest that immigration has served to depress the wages of native low-skill workers by only a small amount.[27]

The tax burden on high earners has also fallen over the past several decades, and the distributive effect of government transfers may have also declined. For example, proportionately the wealthy pay substantially less in taxes than they did a generation ago. The top individual tax rate was reduced from 70 percent at the start of Ronald Reagan's first term to a low of 28 percent by the end of his term in 1988. Through most of the 2000s, it was at 35 percent, and legislation in 2013 increased it to 39.6 percent. Estate taxes, dividend taxes, and capital gains taxes (all of these taxes are paid disproportionately by wealthy individuals) have also been reduced since 1980, whereas Social Security and Medicare taxes, which place a relatively larger burden on the middle class, have increased.[28] The distribution of government transfers has also shifted, moving away from low-income households. In 2007, households in the bottom income quintile received 35 percent of transfer payments, down from 50 percent in 1979.[29] Many growing programs, such as Social Security and Medicare, benefit middle-class Americans.

Several possible reasons account for the spectacular rise in the incomes of the top 1 percent. Some have noted the large increases in pay among corporate executives. The general increase in the size and complexity of businesses may have contributed to this. However, probably more important are changes in corporate governance that have allowed executives to essentially pay themselves more—at the expense of their workers—including with lucrative stock options. Board members who set the pay of CEOs often serve at the pleasure of the CEO, leading to an incentive to provide a high compensation package. As David Grusky and Kim Weeden write, the change in pay-setting practices "[is] rather like asking a professor's students to decide on the professor's pay in advance of receiving their grades. When the fox is guarding the henhouse, one has to believe that the fox's interests are better served than those of the hens."[30]

Some also argue that "superstars," such as actors, athletes, and musicians, make more than they used to, perhaps because globalization and rising living standards have increased consumer demand and the amount that people at successful enterprises can earn. Also more lawyers and financial professionals are in the top 1 percent than in the past, indicating that their specialized services have become increasingly valued and rewarded (in line with more general SBTC arguments above). Lastly, the growing importance of the financial sector in generating profits has led to large pay increases among those working in this sector. Deregulation may have helped increase these profits.[31] As one article noted, "After a down year in 2008, the top 25 hedge-fund managers were paid, on average, more than $1 billion each in 2009, quickly eclipsing the record they had set in pre-recession 2007."[32]

International Comparisons

How does the United States stack up when compared with other relatively wealthy countries? In some respects the United States looks good, but in others, not so good. Starting with a positive indicator, figure 29 shows that GDP per capita is higher in the United States than in most other countries in the OECD. Of the selected countries shown, the United States ranks third, with a GDP per capita of just over $48,000. Only the small, wealthy countries of Norway ($62,500) and Switzerland ($51,200) rank higher, and the overall OECD average is considerably lower, at $35,100. At the bottom of the list are the still developing countries of Mexico ($15,900), Chile ($17,300), and Turkey ($17,500).

However, while average standards of living are higher in the United States than in most other countries, as indicated by GDP per capita, the United States has higher levels of inequality than most other OECD countries. The Gini coefficient in the United States (as measured by the OECD), at 0.38, is higher than in all countries except Chile, Mexico, and Turkey, and it is well above the OECD average of 0.31. Three of the four countries with the lowest levels of income inequality are in northern Europe (Denmark, Norway, and Sweden)—countries with generous safety nets. Higher levels of U.S. inequality naturally translate into higher levels of relative poverty (see figure 30). These poverty rates are calculated by using poverty thresholds set to half of the median income in each respective country. (This means that the poverty threshold is higher in the United

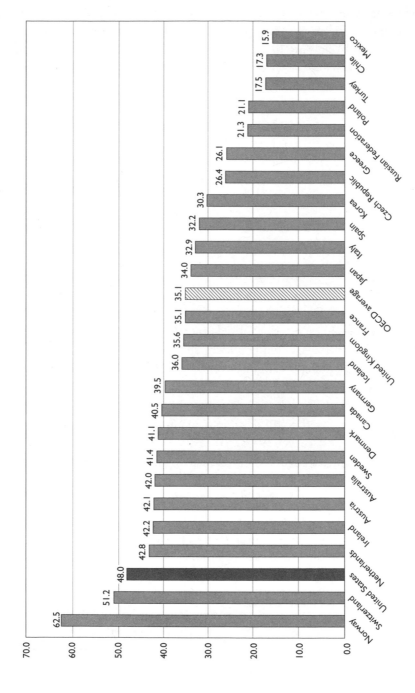

Figure 29. GDP per capita in selected OECD countries, 2011 (in 1,000s of $). Source: OECD 2013a.

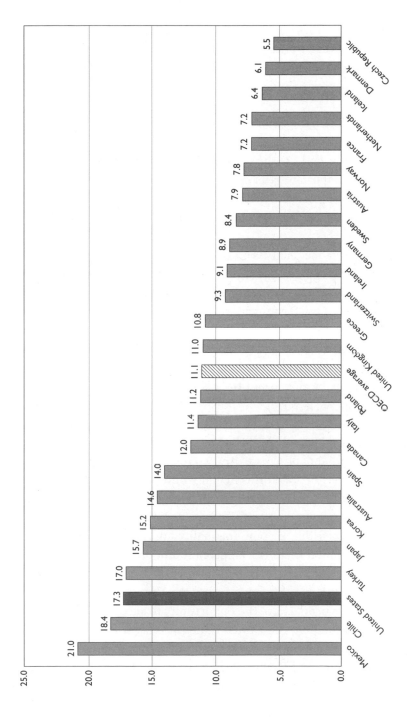

Figure 30. Relative poverty rates in selected OECD countries, late 2000s. Note: The relative poverty threshold used is equal to 50 percent of the median income in each country. Source: OECD 2013b.

States than, say, in Turkey, where the median income is much lower.) These poverty rates are, by design, sensitive to patterns of inequality. Here we see that the relative poverty rate in the United States (17.3 percent) is surpassed only by Mexico and Chile and is significantly above the OECD average (11.1 percent).

Factors that explain the variation in poverty rates across countries are: (1) the amount each devotes to income transfers, (2) how progressive the tax structure is, and (3) the equality in the distribution of earnings. The single most important reason that poverty is relatively high in the United States in particular is that income transfers in the United States are not as well targeted at low-income households as in most other countries.[33]

Notably, however, inequality is on the rise in most OECD countries. For example, household incomes among the top 10 percent of households grew by 1.9 percent annually on average from the mid-1980s to the late 2000s across twenty-seven OECD countries, substantially higher than the 1.3 percent annual growth rate among the bottom 10 percent of households. (The figures for the top and bottom 10 percent of households in the United States were 1.5 percent and 0.1 percent, respectively.) These increases have been driven mainly by changes in the distribution of wages and salaries, rather than changes in government transfers. Many of the forces driving up inequality in the United States discussed above (e.g., the growing importance of skill-biased technological change) are likely to have had the same impact in Europe and other wealthy countries where manufacturing employment has declined. Reforms in many European countries that loosened employer regulations—meant to spur job creation—may have also served to reduce wages at the low end of the income distribution.[34]

Some have argued that income inequality and poverty in themselves may not be troubling if there is a significant amount of opportunity and economic mobility in society. (This issue is discussed in more detail below.) One core American belief and value is that the United States is a vibrant meritocracy, where people have the opportunity to succeed with skill and hard work. Unfortunately, the United States also has lower levels of economic mobility than a number of other wealthy countries in Europe, such as Sweden, Germany, and Denmark. Economic mobility also seems particularly low for the low-income population in the United States.[35]

Among the factors that might explain the relative lack of mobility for the lowest-earnings quintile in the United States is the magnitude of income inequality and the depth of poverty in the country, which leaves poor children starting off well behind others. Inequality is in turn affected by tax policy and the strength of the social safety net.[36] Another explanation could be the high variation in educational quality (where students from poor families often do not have access to good schools) and student performance in the United States, combined with high economic returns to education (i.e., the increase in the positive correlation between education and earnings over time). Indeed, parental background plays a larger role in predicting how students do in the United States than in many other countries—perhaps because schools, which rely considerably on the local tax base, vary considerably across American communities.[37] Racial inequality in the United States and the greater incidence of single-parent families also play some role.[38]

The Great Recession

The Great Recession of 2007–9 was the deepest economic downturn since the Great Depression of the 1930s.[39] Overall, the nation's output (GDP) declined by 8 percent from the end of 2007 to mid-2009. Households lost one-quarter of their wealth over the two-year period, and a third of those losses were attributable to declining home values. (Homes are the most valuable asset for many families.) The nation's economy lost 8.5 million jobs, going from a peak of 138.1 million jobs in December 2007 to a low of 129.6 million jobs in February 2010. The unemployment rate peaked at 10.0 percent.[40]

The precipitating cause of the 2007–9 recession was the bursting of a large housing bubble. This shook the banking system, which then nearly brought all economic activity to a halt.[41] The crisis, however, had a number of other underlying causes, including rising inequality, the loosening of bank lending rules, and the rise of mortgage securitization with too little regulatory oversight. Rising inequality was an important factor, because rising per capita GDP in the 2000s meant that the affluent were enjoying increasing purchasing power even while much of the middle class was not. This helped produce debt-fueled housing consumption, as many households took out large mortgages or borrowed from their home equity.

Deregulation of the banking industry over the years led banks to offer riskier loans at high interest rates to people who could not afford them. The banks would then bundle and sell these mortgages as securities to investors—many of whom did not fully understand the risk associated with these investments. As a rising number of ordinary people defaulted on their home mortgage loans, the housing market collapsed and the value of the securities, and housing, plunged.[42] Banks stopped lending, many businesses went bankrupt, and a deep recession ensued.

In addition to rising unemployment, poverty increased, from 12.3 percent in 2006 to 15.0 percent in 2011, even with an increase in government spending (in the form of unemployment insurance payments, food assistance, and the economic stimulus, among other initiatives) that was aimed at boosting the economy and reducing hardship.[43] Food insecurity rose, and household wealth declined markedly. For example, households saw an average decline of 39 percent in their home equity from 2007 to 2009.[44]

These numbers translated into real hardship for people across the country. As one news story reported:

> The poor stayed poor and the rich got richer, but the middle slipped a few more rungs down the economic ladder. . . . For Ray Bober, 45, of Pittsburgh, whose unemployment benefits ran out this year after a family printing business failed several years ago, the dismal economy takes a toll every time he sends out another resume that goes nowhere. "You have to learn to roll with the punches and laugh a little; it's very depressing," he said. "It takes a toll, especially this long. You want to reach out and shake your fist in the air and blame someone, but you can't. The way it is, is the way it is. There's nothing you can do about it but stay in the fight."[45]

A story on the rise of part-time work after the recession provides another anecdote of the struggles many have continued to face, even years later:

> Some of these new, lower-paying jobs are being taken by people just entering the labor force, like recent high school and college graduates. Many, though, are being filled by older workers who lost more lucrative jobs in the recession and were forced to take something to scrape by.
>
> "I think I've been very resilient and resistant and optimistic, up until very recently," said Ellen Pinney, 56, who was dismissed from a $75,000-a-year job in which she managed procurement and supply for an electronics

company in March 2008. Since then, she has cobbled together a series of temporary jobs in retail and home health care and worked as a part-time receptionist for a beauty salon. She is now working as an unpaid intern for a construction company, putting together bids and business plans for green energy projects, and has moved in with her 86-year-old father in Forked River, N.J. "I really can't bear it anymore," she said, noting that her applications to places like PetSmart and Target had gone unanswered. "From every standpoint—my independence, my sense of purposefulness, my self-esteem, my life planning—this is just not what I was planning."[46]

Implications of Growing Inequality

The growth of income inequality and the long-term effects of the recession have had negative repercussions not only for individuals—many of whom lost jobs, experienced declining wages, lost a home through foreclosure, or faced a significant decrease in their wealth—but also for American society in general. In this section I review arguments about the broader effects of inequality on the economy.

There is some debate about whether inequality is always bad for society. On the one hand, some believe that some measure of inequality can spur people to work harder and be innovative in order to reap greater economic rewards. The profit motive is a basic feature of our market system that can boost the economy as a whole and lead to increases in standards of living for all. For many commentators, what is more important than income inequality is the potential for economic mobility. As long as individuals have the opportunity to work their way up the ladder and achieve success by their talent and hard work, then inequality is acceptable and perhaps even a necessary feature of the economy for helping generate growth. Indeed, the profit motive has likely helped spur the work of some of the most famous American industrialists and inventors. In the nineteenth century, Cornelius Vanderbilt rose from moderate means (his father owned a ferry in New York Harbor) to become a steamboat entrepreneur and then an industrialist who helped build a vast network of railroads across the country. In the early twentieth century, Henry Ford, son a farmer, revolutionized automobile production and made the car affordable for the middle class. Most Americans believe in the fundamental value of meritocracy and what it has meant for the rise of the nation.

Those who are less troubled by income inequality also express concern about policies that aim to reduce inequality, such as through taxation and government transfers, in that they may both dampen the incentive among potential job creators who face high marginal tax rates and foster dependency among people who may wish to rely on welfare benefits rather than income earned through work. Some argue that government spending can also crowd out private investment. The debate on these issues is far from settled, but the evidence from a number of studies confirms that some policies have served to dampen work incentives and economic growth. Most welfare states today thus try to design policies with this issue in mind, and so the debate is more about what conditions cause government spending to reduce long-term economic growth rather than spur it. Many argue that smart government investment and overall growth are compatible goals.[47]

Some observers have offered a number of general objections to inequality, emphasizing that inequality can reduce individual economic well-being, stifle mobility, and in fact hamper long-term growth. On the first of these issues, many have noted that subjective well-being has a relative component. When you are not doing as well as your neighbors, you feel less well off. Robert Frank, an economist and columnist, describes how more people would prefer to live in a 3,000-square-foot house when most other people have 2,000-square-foot houses, than to live in a 4,000-square-foot house when others have 6,000-square-foot houses.[48] This issue does not boil down simply to envy. It is more about fitting in and being able to participate in one's community. Frank relays the following account (by reporter Dirk Johnson) of a low-income student, Wendy, who attended school in an affluent neighborhood: "Watching classmates strut past in designer clothes, Wendy Williams sat silently on the yellow school bus, wearing a cheap belt and rummage-sale slacks. One boy stopped and yanked his thumb, demanding her seat. 'Move it, trailer girl,' he sneered."[49] In another community or in another country, Wendy would not have been considered poor and would not have been denigrated in this way, but in that prosperous community, she stood out.

Frank extends this basic observation by arguing that growing inequality and increased spending at the top of the income distribution have imposed both psychological and even real costs on the middle class. Middle-class families now must pay more in order to purchase housing that is adequate according to community standards, as the kinds of purchases made by those higher in the income distribution help define what is considered necessary and desirable. Indeed, the average size of houses grew 15 percent, to 2,277 square feet, in just ten years between 1997 and 2007.[50] Housing prices, in turn, grew at a steady clip during this time. And because public schools are financed by local property taxes, schools in wealthier neighborhoods are often better than those in poorer neighborhoods. Thus, even if parents did not care so much about the size or quality of their homes, they may still feel the need to purchase more expensive housing in a better neighborhood in the quest for a better education for their children.[51]

Barbara Ehrenreich has described how these processes have driven up housing prices for low-income Americans as well. For example, she reports that a trailer park in Key West (a generally affluent area) located close to hotel jobs was charging $862 a month (in 2011 dollars) for a half-size trailer, forcing lower-wage workers to search for housing farther away in cheaper areas. She argues, "Insofar as the poor have to work near the dwellings of the rich—as in the case of so many service and retail jobs—they are stuck with lengthy commutes or dauntingly expensive housing."[52]

Some have argued that high levels of inequality can also have negative social repercussions in the form of dampening overall economic growth. Economist Joseph Stiglitz, one of the proponents of this view, has offered four arguments. First, if inequality increases and the middle class shrinks, consumer demand suffers. Indeed, much of the strong economic growth in the United States in the twentieth century was fueled by the expansion of consumer markets, and as the demand for new products soared, so did technological innovation, productivity, and wages and benefits. Second, a smaller middle class means lower tax receipts, and hence lower government investment in infrastructure, education, research, and health. All of these investments can spur productivity and growth. Third, high inequality contributes to economic instability. High levels of inequality in developing countries in particular might foster political and social instability, which can lead to violence and economic rifts. Closer to home, income inequality was likely a factor in the housing bubble and subsequent economic bust, as inequality contributed to debt-fueled consumption. Fourth, high inequality means that many low-income people cannot invest in their future, such as by enrolling in college. This reduces individual mobility and overall economic growth, since growth depends on the productivity of a country's workers.[53]

The link between parental socioeconomic status and college attendance and completion remains strong. For example, among those born in the early 1980s, about 54 percent of people whose parents were in the top income quartile ended up completing college, compared with only 9 percent of those whose parents were in the lowest quartile.[54] Moreover, rates of college completion increased by 18 percentage points for children of high-income families born in the 1980s relative to those born in the early 1960s, but only by 4 percentage points among children of low-income families over the same period. In short, the rising cost of college, in real terms, has made pursuing a higher education more difficult than in the past.

One feature story of three young women growing up in south Texas illustrates the challenges many students face:

> Low-income strivers face uphill climbs, especially at Ball High School, where a third of the girls' class failed to graduate on schedule. But by the time the triplets [the three good friends] donned mortarboards in the class of 2008, their story seemed to validate the promise of education as the great equalizer.
>
> Angelica, a daughter of a struggling Mexican immigrant, was headed to Emory University. Bianca enrolled in community college, and Melissa left for Texas State University, President Lyndon B. Johnson's alma mater. "It felt like we were taking off, from one life to another," Melissa said. "It felt like, 'Here we go!'"
>
> Four years later, their story seems less like a tribute to upward mobility than a study of obstacles in an age of soaring economic inequality. Not one of them has a four-year degree. Only one is still studying full time, and two have crushing debts. Angelica, who left Emory owing more than $60,000, is a clerk in a Galveston furniture store.
>
> Each showed the ability to do college work, even excel at it. But the need to earn money brought one set of strains, campus alienation brought others, and ties to boyfriends not in school added complications. With little guidance from family or school officials, college became a leap that they braved without a safety net.[55]

The challenge of obtaining a college degree remains daunting, even as the importance of this kind of education has increased over the past thirty years. Thus, many would argue that we should prioritize reducing income inequality as a way to preserve our meritocracy, enhance economic mobility, and spur investment in future economic growth.

CONCLUSION

The United States has experienced a tremendous amount of economic growth over time. The population has become better educated and more productive, leading to impressive increases in our standards of living. Americans are much better housed, fed, and clothed than a century ago. They have at their disposal many consumer products that would have been unimaginable to their ancestors. Nevertheless, this growth has been punctuated by periods of economic instability and high unemployment, the most notable being the Great Depression of the 1930s, when unemployment reached a peak of 25 percent and the foundations of the entire market system seemed under siege. More recently, increasing inequality, the deep recession of the late 2000s, and the subsequent sluggish recovery have ushered in another period of gloom. Our economic history suggests that periods of economic growth interrupted by sometimes-painful decline will likely continue.

One issue of growing concern is the increase in income inequality since the 1970s. The incomes of middle- and low-income households have stagnated in recent years, even while those at the top have continued to grow; the incomes of the top 1 percent in particular have increased markedly. Levels of wealth inequality are even greater than income inequality, where the top 1 percent of the country owns over 35 percent of its wealth. Growing inequality has likely been propelled by a number of factors, including skill-biased technological change (SBTC), which has prompted a greater demand for workers with high levels of education and skill to fill the kinds of higher-tech jobs that are available. Globalization may have also contributed to growing wage inequality, as many manufacturing jobs—and increasingly other kinds of jobs—have been outsourced to places with lower labor costs, such as China, India, and Mexico. Highly skilled U.S. workers are still faring well because of the high quality of postsecondary education in the United States, along with the fact that many multinational corporations are headquartered in the United States. Declines in unionization, increases in the cost of college, changes in the tax code that have favored the wealthy, the rise of finance, and changes in corporate governance that have produced higher salaries for CEOs (at the expense of workers) may all have played a role in exacerbating inequality in recent years.

The United States has one of the highest GDPs per capita in the world, and it remains well above the average among OECD countries. Nevertheless, inequality is also more prevalent in the United States, indicating that it is a country with larger extremes of wealth and poverty than most of its peers. Economic mobility also appears to be no greater in the United States than in a number of other wealthy countries. It should be noted that increasing inequality is a challenge that most OECD countries are facing, since some of the forces that have increased inequality in the United States (such as globalization) are affecting many other nations as well.

Some argue that inequality is not necessarily a bad thing, because the profit motive of our market system provides an incentive for innovative economic activity. Such activity spurs growth and rising living standards—often for everyone. The opportunity for talented and hard-working people to strike it rich also embodies the ideals of a meritocratic society. Others counter that while some inequality based on these principles is fine, both individuals and society do worse when inequality gets out of hand. Low-income individuals obviously suffer from both the absolute deprivation (in the form of very low wages) and relative deprivation (such as embarrassment and stigma) that can accompany low economic achievement. Society may suffer if inequality is high enough to impede economic growth, given that a significant portion of economic activity is based on the consumption of goods and services by a vibrant middle class. Inequality can also potentially stifle economic mobility if low-income individuals do not have the resources necessary to invest in their own education and skills. This is why inequality coupled with the rising cost of postsecondary education has been so troubling to many Americans.

These issues are often cyclical—often pushed to the background in good economic times and thrust to the foreground during bad ones. How the U.S. economy continues to rebound after the lost decade of the 2000s will thus be of intense interest to all Americans.

5 Immigration and Growing Diversity

The United States is often said to be a land of immigrants—and with good reason. Immigration from a wide variety of other countries has continuously changed the character of this country. The initial wave of colonial settlement from England and around it—along with the large number of involuntary immigrants from Africa sold into slavery—eventually gave way to immigration from the rest of northern and western Europe in the early to mid-1800s. The stream of immigration then shifted to eastern and southern Europe by the end of the nineteenth century. Immigration slowed to a trickle after the passage of restrictive laws in the 1920s, aided and abetted by two world wars and a deep depression, before once again accelerating in the last decades of the twentieth century. During this last wave, immigrants came from an even broader array of countries spanning the globe—millions from Asia, Latin America, and Africa.

For a land of immigrants, however, the subject of immigration has long been a source of considerable political contention in the United States. Debates have generally centered around two issues: (1) the extent to which immigrants are assimilating and (2) the overall social and economic impact of immigration on the nation. New groups of immigrants from differing origins have long been viewed with suspicion by a substantial portion of the native-born population. Many have worried that immigrants weaken the character of the country or that they are too different from the native born to assimilate or, worse yet, indifferent to assimilating altogether. Others have fretted that immigrants are a drain on the economy, or that they bring crime and social disorganization to our nation's cities and communities, or that they take jobs away from native-born Americans. These debates on immigration have echoed across generations.

For example, many nativists reacted with alarm to the increasing immigration of Catholics from Germany and Ireland in the early eighteenth century. Catholics, who were associated with the pope and other monarchies of Europe, were viewed by some as an internal threat who might undermine the republic. As historian Roger Daniels recounts:

> When relatively large numbers of Irish and German Catholic immigrants, many of them desperately poor, began to arrive in the late 1820s and early 1830s, what had been a largely rhetorical anti-Catholicism became a major social and political force in American life. Not surprisingly, it was in eastern cities, particularly Boston, where anti-Catholicism turned violent, and much of the violence was directed against convents and churches. Beginning with the burning down of the Ursuline Convent just outside Boston by a mob on August 11, 1834, well into the 1850s violence against Catholic institutions was so prevalent that insurance companies all but refused to insure them.[1]

By the end of the century, when immigrants from southern and eastern Europe were pouring in, the targets of the nativists changed, though many of the underlying concerns were the same. As Daniels again relates:

> But lurking behind and sometimes overshadowing these [religious and economic] objections to continued immigration was a growing and pervasive racism, a racism directed not against non-white races, but against presumed inferior peoples of European origin. . . . According to one of its founders [of an immigration restriction league], the question for Americans to decide was whether they wanted their country "to be peopled by British, German and Scandinavian stock, historically free, energetic, progressive, or by Slav, Latin and Asiatic races (this latter referred to Jews rather than Chinese or Japanese), historically down-trodden, atavistic and stagnant."[2]

As immigration from non-European countries picked up steam after changes in immigration policy enacted in 1965, many commentators again raised the alarm of immigration's effect on the character of the nation. Writing in 1995, immigration policy critic Peter Brimelow argued that the 1965 law resulted in immigration that is "dramatically larger, less skilled, and more divergent from the American majority than anything that was anticipated or desired . . . is probably not beneficial to the economy . . . is attended by a wide and increasing range of negative consequences, from the physical environment to the political . . . [and] is bringing about an ethnic and racial transformation in America without precedent in the history of the world—an astonishing social experiment launched with no particular reason to expect success." Indeed, he asks, "Is America still that interlacing of ethnicity and culture we call a nation—and can the American nation-state, the political expression of that nation, survive?" Given that his book is titled *Alien Nation: Common Sense about America's Immigration Disaster,* one may not be surprised to find out that Brimelow offers a pessimistic answer to this question.[3]

The rest of this chapter addresses issues raised in these immigration debates by tackling the following basic questions: To what extent is immigration changing the racial and ethnic composition of the country? Are immigrants being successfully integrated into society? What is the economic and social impact of immigration? How does America's experience with immigration compare with those of other countries? A review of the research on these issues can give us a better sense of the types of policies the United States should consider pursuing, keeping in mind that policy is usually driven by a diverse set of constituents with sometimes competing goals.

IMMIGRATION POLICY AND CURRENT IMMIGRATION PATTERNS

From the founding of the country until about 1875 the United States had an open-door immigration policy. The Naturalization Act of 1790 allowed immigrants to acquire citizenship after several years of residence in the United States, and there were no legal restrictions on the number of immigrants or on places of origin. From time to time throughout the nineteenth century there was serious opposition to immigration—or at least to immigrants from certain origins—but these efforts did not have a significant impact on national policy. As noted above, the feeling was sometimes quite vehement, resulting in periodic violence against certain groups, such as Roman Catholics from Ireland.[4]

By the end of the nineteenth century there was considerable debate about the number of immigrants from southern and eastern Europe. In addition, on the West Coast many opposed immigration from China and Japan, as these immigrants were seen as undercutting the economic prospects of the native born.[5] In all cases, racism undoubtedly played a role, for these groups were often considered inferior to the native stock, and the extent to which they could assimilate into American society was also questioned. After the passage of mainly minor laws that barred the entry of convicts and prostitutes in 1875, Congress passed the Immigration Act of 1882, which prohibited immigration from China.[6] Japanese immigration was later limited in 1907 with the "Gentleman's Agreement," in which Japan was pressured to agree not to issue passports to Japanese citizens interested in immigrating to the United States, and the United States agreed to accept the presence of Japanese immigrants already in the country.

The Immigration Act of 1921 was the first law to put a ceiling on the overall number of immigrants allowed entry into the United States, followed by the even tougher Immigration Act of 1924. The 1924 law limited the number of immigrants from any country to 2 percent of the number of people from that country who were already living in the United States in 1890. By using 1890 as the base year for the quotas, the law had the effect of reducing the number of immigrants from southern and eastern Europe, who came in large numbers to the United States especially after that time. Levels of immigration plummeted after these legislative acts and remained low also in part because of the Great Depression in the 1930s and World War II in the early 1940s.[7]

Immigration policy generally became less restrictive in a number of small ways during and after World War II. Perhaps in part a reaction to the racist excesses of Nazism, overt racism in the United States increasingly fell out of favor. In general, many Americans felt that more effort should be made to harmonize policies with basic American ideals of liberty and equality of opportunity.[8] President Franklin Delano Roosevelt, for example, passed an executive order in 1941 that forbade racial discrimination by defense contractors. The Chinese exclusion laws were repealed in 1943, and the Luce-Celler Act of 1946 prohibited discrimination against Indian

Americans and Filipinos, who were accorded the right to naturalization. The Immigration and Nationality Act of 1952 revised the quotas, basing them on the 1920 census (rather than the 1890 census).

In the meantime, immigration from Mexico began increasing in the 1940s and 1950s, largely as a result of the Bracero Program, which aimed to bring contract laborers temporarily to the United States to fill labor shortages, especially in agriculture. Workers were paid low wages, often endured difficult working conditions, and were expected to return to Mexico after their contract expired. The Bracero Program was extended several times before formally ending in the mid-1960s.[9]

At about this time another momentous piece of immigration legislation was passed—the 1965 amendments to the Immigration and Nationality Act (also known as the Hart-Celler Act). This act did away with the discriminatory national quota system and instead set more uniform annual quotas across countries. While supporters of the bill sought to make immigration policy less discriminatory, they did not think it would drastically affect immigration patterns. Senator Edward Kennedy, chair of the Senate Immigration Subcommittee that was managing the bill, asserted, "First, our cities will not be flooded with a million immigrants annually. Under the proposed bill, the present level of immigration remains substantially the same. . . . Secondly, the ethnic mix of this country will not be upset."[10] The bill set an overall cap of 170,000 visas per year, later raised to 290,000. A number of people were, and continue to be, exempt from quotas, including spouses, children, and parents of U.S. citizens, as well as refugees and other smaller categories of immigrants. In 2009, for example, about 47 percent of the 1.1 million people who gained legal permanent residential status in the United States were immediate relatives of U.S. citizens who were exempt from the numerical quotas.[11]

Senator Kennedy's assurances notwithstanding, the most significant effect of the Hart-Celler Act was that it spurred immigration from countries that had little recent history of sending immigrants to the United States, especially Asia and later Africa. (Immigration from Latin America had been in increasing in the years before the passage of the law, so it is not clear whether the law was responsible for spurring any further migration from that region.)[12] Figure 31 shows the number and changing origins of the immigrant population from 1900 to 2009. While the number of immigrants

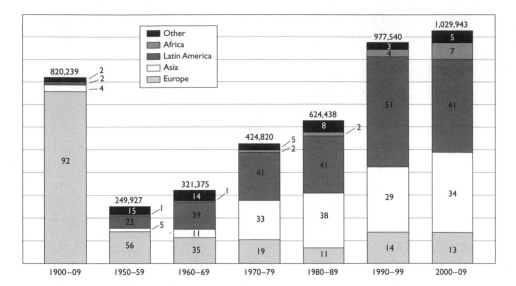

Figure 31. Annual number of legal U.S. immigrants, by decade, and their percentage distributions, by region of origin, 1900–2009. Note: The Y axis demarcates numbers of immigrants in increments of a hundred thousand. The shadings and numbers *within* the graph's bars indicate percentages of immigrants from the different regions of origin. The Latin America category includes Mexico, Central America, the Caribbean, and South America. The Other category consists mainly of immigrants from Canada in the 1950–59 and 1960–69 periods, though it also includes immigrants from Oceania and a small proportion of immigrants whose origin was not known in the 1980–89 and 2000–2009 periods. Source: U.S. Department of Homeland Security 2012.

arriving annually was higher between 1900 and 1909 than in the middle decades of the twentieth century, by the 1990s the number of immigrants arriving surpassed all previous levels. The United States received a historical high of over 1 million legal immigrants annually in the 2000s, with many more undocumented immigrants as well. (About 11 million undocumented immigrants lived in the United States in 2011.)[13] However, because of the smaller population base at that time, the proportion of the population that was foreign born in 1910 (15 percent) was still higher than the proportion foreign born a hundred years later in 2010 (13 percent).[14]

Whereas 92 percent of all legal immigrants were from Europe in the 1900–1909 period, this dropped to just 19 percent in the 1970s and 13

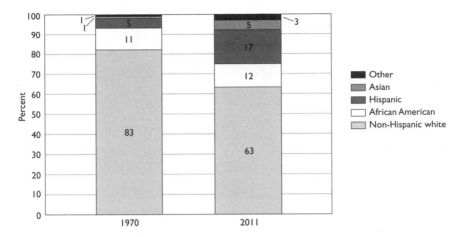

Figure 32. Racial/ethnic composition of the United States, 1970 and 2011. Sources: 1970 data from Martin and Midgely 2010, 3; 2011 data from Motel and Patten 2013, table 1.

percent in the first decade of the 2000s. Meanwhile, the proportion of immigrants from Latin America grew from only 2 percent in 1900–1909 to 23 percent in the 1950s to a peak of 51 percent in the 1990s, before dropping back to 41 percent in the 2000s. The proportion of immigrants from Asia grew rapidly in the 1960s through the 1990s; by the 2000s Asians constituted about a third of legal immigrants. Since 2009, the number of immigrants from Asia has surpassed the number from Latin America.[15] Immigration from Africa was negligible over most of the period, though it has increased in the last couple of decades, such that African immigrants made up 7 percent of all immigrants in the 2000s.[16]

Changing immigration patterns and differential fertility rates (higher fertility rates among minority groups than among whites) have had a major effect on the racial and ethnic composition of the U.S. population. Figure 32 shows that 63 percent of the population was non-Hispanic white in 2011, down from 83 percent in 1970. The percentage of the population that is African American held steady, constituting 12 percent of the total population in 2011. Meanwhile, the percentage of the population that is Hispanic has increased rapidly, from 5 percent in 1970 to 17 percent in 2011. The Asian population has likewise increased significantly, from 1 to 5 percent over the period. The U.S. Census Bureau projects that by 2060, just 43 percent of the population will be non-Hispanic white, 13 percent will be African American, 8 percent will be Asian, and 31 percent will be Hispanic.[17] These projections, however, should be viewed with caution, as they incorporate assumptions about immigration trends, fertility rates, and future patterns of racial and ethnic identification. For example, recent research has shown that Latino fertility rates may not be as high as commonly thought, and that how people view their identity over time and across generations often changes.[18] Nevertheless, it is safe to say that racial and ethnic diversity in the United States will continue to increase in the coming decades.

IMMIGRANT ASSIMILATION

What does assimilation mean in the United States today? Researchers and commentators have struggled with the concept, as have immigrants themselves. A newspaper article from the 1990s relates the following story:

> Night is falling on South Omaha, and Maria Jacinto is patting tortillas for the evening meal in the kitchen of the small house she shares with her husband and five children. Like many others in her neighborhood, where most of the residents are Mexican immigrants, the Jacinto household mixes the old country with the new.
>
> As Jacinto, who speaks only Spanish, stresses a need to maintain the family's Mexican heritage, her eldest son, a bilingual 11-year-old who wears a San Francisco 49ers jacket and has a paper route, comes in and joins his brothers and sisters in the living room to watch "The Simpsons."
>
> Jacinto became a U.S. citizen last April, but she does not feel like an American. In fact, she seems resistant to the idea of assimilating into U.S. society. "I think I'm still a Mexican," she says. "When my skin turns white and my hair turns blonde, then I'll be an American."[19]

The article goes on to argue that the changing demographics of the country challenge the notion that immigrants will be able to assimilate, because many newcomers are visible minorities, and, unlike in the past, many immigrants themselves resist assimilation, not wanting their children to assimilate into a culture that they view as being different from and in many ways inferior to their own.

While debates on these issues are far from settled, the evidence tends to indicate—contrary to the implications of the article above—that immigrants in the newest wave are successfully integrating into American society, though the pace and extent of integration vary significantly across groups. In the next section I delve into these issues by defining assimilation, reviewing the empirical evidence on the issue, and describing why the pessimism expressed in the article above is for the most part unwarranted.

What Is Assimilation?

Assimilation refers to the reduction of ethnic group distinctions over time. In the past the term has sometimes been used to mean Anglo conformity; that is, assimilation occurs when an immigrant group adopts the mores and practices of old-stock native-born white Americans. More recent assimilation theorists emphasize that assimilation need not be a one-way street on which minority members become more like the majority group members. Rather, assimilation involves a general convergence of social, economic, and cultural patterns that typically also involve the upward mobility of immigrants and their children.[20]

Assimilation is often not a conscious decision in which an immigrant decides to shed his or her cultural practices and heritage in the pursuit of another culture's. Rather, as Richard Alba and Victor Nee note, assimilation is a lengthy process that typically spans generations: "To the extent that assimilation occurs, it proceeds incrementally as an intergenerational process, stemming both from individuals' purposive action and from the unintended consequences of their workaday decisions. In the case of immigrants and their descendants who may not intentionally seek to assimilate, the cumulative effect of pragmatic decisions aimed at successful adaptation can give rise to changes in behavior that nevertheless lead to eventual assimilation."[21]

Commentators who believe that immigrants of old were eager to assimilate—unlike contemporary immigrants—are not well acquainted with the historical record. Historian Roger Daniels describes how German immigrants in the nineteenth century came mostly for economic reasons, remained very proud of their homeland, and sought to retain their cultural practices:

> Indispensable for most cultural institutions that were intended to endure beyond the immigrant generation was some way of ensuring that the second and subsequent generations learn and use the ancestral language—what scholars now call language maintenance. . . . Beginning with parochial schools, largely but not exclusively Lutheran and Catholic, Germans eventually turned to the public schools and political action in [an] attempt to make German instruction in all subjects available when enough parents wanted it. In such public schools, English might be taught as a special subject as if it were a foreign language, which, of course, it was and is to many young children of immigrants raised in essentially monolingual homes. And in many parochial schools, English was not taught at all.[22]

Daniels notes that German culture remained very strong and proudly expressed until World War I, when the conflict pitting Germany against England, France, and eventually the United States led to strong anti-German feeling in many quarters. Still, even today many communities in the Midwest have strong German roots and cultural heritage.

Ties to the United States were also, at least initially, weak among many immigrants from a number of other sending countries. For example, of the 4.1 million Italians recorded as entering the United States between 1880 and 1920, anywhere from about 30 percent to nearly half returned to Italy.[23] Over the years, many immigrants have been attracted primarily by economic opportunities rather than by the notion of becoming American. Italians, like many other immigrant groups, were also concentrated in particular neighborhoods of particular cities (such as Little Italy in New York City), and they were concentrated in specific occupations as well, such as in low- and semiskilled trades like construction and pushcart vending. Many native-born Americans stereotyped Italians as criminals, pointing to tight-knit criminal organizations such as the Mafia.[24] Here we see that contemporary concerns with crime in immigrant communities (e.g., Hispanic gangs today) and the stereotyping of immigrant groups are nothing new.

Still, just because immigrants of previous waves of immigration from Europe assimilated does not mean that more recent immigrants from Latin America, Asia, and Africa will have the same experience. Commentators have pointed to a number of differences in the conditions under which these different waves have arrived in the United States.[25] Perhaps the most prominent of the arguments is that immigrants today are racially more distinct than those in the past. The counterview is that despite our perception of previous waves of immigrants from Europe as essentially "white," historical accounts indicate that many among those immigrant groups, including the Irish, Jews, and Italians, were perceived to be racially distinct from the majority of native-born Americans. As Daniels writes: "However curious it may seem today, by the late nineteenth century many of the 'best and brightest' minds in America had become convinced that of all the many 'races' (we would say 'ethnic groups') of Europe one alone—variously called Anglo-Saxon, Aryan, Teutonic, or Nordic—had superior innate characteristics. Often using a crude misapplication of Darwinian evolution, which substituted these various 'races' for Darwinian species, historians, political scientists, economists, and, later, eugenicists discovered that democratic political institutions had developed and could thrive only among Anglo-Saxon peoples."[26] The idea that immigrants from different European countries constituted different races diminished only over time as various groups achieved socioeconomic mobility.[27]

Nevertheless, a number of people remain skeptical about the successful integration of many of today's immigrant groups into American society. A competing theoretical perspective—*ethnic disadvantage*—holds that even if new immigrants learn the language and customs of their new country, they may still not be able to achieve significant socioeconomic mobility or acceptance by the white mainstream. Discrimination, for example, may put many educational opportunities or jobs out of reach for newcomers.

One viewpoint somewhere between the two (assimilation and ethnic disadvantage) is *segmented assimilation*. This perspective focuses on divergent patterns of incorporation among contemporary immigrants.[28] It asserts that the host society offers uneven possibilities to different immigrant groups, some of whom might achieve upward mobility and be successfully assimilated into the mainstream, others who will be marginalized and will adopt harmful cultural practices of disadvantaged native-born groups and experience downward mobility, and yet others who will retain strong ethnic ties and still achieve high levels of socioeconomic success. According to this perspective, racial discrimination and the range of

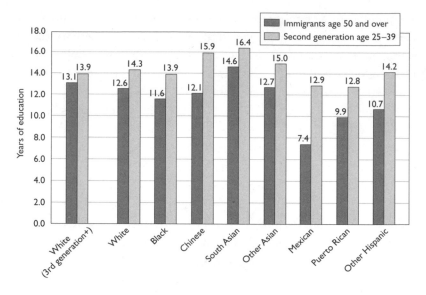

Figure 33. Years of education, by generation, age, and ethnic origin, among U.S. native born and immigrants, 1995–2007. Note: The first set of bars refers to native-born populace; all others refer to immigrants or their offspring. Following the same key that pertains to the other categories, the first bar in the set for 3rd generation+ whites refers to whites 50 and over, and the second bar refers to 3rd-generation whites ages 25–39. Source: Reitz, Zhang, and Hawkins 2011, table 1, using Current Population Survey data.

economic opportunities available in a particular place at a particular time may shape assimilation trajectories of immigrants and their children. A number of studies have tested these perspectives.

Evidence on Assimilation

While one could study many different dimensions of assimilation (social, political, economic, etc.), I will focus on three dimensions of broad interest that are indicative of immigrants' general position in U.S. society: education, earnings, and residential segregation patterns. Taking generational change into account is critical in these comparisons, as assimilation is thought to occur mainly over time and across generations. Beginning with education, figure 33 shows years of education for different ethnic groups by generation and age averaged over the 1995 to 2007 period. (Multiple years of Current Population Survey data were needed to have large enough samples of relatively small groups, such as second-generation Puerto Ricans, to calculate reliable averages.) It should be noted that individuals born in Puerto Rico, although U.S. citizens at birth, are considered to be "foreign-born" in the analysis on the basis of their shared experiences as newcomers to the mainland United States, whereas their children and subsequent generations are "native-born." On the left-hand side of the figure, we see that third- and higher-generation whites age 50 and over have, on average, 13.1 years of education. This number is higher than the figure among similarly aged immigrants of all origins except South Asians, indicating a general educational advantage among the native-white population.

However, we see that the second generation has experienced considerable increases in mean education levels compared with the first generation, and that most groups have closed the gap or surpassed the educational attainment of third- and higher-generation whites of the same age. For example, while the third-generation or more whites of ages 25 to 39 averaged 13.9 years of education, this figure was 14.3 among children of white immigrants, 13.9 among second-generation blacks, 15.9 among second-generation Chinese, and a high of 16.4 among second-generation South Asians. The two second-generation groups that had lower levels of educational attainment than third-generation or more whites were Mexicans (12.9 years) and Puerto Ricans (12.8 years). However, even though these groups did not reach parity with whites, they far surpassed their respective first generations (7.4 years among Mexican immigrants age 50 and over and 9.9 years among similar Puerto Ricans). The second generation of many groups often does better than third-generation whites, because their parents—especially those with high education themselves—are often a "select" group: many immigrated to the United States because they sought economic mobility, and they push their children to excel in school.[29] These general findings about the upward mobility across immigrant generations are in line with the conclusions of other studies that have analyzed this issue with other approaches and nationally representative data. In other words, while many immigrant groups are initially quite disadvantaged compared with the native mainstream, their upward trajectory suggests that some measure of integration is occurring.[30]

These findings do not mean that there is no cause for any concern. First, the immigrants themselves and their children vary considerably in their educational attainment. The United States attracts both very highly educated professionals (e.g., computer programmers and engineers in Silicon Valley) and low-skill laborers who toil away on farms or construction sites across the country. Even among Hispanics we see considerable variation, with Mexicans having the lowest initial levels of education, while education among "Other Hispanics" is considerably higher.

Second, while generational progress among the Mexican-origin population is impressive, Mexican American educational attainment at this time still lags behind other groups. The lack of documentation among many Mexican-origin immigrants tends to impede integration, because such individuals and their children do not have the same means to access the full range of jobs and educational opportunities that others can in the United States.[31] Researchers Michael White and Jennifer Glick find that adolescents from lower socioeconomic backgrounds tend to lag behind their more advantaged peers regardless of racial and ethnic background, and this can serve to slow continued educational progress across generations. White and Glick further note that while the effect of race may be declining in American society, the effect of race and ethnic origin on educational attainment has not disappeared altogether, even after accounting for many other family background factors.[32]

Turning to the second dimension of assimilation, income, figure 34 shows differences in household income by age and generation for the same ethnic groups shown in figure 33. The household income measure is adjusted for household size to produce an "individual-equivalent" measure. Some groups have larger households on average, so this measure provides more of a per capita household income estimate that also takes into account economies of scale enjoyed by larger households.[33] Figure 34 shows that second-generation households have higher incomes, on average, than first-generation ones among all ethnic groups. In addition, whereas all first-generation immigrant groups except South Asians had lower incomes than third-generation+ whites, the second generation of many groups (whites, Chinese, South Asians, other Asians, and other Hispanics) had higher average incomes than third-generation+ whites in the same age range. Second-generation blacks, Mexicans, and Puerto

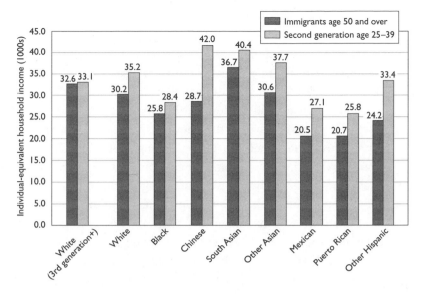

Figure 34. Household income (adjusted for household size), by generation, age, and ethnic origin, 1995–2007 (in 1,000s of dollars). Note: The first bar in the set for 3rd-generation+ whites refers to whites age 50 and over, and the second bar refers to 3rd-generation of whites ages 25–39. Income is in constant 2001 dollars. Household income is divided by the square root of the number of persons in the household. Source: Reitz, Zhang, and Hawkins 2011, table 3, using Current Population Survey data.

Ricans all continued to have lower incomes than whites, even if the gap (as compared with the first-generation white gap) was narrower. More sophisticated analyses that take into account differences in education, marital status, and geographic location across groups tend to find small to negligible differences between whites and Asians but lower incomes among African Americans and Hispanics.[34] Other research confirms lower earnings for African Americans, though more mixed findings for Hispanics once many background factors are taken into account.[35] It is not clear why the gap between whites and African Americans, and perhaps Hispanics, exists, though labor market discrimination might play a role. Some studies have found higher levels of disadvantage particularly among blacks and darker-skinned Hispanics, suggesting the existence of a black-nonblack divide in American society abetted by discrimination.[36]

American color lines are discussed in more detailed in the following chapter.

With respect to the final dimension of assimilation to be discussed, immigrant residential patterns, I previously conducted research on this issue by examining how levels of residential segregation vary by racial/ethnic group and nativity. The conventional wisdom has long been that new immigrants prefer to settle in ethnic enclaves so that they can live near people who share their common history and culture. Living among friends and family can bring comfort to those in a very unfamiliar environment. Immigrants' social networks also draw them to live in particular neighborhoods. According to the assimilation perspective, however, immigrants would be more likely to move out of these enclaves the longer they are in the host country, and certainly we would expect to see later generations living in a broader array of neighborhoods with groups other than immigrants themselves.

I used the most common indicator of residential segregation, the dissimilarity index, to measure the distribution of different groups across neighborhoods in metropolitan areas across the United States. The index ranges from 0 to 100, where 0 indicates complete integration (ethnic groups are evenly distributed across all neighborhoods) and 100 indicates extreme segregation (ethnic groups live wholly homogeneous neighborhoods with co-ethnics). The general rule of thumb is that scores above 60 are considered high in absolute terms, a score between 30 and 60 indicates moderate segregation, and scores under 30 are quite low.

Figure 35 shows average levels of segregation of Hispanics, Asians, and blacks from native-born non-Hispanic whites (hereafter termed "whites") across metropolitan areas in the United States, as calculated with 2000 census data. We see that in general, blacks are highly segregated from whites (an overall dissimilarity score of 67), followed by Hispanics (52) and Asians (43). Of particular relevance to testing the assimilation perspective, native-born Hispanics, Asians, and blacks are less segregated from whites than their immigrant counterparts.[37] In additional analyses, I found that, consistent with the assimilation perspective, some of these differences by nativity are explained by the average characteristics of the foreign born that are generally associated with higher levels of segregation, such as their lower levels of income and English-language fluency, meaning that gains in those attributes generally translate into greater

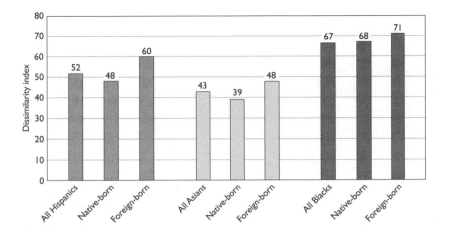

Figure 35. Segregation of racial/ethnic groups from native-born non-Hispanic whites, by nativity, according to the dissimilarity index, 2000. Source: Iceland and Scopilliti 2008, table 1.

residential integration. I also found that immigrants who have been in the United States for longer periods of time were generally less segregated from whites than new arrivals.[38]

Nevertheless, we do see that patterns vary across racial and ethnic groups, with very high levels of segregation between blacks and whites regardless of nativity. On the one hand, this could provide some support for the segmented assimilation perspective. Clearly, blacks tend to live in very different neighborhoods from those of whites, especially in metropolitan areas in the Northeast and Midwest such as Detroit, Milwaukee, Chicago, and New York.[39] On the other hand, as will be shown in chapter 7, black-white segregation has been declining significantly over the years (this also shows up in 2010 census data), such that the residential (and social) distance between blacks and whites will likely continue to narrow in the coming years.

Despite these findings on the generational improvement in education and income and the decline in residential segregation, some commentators remain skeptical about whether all immigrant groups are assimilating. They rightly point out, for example, that Hispanic immigrants have been met with considerable hostility in many communities and question whether Hispanics will eventually be accepted into American society.[40]

Many people also view strict anti-illegal immigration laws passed in states such as Arizona (2010) and Alabama (2011) as condoning racial profiling against Hispanics. Others base their skepticism about assimilation on research; one large study of a sample of Mexican-origin individuals in San Antonio and Los Angeles found that while there was considerable linguistic assimilation among Mexican Americans (i.e., most native-born Mexican Americans were fluent in English), educational and earnings mobility was only modest between the first and second generation, with little additional progress thereafter.[41]

Studies using nationally representative data, however, tend to show slow but steady generational progress among Mexicans. In a careful comparison of assimilation patterns of Mexicans in recent years with Italians and other southern and eastern European groups a century ago, Joel Perlmann concludes that Mexican socioeconomic mobility is slowly progressing such that it may take them "four or five generations rather than three or four to reach parity with the native-white mainstream."[42] That is, the low socioeconomic starting point of Mexican immigrants, combined with the fact that many are in the United States without valid visas (and thus have limited opportunity for upward mobility), suggests that while Mexican Americans will make socioeconomic progress over time, it may take longer for them than for other immigrant groups.[43]

IMPACT OF IMMIGRATION

In addition to concerns about assimilation, some question whether immigrants have a positive impact on U.S. society. While one could potentially examine the impact of immigration on just about any aspect of American life, here I focus on the effects of immigration on three areas of broad interest and concern: the economy, social solidarity and social capital, and crime.

Economic Impacts

One economic issue frequently raised is whether immigrants drive down the wages of native-born workers. The answer comes down to whether immigrants are *complements* to American workers or *substitutes* for them. If they are complements, they are not directly competing for existing jobs. Instead, they work in jobs that employers have trouble filling with existing native-born workers (such as in agriculture in some parts of the country), they work in jobs that only marginally compete with native-born businesses (e.g., bodegas that serve ethnic communities), or they even generate job growth because they are entrepreneurs or consumers of goods and services produced by native-born workers. In these cases, immigrants are complementing the existing native workforce and not taking away their jobs. However, if immigrants are substitutes, they are essentially replacing native-born workers or competing enough with them to drive down their wages.

Economists have debated this issue at length over the years, as different methodological approaches have at times yielded different findings. A number of years ago a National Academy of Sciences panel of accomplished social scientists investigated this issue and concluded that the effect of immigration on the earnings of the native-born workforce is on the whole quite small. Immigration does not reduce the earnings of most native-born workers. Those most susceptible to the negative effects of immigration are low-skill workers, including less-educated African Americans, but even here the effects are small. The evidence suggested that immigrants tend to compete most with immigrants from earlier waves of immigration, for whom the recent immigrants are at times substitutes in the labor market.[44] The findings of the panel have been supported by a more recent review of the research on this topic as well.[45]

The fiscal impact of immigration depends on whether immigrants pay more in taxes than they consume in public services. Calculating the overall impact is quite complicated, as taxes are paid at the federal, state, and local levels via a variety of mechanisms (e.g., income taxes, payroll taxes, sales taxes, etc.), and public services are likewise offered by different levels of government. Moreover, the effects of immigration are both short term and long term, with the latter depending on not only the tax and consumption patterns of current immigrants but also those of the children of immigrants. Both the National Academy of Science panel mentioned above and more recent work have concluded that once all of these elements are balanced, the fiscal effects of immigration are generally small, and they depend on the characteristics of immigrants. Less-educated immigrants tend to consume more public services and contribute less in taxes, as do immigrants over the age of fifty. The federal government tends to benefit from immigration in the form of payroll taxes paid, because even many illegal immigrants with counterfeit Social Security cards have such taxes withheld from their paychecks. Meanwhile, local governments are more likely to bear the brunt of the costs of immigration (at least in the short run), such as in the form of staffing public schools with sufficient support services for immigrant children and health care for a growing local population.[46]

Immigration has a number of other economic benefits to the United States. Immigrants tend to lower the cost of many goods and services as a result of low wages. Higher-income consumers may benefit the most from this because they consume more "immigrant-intensive" products and services, including child care, restaurant food, and landscaping.[47] Among other economic benefits, immigrant entrepreneurs contribute to economic growth, immigration can boost struggling industries and cities, immigrants strengthen America's commercial ties with the rest of the world, immigrants contribute to the United States' engineering and scientific prowess, and immigration counteracts the aging of the native-born population.[48]

Regarding the first of these additional benefits—the contribution of immigrant entrepreneurs—immigrants to the United States have long been economic innovators. Among them, readily recognizable today are Andrew Carnegie (in the steel industry), Alexander Graham Bell (communications), and John Nordstrom (retailing).[49] Even today immigrants are more likely than native-born Americans to start companies. Immigrants, for example, make up 18 percent of all small business owners in the United States, though they are 13 percent of the U.S. population and 16 percent of the labor force.[50] Their impact on the rise of technology businesses and corporations in Silicon Valley in recent years has been immense. One study estimated that immigrants were on the founding teams of just over half of all technology companies in Silicon Valley, including companies such as Google, Sun Microsystems, and SpaceX.[51] In debates about immigration policy, one point many observers agree upon is that high-skill immigrants should be able to get visas to come to the

United States more easily than current policy rules allow. As Alex Salkever and Vivek Wadhwa argued in a column on immigrant entrepreneurs:

> Allowing skilled immigrant entrepreneurs to more easily enter America, where they can create good jobs and pay taxes, is the closest thing to an economic free lunch that we are likely to get. In the words of New York Mayor Michael Bloomberg, we are committing "economic suicide" by making it hard for skilled immigrants to stay in the U.S. and contribute to our economy.... [Foreign-born inventors are most prevalent] in cutting-edge fields such as semiconductor device manufacturing, where 87 percent of patents named an immigrant inventor; information technology, where 84 percent of patents named an immigrant inventor.... Unfortunately, difficulties in obtaining visas are forcing many founders and innovators to either delay their start-up dreams or to relocate to more hospitable countries.[52]

Illustrating this very point, an article in the *Washington Post* recounted the following visa woes of two aspiring entrepreneurs who were postdoctoral mechanical engineers at MIT and, by extension, the impact this problem might have on our economy if it persists:

> Anurag Bajpayee and Prakash Narayan Govindan, both from India, have started a company to sell the[ir water decontamination] system to oil businesses that are desperate for a cheaper, cleaner way to dispose of the billions of gallons of contaminated water produced by fracking.
>
> Oil companies have flown them to Texas and North Dakota. They say they are about to close on millions of dollars in financing, and they expect to hire 100 employees in the next couple of years. *Scientific American* magazine called water-decontamination technology developed by Bajpayee one of the top 10 "world-changing ideas" of 2012.
>
> But their student visas expire soon, both before summer, and because of the restrictive U.S. visa system, they may have to move their company to India or another country. "We love it here," said Bajpayee, a cheerful 27-year-old in an argyle sweater and jeans. "But there are so many hoops you have to jump through. And you risk getting deported while you are creating jobs."[53]

Immigration has also boosted struggling industries, such as the fruit and vegetable industry in California and the garment industry in New York, and has revitalized many inner cities, such as Miami, Los Angeles, New York, and Philadelphia.[54] In Philadelphia, for example, the immigrant population grew by 113,000 just between 2000 and 2006, by which time immigrants constituted 9 percent of the total population. Audrey Singer and her coauthors conclude that immigrants are revitalizing the city by bringing "fresh energy, entrepreneurship, and vibrancy to many parts of the region. They are breathing life into declining commercial areas, reopening storefronts, creating local jobs, and diversifying products and services available to residents. Immigrants are repopulating neighborhoods on the wane and reviving and sustaining housing markets. Across the region, they are helping to make greater Philadelphia a more global, cosmopolitan center, with stronger connections to economies and cultures abroad."[55] On the other hand, Singer also notes that immigration produces challenges for local institutions, such as in the overcrowding of public schools and the need for more services targeted at non-English-speaking individuals. On the whole, however, immigration has been an economic boon for the city. Recognizing the economic potential of immigration, many other places, such as Dayton, Ohio, Michigan, and Iowa, have tried to lure more immigrants.[56] For all of these reasons, the National Academy of Sciences panel concluded that immigration delivers a significant net economic gain for U.S. residents.[57]

Social Cohesion and Social Capital

The arrival of a large number of immigrants naturally changes the dynamics of communities. Many long-standing community members may view the newcomers with distrust and perhaps fear that immigrants are going to change the character of a familiar place. Sometimes animosity can arise in a struggle for power, as established residents may wish to keep their control over resources while new groups fight for recognition and for what they view as their fair share. For example, discussing racial and ethnic tensions in Los Angeles in the 1990s, researcher James Johnson and his colleagues argued, "Tensions, conflicts, and community instability associated with heightened immigration—especially of nonwhite immigrant groups—threaten to balkanize America. . . . We believe that the undercurrent of racial and ethnic intolerance that undergirds the nation's changing demographic realities strongly challenges, and may very well threaten, our ability to establish viable, stable, racially and ethnically diverse communities and institutions."[58]

Johnson and his colleagues provide the example of neighborhood change in the city of Compton, a suburb of Los Angeles. It was initially an all-white community that experienced racial tension and white-to-black population succession in the 1960s. In the following decades, Hispanic migration to the area caused new schisms. On the one hand, black residents resented having to share social services and social institutions with the newcomers. On the other hand, newly arriving Hispanics complained about the lack of access to municipal jobs and leadership positions in the local government and about staffing positions in the school system and the content of the school curriculum.[59]

In 2006, in what was viewed by many as a law targeting Hispanics as a whole, Hazleton, Pennsylvania, passed a law that penalized employers for hiring illegal immigrants and landlords for renting to them. The law was declared unconstitutional in 2010 by a federal appeals courts, but the next year the U.S. Supreme Court upheld a similar law in Arizona and ordered a court of appeals to review Pennsylvania's law. Hazleton is a largely white, conservative community that had experienced a slow demographic decline since the 1940s in large part because of the decline of local industries (coal mining and the garment industry). In the 2000s it became a new destination for immigrants, who have in many ways revitalized the city. Hispanics made up 37 percent of the population in 2010, up from only 5 percent just ten years earlier. But this immigration has also been a source of tension, as it has changed the character of the city.

As a news story looking at relations in Hazleton reported, "Hispanic residents said they felt their entire population was stigmatized by the crackdown on illegal immigrants. Felix Perez, a Walmart employee with two daughters, 2 and 9, recalled a time he hesitated at the wheel of his car, unsure which way to turn, and the non-Hispanic driver behind him got out with a gun in his hand. 'He saw my face, he knew I was Spanish,' Mr. Perez said. 'They believe we are all the same because we look the same.'"[60]

According to the same story, some longtime residents are not entirely happy with the changes in their community. "The people in this town, we're becoming a minority," said Chris DeRienzo, 30, a wedding photographer who opposes a pathway to citizenship for illegal immigrants. "It hurts. I grew up here. It's not what it used to be."

One recent study by the well-known political scientist Robert Putnam examined the effect of diversity on social solidarity and social capital. He found that social cohesion was indeed lower in more diverse communities, at least in the short run. As he puts it, "In ethnically diverse neighborhoods residents of all races tend to 'hunker down.' Trust (even of one's own race) is lower, altruism and community cooperation rarer, friends fewer."[61] For example, survey respondents in relatively homogeneous areas, such as Bismarck, North Dakota, and Lewiston, Maine, were more likely to report that they trust their neighbors "a lot" than those in diverse places like San Francisco, Los Angeles, and Houston. Putnam also cites Richard Alba and Victor Nee, who note, "When social distance is small, there is a feeling of common identity, closeness, and shared experiences. But when social distance is great, people perceive and treat the other as belonging to a different category."[62]

While Putnam's main analysis focuses on this point, he does provide a word of optimism at the end of his published lecture, saying that these low levels of trust might be fleeting. "In the long run, however, successful immigrant societies have overcome such fragmentation by creating new, cross-cutting forms of social solidarity and more encompassing identities. Illustrations of becoming comfortable with diversity are drawn from the US military, religious institutions, and earlier waves of immigration."[63] It should be said that Putnam's analysis should not be taken as the last word on these issues. The results of his study have been criticized on both conceptual and methodological grounds, though empirical studies have tended to support (though not uniformly) his general conclusion about the negative association between diversity and social solidarity.[64] Thus, immigration can lead to a decline in social cohesion, at least in the short run, though a negative long-term impact is far from inevitable.

Regarding a related issue, the effect of immigration on the incidence of crime, conventional wisdom has long held that immigration is associated with social disorganization, ethnic gangs, and many types of criminal activity. However, an emerging consensus among scholars is that immigration to the United States in recent decades has generally not increased crime and in fact has often served to reduce it.[65] For example, sociologist Robert Sampson, one of the leading scholars in this area, found that, controlling for individual and family background characteristics, first-generation Mexican immigrants in Chicago were considerably less likely to commit crimes than later generations. He also found that living in a neighborhood of concentrated immigration was directly associated with lower violence, once a number of other neighborhood attributes were accounted for. More generally, he notes that immigration was increasing in the 1990s just when national homicide rates were plunging. He concludes that the beneficial (or at least unharmful) association between immigration and crime may be due to immigration's role in helping to revitalize many declining inner-city neighborhoods and to the positive influence that many immigrants may have on local cultures, given that immigrants themselves are not prone to crime or violence and for the most part do not come from particularly violent cultures.[66]

INTERNATIONAL COMPARISONS

International migration has been increasing around the globe in recent decades. Most of the discussion below focuses on comparisons between the United States and other peer (mainly wealthy) countries of Europe and the OECD, but it should be noted that many countries in a wide variety of regions have very high net migration rates, ranging from the United Arab Emirates on the Arabian Peninsula to Singapore in Southeast Asia to Botswana in sub-Saharan Africa.[67]

Many European countries that had been senders of migrants (and colonizers) in the nineteenth century became destinations for immigrants in the post–World War II period. Germany, for example, experienced labor shortages in the 1950s as it continued to rebuild and grow after World War II. It first looked to southern Europe, then Turkey, and then North Africa for temporary laborers. Other European countries with guest-worker policies included, among others, Austria, Switzerland, and Sweden. Some countries, particularly Great Britain, France, the Netherlands, and Belgium, also received immigrants from their former colonies. When a sharp recession hit Europe in the early 1970s, countries with guest-worker programs terminated them. However, a significant proportion of supposedly temporary immigrants did not wish to be repatriated to their countries of origin and stayed in their adopted countries. Many European countries have

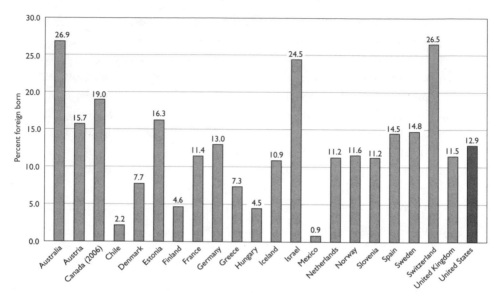

Figure 36. Percentage of the population foreign born in selected OECD countries, 2010. Source: OECD 2013d.

struggled with their growing diversity, and public opinion remains divided on appropriate levels of immigration. Nevertheless, immigration to many European countries both from their neighbors and from non-European countries continues.[68]

The United States continues to attract more immigrants than any other OECD country. For example, the United States had nearly 40 million foreign-born persons in 2010, followed next by Germany, with nearly 11 million.[69] However, because the United States has a much larger total population than any of these other countries, the percentage of its population that is foreign born is lower than in many others, as shown in figure 36. Countries with the highest percentage of foreign-born residents in 2010 were Australia (26.9 percent), Israel (24.5 percent), and Switzerland (26.5 percent). Canada (19.0 percent) also had a higher proportion of foreign-born residents than the United States (12.9 percent). A number of OECD countries had a relatively low percentage of foreign-born residents, such as Mexico (0.9 percent), Chile (2.2 percent), and Hungary (4.5 percent). Overall, however, immigration is both bolstering the populations of many countries that would otherwise be facing the prospect of future demographic decline because of low fertility and also transforming the character of these countries.

A few of the OECD countries, such as Canada and Australia, have long histories of immigration, whereas for others it is a much more recent phenomenon. The extent to which immigrants are assimilating and otherwise affecting OECD countries varies, for the countries themselves vary considerably in terms of the timing of immigration, the composition of the immigrants, their policies toward immigrants, and the economic and social conditions at the time of reception.

In terms of differences in immigration policy, Germany, for example, initially denied citizenship to all immigrants who could not trace their familial roots back to Germany. Over time this became untenable, as many guest workers originally from Turkey and North Africa, and then their children, were clearly in Germany to stay. Thus, laws regarding citizenship were eventually reformed in 1999 to make it easier for immigrants to gain German citizenship.[70] The United Kingdom had more multicultural policies from the 1970s onward, recognizing the rights of different groups and their claims on public resources. In recent years there has been some backlash against multiculturalism—many feeling that it is divisive—and a greater emphasis on promoting integration and community cohesion.[71] France, in contrast, has long had an assimilationist approach to immigration, expecting that immigrants should adopt French customs and culture. This approach informed the 2004 passage of what is sometimes referred to as "the veil law," which forbade any visible sign of religious affiliation in schools, and a 2010 law that banned the wearing of veils that cover the face in public places. Despite policies strongly promoting assimilation, many immigrants and their children in France, especially if they are "visible" minorities (those perceived as different because of skin color, language, accent, self-presentation, or surname), report that others perceive them as not being French, though they do experience at least some measure of integration over time and across generations.[72]

Concerns about immigrant integration in many European countries, such as the United Kingdom, France, the Netherlands, and Sweden, frequently focus on the assimilability of Muslim immigrants in particular.

There is a broad fear of Islamic radicalism and a skepticism about whether the values of religious immigrants are compatible with the culture of secular humanism that predominates in many European countries.[73] Muslim immigrants in turn often feel that they are viewed with suspicion and discriminated against by the native-born mainstream.[74]

Studies that have systematically investigated immigrant incorporation into Europe and other OECD countries for the most part find that the second generation often does better than the first, as in the United States, though significant variation occurs across immigrant groups. One study of education, unemployment, and occupational attainment outcomes among the second generation in ten countries in Europe (Austria, Belgium, Great Britain, Denmark, France, Germany, the Netherlands, Norway, Sweden, and Switzerland) finds that upward mobility occurs among the second generation but that second-generation minorities from non-European countries still tend to experience some disadvantage, such as those of Turkish ancestry in Belgium, Germany, and the Netherlands; those of Moroccan or other North African ancestry in Belgium, France, and the Netherlands; individuals of Caribbean or Pakistani ancestry in Britain; and those of Surinam ancestry in the Netherlands.[75]

Another cross-national comparison of immigrant integration into the United States, Canada, and Australia finds common patterns of high achievement among the Chinese and South Asian second generation in these countries. Children of black immigrants tend to fare less well in all contexts, though the second generation still does better than the first. Across these host countries, some specific differences appear in relation to the starting points of the immigrants and the extent of generational change, but on the whole the similarities among these countries seem to outweigh the differences.[76] In short, in many different contexts, children from low-status immigrant families lag behind the children from native families, but immigrant incorporation is the dominant trend.[77]

A FINAL NOTE ON IMMIGRATION POLICY

Immigration reform has been discussed from time to time in recent years in the United States, mostly focusing on reducing the number of illegal immigrants currently in the country and attracting immigrants that would boost our economy. In some quarters, support for an expanded guest-worker program in the United States is considerable, especially among large businesses that would like to recruit low-wage workers for agricultural work or other labor-intensive work. While there may be good short-term economic reasons to have a guest-worker program, the entry of a large number of temporary, low-skill workers with relatively few rights or prospects for legal incorporation through citizenship may result in the growth of a socially, economically, and politically marginalized constituency. As indicated above, the record of guest-worker programs in western European countries suggests that such immigrants are not usually content to simply go home after they are no longer needed. In fact, approximately 25 to 40 percent of undocumented immigrants in the United States are visa overstayers rather than people who crossed the border illegally.[78] For similar reasons, providing the means for current undocumented immigrants to eventually attain citizenship will likely help them and their children more easily integrate into American society.

On the other hand, policies that favor admitting more immigrants on the basis of education and skills could serve to boost our economy, as such immigrants often engage in highly productive work. They are also more likely to have a positive fiscal impact on national, state, and local budgets through the higher taxes that they pay as compared with lower-skill immigrants. As noted above, the children of high-skill immigrants are also more likely to do well in school and in the labor market and are thus less likely to be marginalized and isolated. Of course, it should be said that immigration policy should not be shaped only on the basis of economic cost-benefit analyses. Immigration policy has long had an important humanitarian component that should help inform policy decisions as well. For example, many countries, including the United States and those of Europe, have policies that allow refugees from dangerous, war-torn countries to immigrate, believing that it would be inhumane to allow them to face extreme hardship or death if they remained. Over the years, such groups have included Jewish refugees during World War II, Vietnamese refugees from the Vietnam War, and Somali refugees in the 2000s seeking to escape the anarchy and clan warfare occurring in many parts of the country.

CONCLUSION

Immigration has contributed to increasing racial and ethnic diversity in communities across the United States. While the United States is a land of immigrants, fears about the impact of immigration and whether new immigrants are capable of assimilating have been frequently expressed over the years and continually crop up in policy debates on the issue. Research on the recent, post-1965 wave of immigration tends to show that immigrants are by and large being integrated into American society. The second generation tends to have higher levels of education and earnings than their immigrant parents, and that generation also achieves greater parity with whites. The native-born second generation also tends to be less residentially segregated than the first generation. Nevertheless, there is significant variation across immigrant groups, with Asians having the highest levels of attainment. Asian immigrants tend to have relatively high levels of education, and this confers advantages to their children in school and in the labor market. Hispanic immigrants come with relatively low levels of education, and while their children tend to do better than their parents, on average they do not achieve parity with whites. The children of black immigrants likewise achieve some measure of mobility but remain disadvantaged relative to the mainstream; racial discrimination may impact their life chances.

Many studies have also examined the economic and fiscal impacts of immigration. They have generally found that immigrants do not have much of an impact on the employment or wages of most of the native born, though there might be a small negative effect on the wages of low-skilled native-born workers. This effect is generally small because immigrants are often complements of rather than substitutes for American workers; also immigrants often create jobs and are consumers too, which can spur economic growth. Indeed, immigrants are more likely to be entrepreneurs than native-born workers, and high-skill immigrants have been crucial in spurring innovative economic activity in science and technology, such as in Silicon Valley.

The fiscal impact of immigration is small in the aggregate. Immigrants consume government services (such as public education), but they also pay taxes. Highly educated immigrants tend to pay more than they consume in public services. The federal government budget may benefit from immigration, because a large majority of immigrants (including many illegal immigrants with fake Social Security cards) pay federal payroll taxes, though some local governments are harder hit because of small tax collections from immigrants and the cost of locally financed services (such as schools).

More diverse areas sometimes experience intergroup conflict and have less social cohesion and social capital than more ethnically homogeneous areas, at least in the short run, but communities that can successfully incorporate immigrants often forge larger, more inclusive identities over the long run. In the United States at least, immigration in recent decades has not been associated with more crime; immigrants themselves often contribute economically to poor communities and are not particularly prone to criminal activity or violence.

International migration is increasing worldwide. Many European countries that used to send migrants elsewhere in the nineteenth century have, in the post–World War II period, received many immigrants from abroad. These countries struggle with many of the same issues that immigration raises in the United States, such as the considerable concern about whether immigrants and their children—particularly those who are "visible minorities"—will integrate into society. While different host countries and different immigrant groups experience considerable variation, there are signs that integration is occurring in many European countries as well. These trends have not silenced debates on immigration in the United States or abroad, as many are still concerned about how immigration will continue to change the character of their country and how immigrants of the future will fare.

6 Racial and Ethnic Inequality

Racism has a long history in the United States. The country's Founding Fathers were deeply ambivalent about the institution of slavery. On the one hand, slavery stood in opposition to the ideals famously expressed in the Declaration of Independence: "We hold these truths to be self-evident, that all men are created equal, that they are endowed by their Creator with certain unalienable Rights, that among these are Life, Liberty and the pursuit of Happiness." On the other hand, the founders did not advocate for immediate emancipation of slaves for at least three reasons: their need to compromise with pro-slavery advocates to maintain the American republic, their view of slavery as a form of property protected by the Constitution, and their own attitudes about the racial superiority of whites.[1]

The founders themselves had varying views of slavery. George Washington owned hundreds of slaves but generally opposed the institution of slavery and provided for the freeing of his slaves upon the death of his widow. John Adams (the nation's second president) never owned slaves and was against slavery but generally did not take a strong political stand on the divisive issue. Notably, his son, John Quincy Adams, the sixth president, became a strong anti-slavery advocate during his postpresidency congressional career in the 1830s and 1840s. He accused slaveholders of immorality and stridently called for slavery's abolition.

Thomas Jefferson is perhaps the best personification of the nation's ambivalence on the issue. On the one hand, he was the primary author of the lofty language in the Declaration of Independence, and he believed that slavery was an evil stain on the nation's character. As president in 1807, he signed into law a bill that banned the importation of slaves into the United States. In an 1814 letter to Thomas Cooper, he wrote, "There is nothing I would not sacrifice to a practicable plan of abolishing every vestige of this moral and political depravity."[2] On the other hand, he remained a slave owner to his death (at which time his 130 slaves were auctioned off to cover his family's debts), and he believed in the biological inferiority of African Americans. He also believed that freed slaves and their former masters could never live in harmony and that racial mixing would be degrading to whites and to the country. As historian Stephen Ambrose writes, "Jefferson, like all slaveholders and many others, regarded Negroes as inferior, childlike, untrustworthy and, of course, as property."[3] For these reasons, he preferred to gradually free slaves but then deport them to Africa or the West Indies.[4]

Disagreements about slavery festered for decades after the founding of the country, at times threatening to break it apart. The tenuous compromise between slaveholding states of the South and free states of the North finally buckled with the election of Abraham Lincoln, who was feared by many for his anti-slavery convictions. The military victory by the North in the Civil War and the passage of the Thirteenth Amendment to the Constitution that outlawed involuntary servitude settled the issue once and for all. However, despite the abolition of slavery, black subjugation continued for another century in the South in the form of Jim Crow segregation. Northern blacks often fared only a little better, increasingly crowded into ghettos as the twentieth century progressed and facing strong discriminatory barriers in the labor market. Legal barriers to equality final fell during the civil rights movement, which culminated with the passage of a number of laws in the 1950s and 1960s forbidding racial discrimination in many walks of life. Americans attitudes toward race have also continued to liberalize steadily since then.

Many argue that race therefore has a different meaning and significance for the generation coming of age today than for previous ones. For example, National Public Radio (NPR) conducted a series of conversations about race (The Race Card Project), for which thousands of people submitted their thoughts on race and cultural identity today in six words. One respondent that NPR highlighted, George Washington III, an African American married to a white woman in North Carolina, submitted the following entry: "My mixed kids have it differently." By this, he meant that unlike in the past when anyone with any African American ancestry was considered black (the "one drop" rule), his children now have the freedom to identify as mixed race and can celebrate both sides of their family.[5]

With the election of Barack Obama as president in 2008 (and his reelection in 2012), some have argued that the United States is now postracial—that race no longer plays a very meaningful role in people's lives. Others scoff at this notion, arguing that race still plays a central role in determining people's life chances. The goal of this chapter is to examine the role of race in contemporary American society. I describe differences in socioeconomic outcomes across racial and ethnic groups, discuss the factors that contribute to these differences, and reflect on the trajectory of the American color line today.

WHAT IS RACE AND ETHNICITY?

Race commonly has been thought of as a biological concept that distinguishes groups by physical, mental, and genetic traits. While some research activity continues today exploring genetic differences between races, most contemporary social and biological scientists do not believe any evidence exists indicating that racial differences have a deep biological or genetic origin. Instead, most accept the notion that race is a social construction, and as such, meaningful social distinctions between racial groups vary across time and place. During the Enlightenment in the 1700s, many European scholars became interested in understanding racial differences and created all sorts of classification schemes that included anywhere from three to thirty categories of race. Some of these scholars, for example, divided Europeans themselves into four races:

Nordic or northern, Alpine or central, Mediterranean or southern, and Slavic or eastern.[6]

Many southern and eastern European immigrants to the United States in the late nineteenth century and the early twentieth were initially viewed as racially distinct, stoking the fears of nativists and public officials, as previously discussed. Theodore Roosevelt warned of "race suicide" and bemoaned the higher fertility rate among inferior immigrant women compared with that of Anglo-Saxon women. Notions of race were legitimized by scientists who developed theories of eugenics and the role of genes in explaining broad social differences across populations.[7] One of the earliest applications of IQ testing was to show that southern and eastern European immigrants were not as smart as the native stock—a hypothesis that was believed to have been confirmed.[8]

The sociologist Mary Waters notes, "At the peak of immigration from southern and central Europe there was widespread discrimination and hostility against the newcomers by established Americans. Italians, Poles, Greeks, and Jews were called derogatory names, attacked by nativist mobs, and derided in the press. Intermarriage across ethnic lines was very uncommon. . . . The immigrants and their children were residentially segregated, occupationally specialized, and generally poor."[9] Assimilation occurred only gradually through the twentieth century as immigration ebbed, the country's attention turned to two world wars and a depression, and social and economic changes in the post–World War II period further facilitated the upward mobility of the descendants of these immigrants.[10]

Illustrating differences in views about the meaning of race across places, conceptions of race have been more fluid in Latin American societies, where skin color is seen along a continuum, than in the United States, where the division between black and white racial identities has long been sharply defined (perhaps at least until recently). The Brazilian census, for example, has the following categories: white, brown, black, yellow, indigenous, and undeclared. More generally, different societies use different physical attributes to construct racial categories.[11] Skin color seems like an easily observable way to divide people, but is it any more important than eye color, curliness of hair, or any other physical characteristic? Thus, social scientists today see race as representing social relations embedded in a society's specific historical context.[12] Racial distinctions are real and meaningful in a given place to the extent that people are treated differently and have different kinds of life experiences and outcomes.

There is often some confusion about the distinction between "race" and "ethnicity." *Race* typically refers to a group of people who are perceived, by both themselves and others, as possessing distinctive hereditary traits. In the U.S. context, phenotypical difference (skin color) has been the most salient marker of racial difference. In contrast, *ethnicity* refers to a group of people who are differentiated by culture rather than by perceived physical or genetic differences. Nevertheless, the terms *race* and *ethnicity* are often used interchangeably in public conversations today, especially given the growing diversity of the U.S. population, increasing intermarriage, and the changing meaning and importance of group differences. There is also some ambiguity about whether some groups, such as Hispanics or Middle Easterners, are distinct races or ethnicities.[13]

The U.S. Census Bureau has collected data on race/ethnicity in a variety of ways over the years, reflecting changing notions of salient social divisions. It currently collects such information with two questions. The first question asks, "Is this person Spanish/Hispanic/Latino?" There is an answer box for "no" and additional "yes" boxes for people to indicate if they are Mexican, Puerto Rican, or Cuban. There is also a write-in box where respondents can identify other origins. The next question on the form asks, "What is this person's race?" There are answer boxes for White, Black, American Indian, or Alaska Native, and a series of boxes for various Asian groups and Native Hawaiians. People can also mark "some other race," as well as (beginning in the year 2000) two or more races. When disseminating data on race and ethnicity, the Census Bureau essentially uses five race categories (White, Black, American Indian and Alaska Native, Asian, and Native Hawaiian and other Pacific Islander) and one ethnicity (Hispanic origin). A number of respondents are confused by these questions and wonder why Hispanic origin is asked separately.[14] Some advocate using a single combined question that asks more simply about ethnic origins, with the view that "race" has little or no objective basis.[15] Given the fuzziness in the use of these concepts, I often use the terms *race* and *ethnicity* either together (as in the title of this chapter) or interchangeably.

CONTEMPORARY PATTERNS OF RACIAL AND
ETHNIC INEQUALITY

U.S. society has become increasingly racially and ethnically diverse. The proportion of the population that was non-Hispanic white decreased substantially from 83 percent in 1970 to 63 percent in 2011. Meanwhile, the relative size of the black population stayed fairly steady (12 percent in 2011), and the representation of Hispanics (5 to 17 percent) and Asians (1 to 5 percent) increased significantly over the period. In this section we examine changes in the educational attainment, income, poverty, and wealth of different groups to shed light on the extent of racial and ethnic socioeconomic inequality in American society.

Figure 37 shows that college completion has increased markedly for all racial/ethnic groups over time, but significant disparities remain. In 2012, only about 1 in 7 Hispanics who were 25 years old and over had completed college, compared with over a fifth of blacks, over a third of non-Hispanic whites, and over half of Asians. In 1940, only 5 percent of the total population age 25 years and older had a college degree, including 5 percent of whites and just 1 percent of blacks. As one would expect, educational attainment disparities show up in high school graduation rates as well, though the white-black gap is narrower, with 93 percent of non-Hispanic whites and 85 percent of blacks graduating from high school among those age 25 and older in 2012. Hispanics have the lowest levels of high school completion at 65 percent. About 89 percent of Asians had completed high school in 2012.[16]

Racial and ethnic differences persist when looking at median household income (see figure 38). All groups experienced real increases in income over time, with all groups also taking a tumble during the Great Recession. Consistent with the educational differences described above, the median household income was highest among Asians at $65,129, followed by non-Hispanic whites ($55,412). However, even though African Americans had higher levels of education than Hispanics, median household income was higher among Hispanics ($38,624) than blacks ($32,229).

Unsurprisingly, racial and ethnic differences also show up in poverty statistics (figure 39). In 2011, 10 percent of non-Hispanic whites and 12

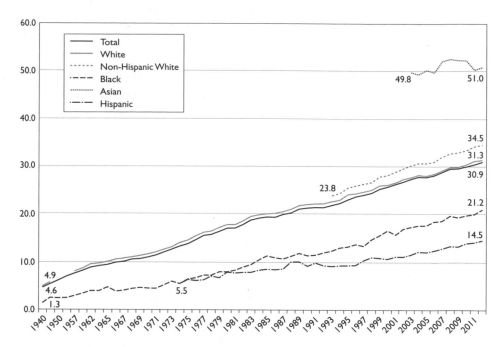

Figure 37. Percentage of people age 25 years and older who have completed college, by race and ethnicity, 1940–2012. Note: Data were collected for different groups at different points in time, which accounts for the various gaps in the graph, including that for whites between ca. 1947 and 1957. Please refer to U.S. Census Bureau 2013d for more information. Source: U.S. Census Bureau 2013d.

percent of Asians were poor, compared with 25 percent Hispanics and 28 percent of African Americans. Notably, the black poverty rate declined significantly over time, from a high of 55 percent in 1959. Nevertheless, the 2000s were a difficult decade for low-income Americans, with blacks experiencing the largest absolute increase in poverty. Finally, racial and ethnic inequality in wealth is even larger than in education, income, or poverty. The mean net worth of white households was $593,000 in 2010, whereas the mean net worth of African American and Hispanic households was only $85,000 and $90,000, respectively. Part of this reflects the fact that non-Hispanic whites are much more likely to be homeowners (75 percent) than African Americans (48 percent) and Hispanics (47 percent), and the value of one's home is most often a household's greatest single asset.[17]

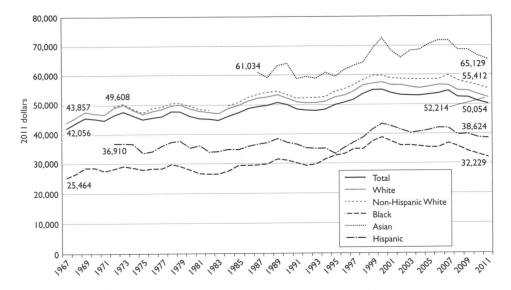

Figure 38. Median household income, by race and ethnicity, 1967–2011 (in constant 2011 dollars). Note: No published data are available for non-Hispanic whites in 1984. Source: U.S. Census Bureau 2012k.

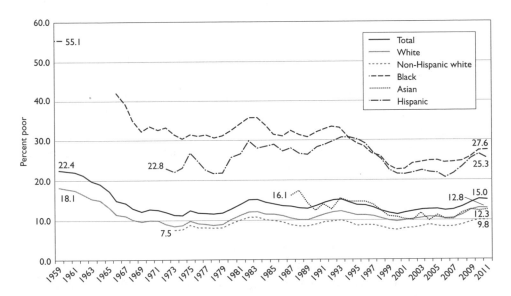

Figure 39. Poverty rates, by race and ethnicity, 1959–2011. Note: No published data are available for blacks between 1959 and 1966. Source: U.S. Census Bureau 2012g.

What factors help explain these disparities? Broad social inequalities in multicultural societies are often a function of what sociologists refer to as "social stratification," which involves members of one group in power seeking to maximize their position by restricting others' access to resources such as jobs, education, health services, and political power. Max Weber noted that usually a social group "takes some externally identifiable characteristic of another group—[such as] race, language, religion, local or social origin, descent, residence, etc.—as a pretext for attempting their exclusion."[18] In this way, broad social boundaries are drawn and maintained.[19] African Americans, Asian Americans, Hispanics, Native Americans, and even many white ethnic and national groups, such as Jews and the Irish, have all at times had to cope with limited opportunities, though their experiences have differed in very important ways. Below I discuss the experiences of contemporary racial and ethnic minority groups in more detail.

African Americans

African Americans have long struggled against racial oppression. They first arrived in the United States in large numbers as involuntary immigrants during the slave trade and were heavily concentrated in southern states. The Civil War and accompanying constitutional amendments ended slavery and conferred citizenship upon African Americans. Nevertheless, after some hope of equality during Reconstruction, from about 1865 to 1877, when blacks gained the right to vote and a number were elected to state legislatures, the U.S. House of Representatives, and even the U.S. Senate, they were relegated to second-class citizenship by the late 1870s, with southern whites reestablishing their own supremacy. Through violence and intimidation, southern whites denied blacks the power to vote. As many as two thousand to three thousand lynchings were perpetrated in the last decade and a half of the nineteenth century.[20] In the economic sphere, blacks in the South often worked as sharecroppers, mainly because they were barred by law or custom from most other full-time jobs outside the black community. Jim Crow laws mandated segregation in all public facilities, ensuring inferior services, including education, for the black community.[21]

Gunnar Myrdal, in his book *An American Dilemma: The Negro Problem and Modern Democracy*, published in 1944, described the nature and extent of black subjugation in the South:

> Violence, terror, and intimidation have been, and still are, effectively used to disfranchise Negroes in the South. Physical coercion is not so often practiced against the Negro, but the mere fact that it can be used with impunity and that it is devastating in its consequences creates a psychic coercion that exists nearly everywhere in the South. A Negro can seldom claim the protection of the police and the courts if a white man knocks him down, or if a mob burns his house or inflicts bodily injuries on him or on members of his family. If he defends himself against a minor violence, he may expect a major violence. If he once "gets in wrong" he may expect the loss of his job or other economic injury, and constant insult and loss of whatever legal rights he may have had.[22]

During the twentieth century many blacks left the oppressive conditions in the South to look for opportunity in the North, especially in booming industries in many northeastern and midwestern cities such as Chicago, Detroit, and New York. This Great Migration resulted in a striking regional redistribution of the black population in the United States. In 1900, about three-quarters of all African Americans lived in rural southern areas; a century later, that figure had declined to about 12 percent. By 1950, more than 2.5 million southern-born African Americans were living outside the region, a number that increased to more than 4 million by 1980.[23] While economic opportunities were better in the North, and the racial climate was not as oppressive (northern blacks, for example, could for the most part vote), blacks still faced a wide range of discriminatory barriers in the labor and housing market and were segregated in congested northern ghettos.

The civil rights movement in the 1950s and 1960s overturned the legal framework that supported the unequal treatment of blacks. In 1954, for example, in the case *Brown v. Board of Education of Topeka*, the Supreme Court ruled that the separate-but-equal doctrine underlying the Jim Crow system was invalid. In the 1960s several laws were passed in Congress (including the far-reaching Civil Rights Act of 1964) that prohibited racial discrimination in employment practices, public accommodations, and housing market transactions. The civil rights movement itself was propelled mainly by nonviolent protest and civil disobedience. The Montgomery Bus Boycott in Alabama in 1955–56, for example, protested racial segregation in the city's public transit system, which relegated blacks to seats in the back of the bus. The campaign began when Rosa Parks, an African American woman active in the movement, refused to give up her seat to a white person. The boycott was a success, and the Supreme Court eventually declared segregation laws to be unconstitutional.

Legal changes have also been accompanied by gradual changes in public opinion. The proportion of whites holding blatantly racist attitudes has dropped considerably over the decades according to national polls. For example, in the 1940s and 1950s, fewer than half of whites surveyed believed that white and black students should attend the same schools or that black and white job applicants should have an equal chance of getting a job. By the 1990s, however, over 90 percent of whites said they believed that schools and employers should treat whites and blacks equally.[24]

The removal of legal barriers and the slowly changing social norms, however, did not translate into immediate social and economic equality. Civil rights legislation was being passed during a time of deindustrialization— when the share of people employed in manufacturing was declining—and when many northeastern and midwestern cities were losing jobs and people through outmigration to the Sun Belt. (Many jobs also went abroad.) For example, in the twenty-year period between 1967 and 1987, Philadelphia lost 64 percent of its manufacturing jobs, Chicago lost 60 percent, New York City lost 58 percent, and Detroit 51 percent. This hurt blacks as well as whites living in those cities and contributed to the increasing poverty of blacks concentrated in inner cities.[25]

Some commentators, such as William Julius Wilson, have argued that race has become less important in determining the labor market success of African Americans and that class position has become more important.[26] From colonial times through the first half of the twentieth century, racial oppression was deliberate and overt. By the latter half of the twentieth century, many traditional barriers were dismantled as a result of political, social, and economic changes of the civil rights era. Wilson emphasizes that although discrimination has become less common though not eliminated, economic conditions have come to play an increasingly important role in shaping opportunities available to African Americans.

He argues that deindustrialization and class segregation in particular have hampered the economic mobility of less-skilled blacks.[27]

Studies show that the economic "penalty" of being African American has declined since the 1960s, in that occupational mobility has increased, as has wage parity.[28] Racial differences in economic outcomes are significantly reduced when one accounts for educational achievement.[29] Measuring the direct effects of discrimination is difficult, because it is not always clear when a discriminatory action has occurred or if general observed differences between whites and blacks are a result of unmeasured differences (e.g., quality of schooling received) or of discrimination itself. Careful examinations of this issue tend to indicate that discrimination still occurs in labor markets and in other areas. For example, "paired-test studies," in which minority job applicants were paired with white applicants with similar backgrounds and trained to be as similar as possible in behavior, have shown that minorities, particularly African Americans and foreign-sounding Latinos, were less likely to be given job interviews and offers, at least in the low-wage labor market.[30] Economists have estimated that perhaps one-quarter of the black-white wage gap is due to prejudice, suggesting that racism continues to contribute to African American economic disadvantage.[31]

Other factors have also contributed to relatively low levels of socioeconomic attainment among African Americans, some related to race and others more nonracial in origin. One race-related factor is residential and social segregation. Because African Americans often live in segregated and disadvantaged communities, they may have fewer economically useful contacts ("social capital") on which to draw to help achieve success. Many people, for example, find a job via word of mouth through friends and neighbors. Those with affluent friends and neighbors typically have access to more and better opportunities.[32] Residential segregation also affects educational disparities because a significant portion of school funding comes from local taxes. Schools in poor neighborhoods often have inferior resources and fewer enrichment programs. High neighborhood poverty rates are strongly correlated with lower student test scores.[33] Declining levels of black segregation in recent decades, along with rapid black suburbanization, has likely reduced the effects of segregation in contributing to racial inequalities over the past couple of decades. However, many cities—particularly some in the Northeast and Midwest such as Chicago, New York, Detroit, and Milwaukee—still have very high levels of black segregation.[34]

Another factor that contributes to higher poverty rates among African Americans is differentials in human-capital skills. Human capital refers to education attainment and subsequent work experience and skills. The gap in average levels of education has declined over the past few decades. Nevertheless, the quality of schooling received by children in the United States still varies widely, and, as mentioned above, African Americans are more likely to attend inferior schools with fewer resources and have lower test scores. Lower employment levels among young African Americans subsequently contribute to earnings differentials. High black incarceration rates (black men are eight times more likely to be incarcerated than white men) translate to a relatively high proportion of young black men entering the labor force with a criminal record, which further dampens their employability. The rapid growth in the prison population from the late 1970s through the mid-2000s exacerbated this problem. Many contend that high black incarceration rates are in part due to racial profiling by law enforcement and racial biases in the sentencing process.[35]

Differences in family structure affect ethnic socioeconomic differentials as well. While 36 percent of white births were to unmarried women, the figure was double (72 percent) among African Americans.[36] This contributes to socioeconomic inequalities because single-parent families are considerably more likely to be poor: about 4 in 10 (41 percent) female-headed families with children were poor in 2011, compared with fewer than 1 in 10 (9 percent) of married-couple families with children.[37] Single parents often struggle to earn sufficient income for their family while also providing an attentive, nurturing environment for their children.

Thus, some have emphasized that an African American disadvantage has persisted across generations because of *cumulative disadvantages*. Racial gaps show up early in childhood and widen through the life course. As author Michael Wenger puts it:

> On average, African Americans begin life's journey several miles behind their white counterparts as a result of the legacy of our history of racial oppression. This disadvantage is compounded by institutional hurdles they encounter at every stage of the journey: the socioeconomic conditions into

which they're born, the system of public education through which they pass, the type of employment they are able to secure, the legacy they are able to leave behind. These hurdles, arduous, relentless, and often withering to the soul, do not confront many white people as they pursue their hopes and dreams.[38]

The importance of cumulative disadvantages suggests that ending inequality has no single easy solution and helps explain why progress has been slow—though some suggest that early childhood interventions revolving around schooling could be the most effective approach to reducing racial disparities.[39] Even as race has become less important in American society, economic inequality and class background have become more important. For example, while the black-white reading gap used to be substantially larger than the rich-poor reading gap in the 1940s, by the 2000s the reverse was true.[40] As a result, while we have seen considerable growth in the black middle class in recent decades, the economic challenges faced by poor African Americans remain daunting.[41]

Hispanics, Asians, and the Role of Immigration

The many racial and ethnic dividing lines in American society have historically reserved privilege for whites. Through much of the twentieth century, some of the factors that impeded African American mobility—discrimination and segregation—also affected Hispanics and Asian Americans. Some of the traditional racial dividing lines have eased, however, mainly since the civil rights era, enabling many members of these groups to achieve socioeconomic mobility and broader incorporation into mainstream society, though people still debate the extent to which racial dividing lines continue to inhibit opportunity.

Hispanics have a long history in the United States, dating at least as far back as the annexation of territory in Florida in the early 1800s. At the request of a growing number of U.S. settlers in what had been Mexican territory, the United States annexed Texas in 1845, precipitating the Mexican-American War. After defeating the Mexican army in 1848, the United States annexed California, New Mexico, Nevada, Arizona, Utah, and Colorado as well. The Mexican-origin population in the American Southwest in 1848 was likely about 80,000 people—roughly one-fifth of

the total population of that area.[42] Mexican Americans living in these territories were often treated as second-class citizens. In subsequent decades
Mexicans were used as cheap labor in the building of railroads, in mining,
and in agriculture. During labor shortages they were often recruited, but
at other times they were encouraged to return to Mexico, often with force.
Between 1930 and 1960, almost 4 million Mexicans were deported.[43]

The presence of other Hispanic groups is more recent. Puerto Ricans
migrated to the U.S. mainland in large numbers in the 1950s and 1960s.
Reflecting Puerto Rico's status as a U.S. territory (Spain ceded Puerto Rico
to the United States in 1898 as a result of its defeat in the Spanish-
American War), Puerto Ricans are U.S. citizens at birth. The Puerto Rican
population is generally very mixed, and in the past the darker-skinned
Puerto Ricans in particular encountered significant racial barriers.[44]
Cubans entered the United States in significant numbers after the Cuban
Revolution in 1959. Many of these immigrants were highly educated pro-
fessionals who had been supporters of the deposed president and dictator,
Fulgencio Batista. Another wave entered in 1980 as part of the Mariel
Boatlift; this group was decidedly more socioeconomically mixed. Cubans
overwhelmingly settled in Miami, and many found success as entrepre-
neurs and small business owners.[45]

As of 2010, there were 31.8 million Mexican-origin people in the United
States (63 percent of the Hispanic population), up from 8.7 million in
1980. The next two traditionally largest groups—Puerto Ricans and
Cubans—have been falling as a fraction of the total Hispanic population,
from 14 percent and 6 percent, respectively, in 1980 to 9 percent and 4
percent in 2010. In the meantime, the number of Salvadorans, Dominicans,
and Guatemalans in the United States has grown rapidly in recent years,
though each of these groups still made up no more than about 2 to 3 percent of the Hispanic population nationally in 2010.

Among Asian groups, the Chinese were the first to immigrate in significant numbers around the time of the California gold rush in 1848. In the
1860s, an estimated 12,000 to 16,000 Chinese laborers were employed to
build the western leg of the Central Pacific Railroad. Some Chinese also
worked in agriculture, and others were entrepreneurs in San Francisco.[46]
The Chinese experienced a good deal of discrimination and violence as the
community grew; they were viewed as economic competitors who would

drive down the wages of native-born Americans. The Naturalization Act of 1870 limited naturalization in the United States to "white persons and persons of African descent"; this meant that the Chinese were aliens ineligible for citizenship and remained so until 1943. The 1882 Chinese Exclusion Act went further, barring the immigration of all Chinese laborers. Because Chinese immigration was so heavily male, the Chinese population in the United States began to gradually decline until about 1920, after which it slowly rebounded as a result of natural increase.[47]

The first group of Japanese arrived in California around 1869 but began to increase more markedly in the 1890s. Initially, most Japanese worked in agriculture, filling a large demand for labor, though many went on to live in larger cities, including San Francisco and Los Angeles, and others became successful farm owners and entrepreneurs. However, white California workingmen and others eventually lobbied for their exclusion. Cognizant of the military might of Japan, which was a considerably more powerful country than China at the time, and not wishing to offend it, the Gentleman's Agreement of 1907 was negotiated between the United States and Japan, ending most kinds of immigration from Japan to the United States, except for family-reunification purposes. In 1913 and 1920 California enacted anti-alien land laws aimed at Japanese farmers, barring "aliens ineligible for citizenship" from purchasing and leasing agricultural land. The resident Japanese population, however, found ways to get around some of these obstacles, and many continued to prosper. Japanese immigration was later completely halted in 1924.[48] Many Japanese on the West Coast were infamously interned in camps during World War II—a fate not suffered by the German American and Italian American communities—indicative of the racism of the time.

Initial migration of Filipinos to the United States came shortly after the American annexation of the Philippines in 1898. In the 1920s and 1930s larger numbers came as farmworkers, filling in the kinds of jobs held by the Chinese and Japanese immigrants in previous years. As Asians, Filipinos were aliens ineligible for citizenship until the 1940s. Filipinos faced a significant amount of prejudice and discrimination. As writer Carlos Bulosan wrote in 1946, "Do you know what a Filipino feels in America? . . . He is the loneliest thing on earth. There is much to be appreciated . . . beauty, wealth, power, grandeur. But is he part of these luxuries? He looks, poor man, through the fingers of his eyes. He's enchained, damnably to his race, his heritage. His is betrayed, my friend."[49] Another time he wrote, "I feel like a criminal running away from a crime that I did not commit. And that crime is that I am a Filipino in America."[50] Filipinos, like other Asians and other minorities, were excluded from a broad array of economic opportunities and were viewed as unwelcome aliens by the native white majority population.

The second wave of immigration after the elimination of discriminatory national-origin quotas in 1965 included Asians from a variety of other countries, including India, Vietnam, and Korea. In 2010, the largest Asian subgroup was Chinese (24 percent of the Asian population), followed by Asian Indians (19 percent) and Filipinos (17 percent). The fraction of the Asian population that is Chinese has stayed roughly the same over the past three decades, with the percentage of Asian Indians growing substantially (they were 10 percent of the Asian population in 1980) and the percentage of Filipinos declining, but slowly (they were 22 percent of the Asian population in 1980). The percentage of Japanese as a share of the Asian population has fallen considerably, from 20 percent in 1980 to 5 percent in 2010, and Korean and Vietnamese each made up 10 percent of Asians in 2010.[51]

In some respects Latinos and Asian Americans share certain experiences, because both groups have been historically discriminated against, both have experienced substantial increases in their population resulting from immigration since the 1960s, and both are heterogeneous in terms of their national origins (though Mexicans are by far the largest group among Latinos and overall). Nevertheless, as figures 37 through 39 indicate, socioeconomic outcomes of Hispanics and Asians differ substantially. For the most part Asians are on equal socioeconomic footing with native-born whites, and in fact their outcomes exceed those of whites in some respects. Because nearly two-thirds of Asians and about 2 in 5 Hispanics are foreign born and many more of both groups are of just the second generation, we need to investigate the characteristics of immigrants from Latin America and Asia to understand their disparate outcomes.[52]

Chapter 5 described patterns of assimilation among Asians and Hispanics and noted important differences in characteristics of the immigrants from different origins, especially in levels of education. Specifically, immigrants from Asia tend to constitute a more "select" group than immigrants from Latin America. Immigrants from Korea, India, and the Philippines achieve higher average levels of education than both Latinos and native-born whites. For example, about 80 percent of immigrants from India have a bachelor's degree or more, compared with 6 percent from Mexico.[53] One factor explaining these differences is that while many immigrants from Asia become eligible to migrate to the United States because of their work-related skills, a larger proportion of immigrants from Latin America immigrate because they have relatives who are U.S. citizens.[54]

It is important to note of course that poverty among immigrants also varies considerably by country of origin; not all subgroups among Asians and Hispanics are similarly advantaged or disadvantaged. Among foreign-born Hispanics, for example, poverty rates in 2007 were high among Dominicans (28 percent) and Mexicans (22 percent) but more moderate among Cubans (16 percent) and Colombians (11 percent).[55] South Americans have nearly reached parity with non-Hispanic whites in terms of both the proportion having a college education and median household income.[56] Among Asian immigrant groups, poverty rates were a little higher for Koreans (17 percent) than for immigrants from Japan (9 percent), India (7 percent), and the Philippines (4 percent).[57] Many of these differences are explained by the average characteristics of the immigrants themselves (especially educational attainment), though as noted above each group has a unique history of immigration to the United States.

Initial disadvantages tend to persist over time and across generations. Native-born Hispanics obtain on average higher levels of education than immigrant Hispanics, but their educational levels still lag behind those of native-born whites, largely because of the lower initial level of family resources of Hispanics.[58] In contrast, native-born Asian Americans tend to achieve high levels of education, which translate into better jobs, higher incomes, and less poverty. Once family characteristics are taken into account, there is little difference in the poverty rates between native-born Asians and native-born non-Hispanic whites.[59] While Latinos are less likely to have a college degree and tend to work in lower-skill, lower-wage jobs, once human capital differences are accounted for (especially education and English-language proficiency), there is not that much difference between whites and Hispanics in terms of occupational status and earnings.[60]

The research literature does not offer a definitive answer as to the extent of racial/ethnic discrimination faced by Asians and Latinos in the labor market. For Asians, it is probably safe to say that discrimination is not widespread enough to significantly affect average levels of socioeconomic achievement. For Latinos, family background characteristics (such as education and income) are likely to play the most prominent role and ethnicity a more minor one. Race appears to continue to play a significant role in explaining lower wages and higher poverty among blacks and darker-skinned Latinos.[61]

Native Americans

The experience of Native Americans, as the original inhabitants of the North American continent, differs from that of all the other groups. At the time when Jamestown was established in 1607, estimates of the number of Native Americans living in what is now the United States is estimated to have varied from about 1 million to 10 million.[62] The population declined substantially over the course of the seventeenth through the nineteenth century, reaching an estimated low of 250,000 in 1890. The most important factor contributing to the decline in population was the diseases brought by American colonists to which Native Americans had little immunity or resistance, including scarlet fever, whooping cough, bubonic plague, cholera, and typhoid. Other causes for population decline include warfare, displacement, the slaughter of buffalo on which some tribes depended, and alcoholism.[63] The Native American population has grown rapidly since the 1970s, not just from natural increase but also in part because a greater number of Americans have asserted some Indian heritage. The civil rights movement and the decline in negative stereotyping of Native Americans—as well as the increase in positive representations of Native Americans in popular culture, such as the movie *Dances with Wolves*—help explain the increase in self-reported Native American identity.[64] As of 2010, 2.9 million Americans identified as solely Native American (0.9 percent of the total U.S. population), and another 2.3 million (0.7 percent) said they were at least part Native American.[65]

Despite this demographic growth, Native Americans tend to have low levels of educational attainment and income and high levels of poverty. In 2010, among the Native American population age 25 years and older, 13 percent had a college degree or more (compared with 30 percent among the population as a whole). Median household income was $35,000 (the national average was $50,000), and their poverty rate was 28 percent (the national average was 15 percent), placing their level of disadvantage near that of African Americans.[66] Native Americans have long had to overcome a dearth of job opportunities in and around reservations and also poor schooling. Although some evidence indicates a decline in the net negative effect of being Native American on wages over the last half of the twentieth century, Native Americans still have lower levels of educational attainment and earnings than otherwise comparable whites.[67] It is not clear whether these differences are explained by discrimination or by other difficult-to-observe factors correlated with being Native American.[68] Research on Native Americans tends to be more limited than that of other groups, in part because of the relatively small Native American population. Additional research on Native Americans, not to mention the other groups, would help shed further light on the complex interrelationship between race and socioeconomic disparities.

MULTIRACIAL AMERICA: ARE WE POSTRACIAL?

The number of mixed-race marriages and multiracial individuals has grown considerably in recent years. The multiracial population grew by 50 percent between 2000 and 2010, from 1.8 million to 4.2 million, making it the fastest growing group of children in the country. Despite this growth, the overall proportion of Americans who report two or more races is still small, at 2.9 percent, according to the 2010 census (the races consist of white, black, American Indian, Asian, and Native Hawaiian). The most common multiracial combination is black and white. Nevertheless, only 2.5 percent of non-Hispanic whites reported more than one race (i.e., among those who reported being white either alone or in combination with another racial group), compared with 6.1 percent of blacks, 13.5 percent of Asians, and 44 percent of Native Americans.[69]

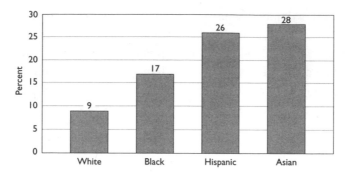

Figure 40. Percentage of newlyweds married to someone of a
different race/ethnicity, 2010. Source: Wang 2012, 8.

The number of Americans identifying as multiracial will likely grow
rapidly in the coming years because of recent increases in intermarriage.
According to one study, about 15 percent of all new marriages in the
2008–10 period involved spouses of different races or ethnicities—more
than double the percentage (6.7 percent) in 1980. (In this same study
Hispanic origin was considered as a separate race/ethnicity from white.)
The percentage of marriages involving a mix of differing races/ethnicities
varies across groups, with a low of 9 percent of newlywed whites who married someone of a different race/ethnicity, compared with 17 percent of
blacks, 26 percent of Hispanics, and 28 percent of foreign-born and U.S.-
born Asians (see figure 40). In fact, nearly half of all U.S.-born Asians
marry whites.[70] Overall, about 7 in 10 of mixed-race/ethnicity marriages
still involve a white spouse, reflecting the fact that whites constitute the
largest racial/ethnic group in the United States. The median household
income of mixed-race newlywed couples tends to fall somewhere between
the median incomes of couples in the same-race groups.[71]

Americans have become more accepting of intermarriage. In 2011,
nearly two-thirds of Americans (63 percent) said they "would be fine" if a
family member married someone of a different race. In contrast, in 1986
(when the question was asked differently), about a third of the public
viewed intermarriage as acceptable for everyone, 37 percent said it was
acceptable for others but not themselves, and 28 percent said different
races marrying one another was not acceptable for anyone. Younger

respondents were more accepting of intermarriage than older ones, suggesting differences in views about race over time and across age cohorts.[72]

One news story reporting on the rise in intermarriage told the story of seventeen-year-old Kayci Baldwin of Middletown, New Jersey, who was the daughter of a mixed-race couple:

> She remembers how her black father and white mother often worried whether she would fit in with the other kids. While she at first struggled with her identity, Baldwin now actively embraces it, sponsoring support groups and a nationwide multiracial teen club of 1,000 that includes both Democrats and Republicans.
>
> "I went to my high school prom last week with my date who is Ecuadoran-Nigerian, a friend who is Chinese-white and another friend who is part Dominican," she said. "While we are a group that was previously ignored in many ways, we now have an opportunity to fully identify and express ourselves."[73]

One blogger, Leighton Woodhouse, describes broader social changes and his own experiences in a similar way:

> My girlfriend and I are both of mixed racial heritage. I'm half Japanese and half Anglo. She's half Salvadoran and half Jewish. If and when we have children, they'll be a quarter Asian, a quarter Latino and half white, with the white side split WASP/Jewish. When our kids become 18 and fill out their first voter registration forms, the only ethnic category that will make any sense for them to check off is "Multiracial." Today, checking off that box feels pretty close to checking off "Other" or "None of the above" on a questionnaire on any given topic; it's a throwaway category for misfits that has little if any analytical value to the researchers who review the data, but that has to be in there to get the respondent to the next section. When enough Americans start checking off that box, however, it's going to be impossible to ignore.[74]

So are we postracial? The short answer is no. Changes in American society since the 1950s and 1960s have been momentous. The fall of legal barriers and changes in attitudes have opened up many opportunities that were previously closed, if not unimaginable. African Americans, Hispanics, and Asians hold more high-level jobs in government and in the private sector than they used to, and this pattern is more pronounced among younger cohorts.[75]

However, as long as the socioeconomic disparities highlighted in figures 37 through 39 persist, it will be hard to claim that we are "beyond race." The disparities are caused in part by factors directly related to race (especially in the case of African Americans), such as discrimination. As Woodhouse goes on to say in his blog about the growing multiracial population and its consequences, "That's not to suggest that the age of the generation that follows the Millennials will be some sort of post-racial paradise. Countries like Brazil have had broad racially mixed populations for generations; that hasn't lessened their citizens' propensity for bigotry."[76]

Racial inequality is also exacerbated by factors that are not specifically racial, and they have disparate impacts. Of note, growing economic inequality in American society is serving to hamper the opportunities of low-income Americans and their children. The soaring cost of college has made it more difficult for poor families to utilize a traditionally important avenue to upward mobility. The overrepresentation of blacks and Hispanics among the poor exacerbates racial inequalities and will serve to lengthen the time until racial and ethnic parity is achieved.

INTERNATIONAL COMPARISONS

Examining the experience of minorities around the globe can provide a broader perspective for understanding race relations in the United States. However, rigorous international comparisons of racial and ethnic inequality can be challenging for a number of reasons. For one, ethnic divisions vary widely across countries, making it important to have a deep understanding of local social relations and institutions. In Rwanda, for example, there have been major fault lines between the Tutsi and Hutu people, leading to genocide in 1994. Even though these groups would both be referred to as "black" in the United States, some commentators view them as racially distinct, differing in physical appearance, such as in skin tone and nose width.[77] In some countries, social stratification occurs among religious groups rather than ethnic ones—for example, the Shia-Sunni split in parts of the Middle East and elsewhere in Asia. In other countries, such as many in Europe, ethnic divisions are of relatively recent origin, resulting from the increase in international migration. In these contexts—

as in the United States when discussing outcomes among some groups—separating the effect of nativity from race and ethnicity is difficult.

Chapter 5 discussed the variation in the extent to which immigrants of different origins are integrating in Europe. Immigrants of Muslim and North African origins are often disadvantaged in a number of countries. Various factors contribute to this, including the social background (e.g., level of education and language fluency) of the immigrants and their children and racism and discrimination in the host society.[78] For example, the 1999–2000 European Values Study indicated that between 8 and 33 percent of respondents in various European countries reported to be unwilling to have Muslims as neighbors, with a mean of 15 percent in western European countries and 19 percent in eastern European countries. Although the World Values Survey indicates that racial intolerance extends to all corners of the globe, the degree of intolerance differs from place to place. People in Anglo countries (the United States, Canada, and Australia) and Latin American ones tended to be more tolerant and were less likely to reject a racially different neighbor, while racial intolerance was relatively high in many Middle Eastern and other Asian countries, such as India, Jordan, and Indonesia, where people often reported not wanting to live near a racially distinct neighbor.[79] A caveat of these results is that the question on tolerance might be understood differently in different countries, and in some countries (such as Western democracies) expressing racially intolerant views is more taboo.

More generally, while the groups in conflict vary across countries, a common theme is that ethnic antagonisms are typically based on prejudices and stereotypes that serve to magnify the differences across groups and justify discriminatory behavior. That is not to say that stereotypes have no basis (groups often exhibit different characteristics and practices), but the role of structural factors—such as educational inequalities—in reinforcing disadvantage often goes unacknowledged. One news story on ethnic inequality in Slovakia describes the social and institutional relations between the dominant Slovaks and the disadvantaged Roma (often known as Gypsies), who arrived as migrants in Europe from the Indian subcontinent about fifteen hundred years ago. The Roma have high rates of unemployment, illiteracy, and are often targets of abuse, and many Europeans associate them with criminality. Some activists in Slovakia are pressing for equal rights for the Roma. A lawsuit was brought against one school in which Roma children were segregated into their own playground, did not have access to the school canteen, and were divided into different classes along ethnic lines. The lawsuit was successful, but some are not sure it will solve all problems. The article reports that there is still much wariness of the Roma among the school's faculty: "'These people are interested in only two things: money and sex,' said Vladimir Savov, an English teacher. 'They are lazy and don't want to learn.' Like other teachers, Mr. Savov now accepts that change is necessary, if only to satisfy the court, but he is deeply skeptical about abandoning segregated teaching. 'Mixed classes are a good idea in principle, but the question is how will they work in real life,' he said."[80]

In many immigrant societies the alienation of native-born minority groups is a function of their feeling left out of prosperity. Even Sweden, widely known for its commitment to equality, generous social safety net, and liberal immigration policies, has been the site of ethnic unrest. In May 2013 riots broke out in Stockholm, precipitated by the fatal shooting of a sixty-nine-year-old immigrant wielding a knife. The riots lasted for a few days and mainly involved rock throwing at police and the burning of cars and a school, though with no fatalities. Some attributed the riots to discrimination, high unemployment among the young, and growing income inequality. As one observer, Barbro Sorman, an activist of the opposition Left Party declared, "The rich are getting richer and the poor are getting poorer. Sweden is starting to look like the U.S.A." In contrast, those who viewed the riots with dismay feel the immigrants and their children are ungrateful for the opportunities they have received. One person who was generally sympathetic to immigrants' complaints of discrimination noted, "There are a lot of people aged from 20 to 22 who say, 'I want a job, I want it now, and I want to stay here.' . . . This is their problem, but it becomes a government problem."[81]

In short, many countries around the world are grappling with ethnic diversity. For some, ethnic divisions have long historical roots. For others, diversity is a more recent phenomenon resulting from increases in international migration and the gap between the aspirations of immigrants and their children and the opportunities available. Because racial and ethnic inequalities often have complicated origins, they frequently defy easy solutions.

CONCLUSION

Despite the decline in racial inequality and overt prejudice in the United States in recent decades, we still see significant differences in socioeconomic outcomes across racial and ethnic groups, such as in educational attainment, income, poverty, and wealth. Some of the continuing differences, particularly among blacks and perhaps Native Americans, can be explained by prejudice, stereotypes, and discrimination. However, the importance of race alone in determining life chances has declined substantially in recent decades, and the importance of socioeconomic background has increased. Unfortunately, the increasing importance of socioeconomic background serves to slow progress in reducing racial disparities, as initial disadvantages among groups often persist across generations because of these economic inequities.

7 Migration and Residential Segregation

In the first decades of the twentieth century cities such as New York, Chicago, Detroit, Philadelphia, and Cleveland—all in the Northeast and Midwest—were magnets for jobs and people. The population of New York, for example, doubled from 3.4 million to 6.9 million between 1900 and 1930; Chicago did the same, from to 1.7 million to 3.4 million. The past thirty years or so have produced a decidedly different pattern. While New York still managed to grow from 1980 to 2010, the populations of Chicago, Detroit, Philadelphia, and Cleveland all declined. These are just some of the cities of the Rust Belt—once vibrant industrial centers bruised and bloodied by the gradual and long-term decline of manufacturing in the United States. Detroit's fall has been precipitous, as it shrank from 1.2 million people to just 700,000 between 1980 and 2010. (It had 1.8 million people at its peak in 1950.) Local planners in Detroit now grapple with yawning budget deficits and how to shrink the footprint of the city to avoid block after block of abandoned buildings and desolate neighborhoods. The city even declared bankruptcy in 2013. Growth has instead occurred in cities mainly in the South and West—the Sun Belt—such as Houston (from 1.6 million in 1980 to 2.1 million in 2010), Phoenix (800,000 to 1.4 million), and San Antonio (800,000 to 1.3 million).[1]

What explains these regional patterns? Natural increase (or decrease)—the difference between births and deaths in the existing population—is only part of the story. A more important factor is large-scale migration trends. A story in the *Austin Statesman* newspaper discussed the rapid population growth in Austin in recent years,[2] noting, "With its high-tech industry and universities, its good economic health compared with other places, and its reputation as a vibrant hot spot for young people, the Austin metro area scores well with job seekers and young adults." The story also highlighted the experiences of two recent migrants to the area:

> The first time she set foot in Austin in 2010, [Julie] Wernersbach found herself basking on the upstairs patio at Whole Foods. It was a shimmery, sun-dappled day. She wore a tank top. It was December. . . . Just four weeks after that Shangri-La moment, Wernersbach packed up her belongings and left her home in frosty Long Island, N.Y., to take a job in Austin as a publicist for BookPeople. "Austin was a place I wanted to be and a place I wanted to work," Wernersbach said. Austin just felt comfortable, Wernersbach said, and she liked its creative culture and its appreciation for a locally owned bookstore. "And I'm having a little fun," Wernersbach added, laughing again.
>
> [One] Washington transplant, Yahaira Rodriguez, a 35-year-old Puerto Rico native, came to Austin for the first time in early 2011 for a national meeting of the home-grown Las Comadres, a social and professional networking organization for Latinas that has members across the world. "I fell in love with the city and with the people," Rodriguez said. By that summer, Rodriguez had made a new home in Austin, drawn, she said, by the city's diversity and what she considered its strong sense of community. Rodriguez thinks Austin is a place where entrepreneurs can flourish. That was something she was looking for, and she is putting it to the test, starting up a private practice here as a life coach and as a consultant working with nonprofits.[3]

These stories highlight the role of economic conditions in drawing people to places. Few people would choose to move to Austin if there were no jobs there. Likewise, social networks are instrumental in shaping migration streams. People hear about places from others whom they know. They are drawn to these locations because they offer a type of community in which they believe they can find comfort and thrive.

Economic factors and networks, along with constraints faced by individuals and the groups to which they belong, help explain not only broad regional trends in population growth and decline but also why different people choose to settle in different neighborhoods within cities. It is no coincidence that African Americans in Chicago live in neighborhoods that are mostly African American, and whites live in neighborhoods that are mostly white, nor are high levels of residential segregation by income in many metropolitan areas arbitrary. These patterns are rooted in social structure and are shaped by sociodemographic changes in American communities.[4]

The rest of this chapter explores these themes, describing patterns of regional growth and decline, the rise of American suburbs, and trends in neighborhood-level racial/ethnic and economic segregation, and offers explanations for these trends. I also draw international comparisons to further help understand patterns of migration and residential segregation in the United States and other developed countries around the world.

PATTERNS OF REGIONAL, STATE, AND METROPOLITAN AREA GROWTH AND DECLINE

Since the middle decades of the twentieth century, the population of the United States has shifted from the Rust Belt to the Sun Belt (see figure 41). Whereas only 13 percent of the population resided in the West in 1950, by 2010 nearly a quarter did. Likewise, the percentage of the population in the South rose from 31 percent to 37 percent. The Northeast and Midwest experienced corresponding relative declines, such that by 2010 about 40 percent of Americans lived in these two regions combined, down from 55 percent in 1950.

At the state level, we see that, unsurprisingly, those with the largest growth in relative terms are in the South, such as Texas, and the West, including Nevada, Utah, Arizona, and Idaho (see figure 42). While California continually received migrants from other states throughout the twentieth century, by the late 1990s large numbers of Californians were migrating out, to states such as Nevada and Arizona.[5] California's population nevertheless still continued to grow in the 1990s and 2000s because of international migration to the state and natural increase. Michigan was the only state that lost population between 2000 and 2010 (Puerto Rico also lost population), while other

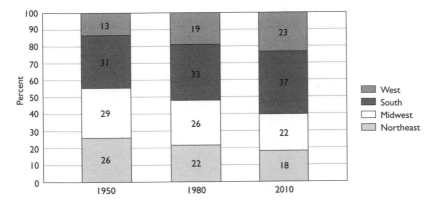

Figure 41. Population percentage distribution, by region, 1950–2010. Source: U.S. Census Bureau 2012a.

midwestern and northeastern states grew slowly as a result of natural increase and some immigration from abroad and despite migration of many of their residents to other states.

Table 3 provides a geographically more detailed look at changes by showing the ten metropolitan areas with the fastest rates of growth and decline in the 2000s. Again reflecting broader trends, those with the fastest growth are Sun Belt metropolitan areas, including larger ones such as Las Vegas and Austin. Those experiencing the largest declines in population are in the Northeast and Midwest, with the exception of New Orleans, which suffered enormous population loss as a result of the hurricane that submerged much of the city in 2005, and Pine Bluff, Arkansas. Pine Bluff is an area with high levels of unemployment, poverty, and crime. Many of the local manufacturing jobs have been outsourced abroad over the years.[6] The midwestern and northeastern cities on the list have likewise suffered from the departure of manufacturing jobs to other regions and to other countries with lower labor costs.[7] It should be noted that the Great Recession, which began in 2007, affected patterns of growth in the late 2000s, with fast-growing places such as Las Vegas and Phoenix experiencing considerably slower growth after the housing bubble burst and foreclosures soared in those areas.[8]

Immigration from abroad is also helping fuel the population growth of many Sun Belt areas. One striking trend of the 1990s and 2000s is that

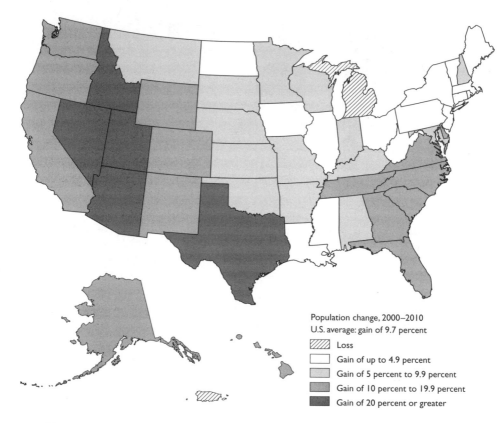

Figure 42. Percentage of change in population, by state, 2000–2010. Source: Mather, Pollard, and Jacobsen 2011, 10.

immigrants increasingly settled in untraditional ports of entry. For example, the share of immigrants in the five U.S. metropolitan areas with the largest foreign-born populations—New York, Los Angeles, Miami, Chicago, and Houston—declined from 43 percent in 2000 to 38 percent in 2010. New immigrant destinations include places such as Orlando, Las Vegas, and Atlanta. Many smaller areas that traditionally have had very few immigrants also saw tremendous growth in their foreign-born population, such as Knoxville, Tennessee, Louisville, Kentucky, and even a few cities in the Northeast and Midwest, such as Scranton, Pennsylvania, and Indianapolis, Indiana.[9]

Table 3   Metropolitan Areas Ranked according to the Fastest Rates of Growth and Decline, 2000–2010

		Population		Change	
RANK	METROPOLITAN AREA	2000	2010	NUMBER	PERCENT
	Fastest Rate of Growth				
1	The Villages, FL	53,345	93,420	40,075	75
2	St. George, UT	90,354	138,115	47,761	53
3	Las Vegas–Henderson–Paradise, NV	1,375,765	1,951,269	575,504	42
4	Raleigh, NC	797,071	1,130,490	333,419	42
5	Cape Coral–Fort Myers, FL	440,888	618,754	177,866	40
6	Provo–Orem, UT	376,774	526,810	150,036	40
7	Greeley, CO	180,926	252,825	71,899	40
8	Myrtle Beach–Conway–North Myrtle Beach, SC–NC	269,772	376,722	106,950	40
9	Austin–Round Rock, TX	1,249,763	1,716,289	466,526	37
10	Bend–Redmond, OR	115,367	157,733	42,366	37
	Fastest Rate of Decline				
1	New Orleans–Metairie, LA	1,337,726	1,189,866	-147,860	-11
2	Pine Bluff, AR	107,341	100,258	-7,083	-7
3	Youngstown–Warren–Boardman, OH–PA	602,964	565,773	-37,191	-6
4	Johnstown, PA	152,598	143,679	-8,919	-6
5	Weirton–Steubenville, WV–OH	132,008	124,454	-7,554	-6
6	Ocean City, NJ	102,326	97,265	-5,061	-5
7	Saginaw, MI	210,039	200,169	-9,870	-5
8	Springfield, OH	144,742	138,333	-6,409	-4
9	Charleston, WV	235,938	227,078	-8,860	-4
10	Detroit–Warren–Dearborn, MI	4,452,557	4,296,250	-156,307	-4

SOURCE: U.S. Census Bureau 2013a.

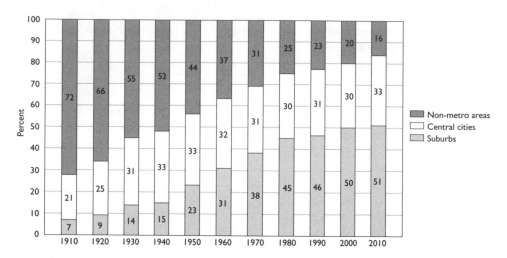

Figure 43. Percentage of the population in suburbs, central cities, and nonmetropolitan areas, 1910–2010. Source: Mather, Pollard, and Jacobsen 2011, 15.

Within metropolitan areas, the U.S. population has become increasingly suburban. In 1910, only 7 percent of the total U.S. population lived in suburban areas, another 21 percent lived in central cities, and nearly three-quarters did not live in metropolitan areas at all. However, by 2010, over half (51 percent) of the U.S. population lived in the suburbs, another third in central cities, and only 16 percent lived outside metropolitan counties (see figure 43). The long-term growth of the suburbs is explained by the general movement of the population from rural to metropolitan areas over the period, plus the growing number of people within metro areas choosing to live outside central cities. The rise of the automobile industry in the early part of the twentieth century and the tremendous growth in the country's highway infrastructure later on allowed more people to commute to work across longer distances.

Early suburban residents were mainly white and affluent. Over time suburbs have become substantially more diverse. While the share of whites in suburbs increased slightly from the 1990 to 2010 period (from 74 to 78 percent), the increase was more substantial for blacks (44 to 51 percent), Asians (54 to 62 percent), and Hispanics (47 to 59 percent).[10] Suburbs are also more socioeconomically diverse than they used to be. In the 2000s the suburban poor population grew much faster than the central city poor population.[11]

While the share of the population in the suburbs grew every decade over the last century, the rate of suburban growth slowed in the 2000s, and there are at least some signs of a central city revival. Suburbs located in the outer ring of central cities, sometimes termed "exurbs," were the hardest hit by foreclosures when the housing bubble burst at the onset of the Great Recession.[12] In fact, central cities grew at a faster rate than suburbs during 2010 and 2011—the first time this had happened in decades. While some of this is due to the continued after-effects of the recession, cities are more generally experiencing more success in attracting and retaining young people, families, and professionals.[13] Alan Ehrenhalt, a journalist who has written a book on the topic, argues that cities such as New York, Chicago, and Philadelphia are now beginning to resemble European cities, where the wealthy live downtown and the working class and poor live in suburban fringe areas: "The late 20th century was the age of poor inner cities and wealthy suburbs; the 21st century is emerging as an age of affluent inner neighborhoods and immigrants settling on the outside."[14] As one blogger who was interviewing Ehrenhalt noted:

> New York isn't what it used to be. The vacant urban streets depicted in films like *The French Connection* and *Taxi Driver* are long gone. Today, families with strollers now compete for sidewalk space near Wall Street. Central Park has become "boringly safe." Even the hipster capital of Williamsburg, Brooklyn, will soon be getting a Whole Foods. This phenomenon is not unique to New York. From Phoenix, Arizona to Stapleton, Colorado, cities have begun to change. The urban centers that people used to run from are now a magnet for the upwardly mobile, while the suburbs and exurbs are increasingly host to poorer populations. This shift, known as a demographic inversion, is rapidly turning America inside out.[15]

While some signs indicate that central cities are indeed faring well in recent years, this inversion should not, as yet, be overstated. After all, despite increasing poverty in suburbs, the overall suburban poverty rate, at 11 percent in 2011, was lower than that in central cities (15 percent) and nonmetropolitan areas (17 percent).[16] Nevertheless, it does appear that the traditional dichotomy of wealthy white suburbs on the one hand and poor, minority central cities on the other has softened considerably in recent years.

RESIDENTIAL SEGREGATION

While the distinction between cities and suburbs may be declining, this does not necessarily mean that individual neighborhoods themselves (in either central cities or suburbs) are becoming more racially and socioeconomically integrated. This section explores this issue by analyzing the extent to which different racial/ethnic and socioeconomic groups share neighborhoods with each other—usually discussed in terms of "residential segregation." The basic trend is that while racial and ethnic segregation has generally been declining over the past few decades, economic segregation has increased.

Racial and Ethnic Residential Segregation

Many social scientists have examined the residential patterns of immigrants and minority groups over the years. In 1925, sociologist Ernest Burgess described how new immigrants tended to settle in central city ethnic enclaves close to employment opportunities but would often then move to farther, less dense residential areas as they became more familiar with their surroundings and their incomes rose.[17] Many other studies have also documented the very high levels of black-white segregation. The black-white color line has been a very rigid one, reinforced by discrimination and sometimes violence directed toward blacks.[18] Since the 1980s interest in the residential patterns of other groups—mainly Asians and Hispanics—has grown following the increase in immigration from non-European countries in recent decades.

Focusing on this more recent period, figures 44 and 45 show trends in racial/ethnic residential segregation for whites, blacks, Hispanics, and Asians from all who were not group members over the 1970 to 2010 period averaged across all metropolitan areas. Figure 44 employs the *dissimilarity index*, the most commonly used measure of segregation, which indi-

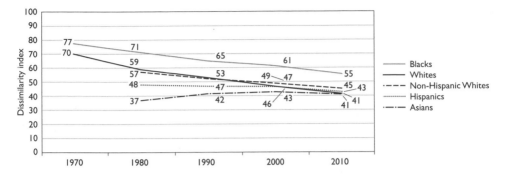

Figure 44. Mean dissimilarity by group, 1970–2010. Note: The reference group is all nongroup members, according to the definition of the group used. Segregation calculations are weighted by the size of the group population of interest and include only those metros with at least 1,000 members of the group of interest. Sources: 1980–2010 numbers from Iceland and Sharp 2013; 1970 numbers from Iceland et al. 2010.

cates the evenness in the distribution of people across neighborhoods in a metropolitan area. If the metropolitan area is, for example, 20 percent black, then each neighborhood should be 20 percent black if that metropolitan area were considered to exhibit no segregation of blacks. The index varies from 0 to 100, with higher numbers indicating more segregation. Figure 45 uses the *isolation index*, which is a measure of exposure of one group to others. This index also ranges from 0 to 100, with 100 indicating the highest level of isolation. It measures the average percentage of group members in the neighborhood where the typical group member lives. Holding other factors equal, larger ethnic groups will be more isolated than smaller ones simply because of the presence of more co-ethnics with whom to share neighborhoods.

Figure 44 indicates that white and black dissimilarity from others not of their own group has continuously declined over the 1970 to 2010 period. Among blacks, the drop was from 77 to 55, and among whites, it was from 70 to 41. A common rule of thumb is that dissimilarity scores over 60 are high, those from 30 to 60 are moderate, and those below 30 are low. Thus, black and white segregation fell from very high levels to more moderate ones. Nevertheless, black and white segregation remains very high in some midwestern and northeastern metropolitan areas,

where racial divisions are more entrenched than in growing Sun Belt metropolitan areas. For example, black-white dissimilarity scores in Detroit,
Milwaukee, New York, and Chicago range from 76 to 80 (this is indicative
of extreme segregation), while those in Las Vegas, Phoenix, Charleston,
South Carolina, and Raleigh all range between 36 and 41.[19] Low-income
blacks in particular face very high levels of segregation.[20]

Figure 44 also shows that Hispanic dissimilarity declined slightly from
1980 to 2010 (from 48 to 43), and Asian segregation increased slightly
(from 37 to 41). Findings from other studies suggest that the relative stability of Hispanic and Asian segregation is a function of new immigrants
fortifying ethnic enclaves even as longer-term immigrants and their children seek out more integrated environments.[21] One notable finding is that
by 2010, levels of segregation of whites, Hispanics, and Asians from those
who were not group members had nearly converged to the 41 to 44 range.
Black segregation remains higher, though it nevertheless declined significantly over the 1970 to 2010 period.

Figure 45 shows trends using the isolation index. Here we see a bit of a
different story, with whites standing out as being considerably more isolated than any other group. The isolation index of 79 for all whites in 2010
indicates that the typical white individual lived in a neighborhood that
was 79 percent white. This figure is down from 94 percent in 1970, indicating that whites live in more diverse neighborhoods than they used to,
which in turn reflects the growing diversity in the nation as a whole.[22]

Among other groups, we see that black isolation steadily declined over
the period, from 66 in 1970 to 46 in 2010, even though the relative size of
the black population in the United States has not changed much. This
indicates that the typical African American individual no longer lives in a
neighborhood that is majority black. It should be noted that declines in
black isolation are in large part a function of blacks living in neighborhoods with other minorities, such as Hispanics, as blacks are only modestly more likely to live in neighborhoods with whites than they used to
be.[23] Black isolation levels have nearly converged with Hispanic isolation
levels, in part reflecting the similarity in the size of the two groups. Asian
isolation has increased steadily but remains below that of other groups,
reflecting this group's relatively small, though growing, population.
Isolation of each group tends to be highest in areas with the high concen-

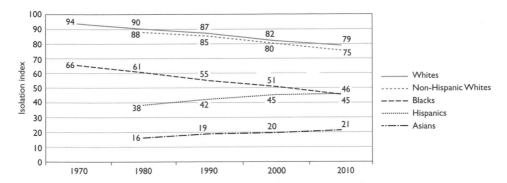

Figure 45. Mean isolation, by group, 1970–2010. Note: The reference group is all nongroup members, according to the definition of the group used. Segregation calculations are weighted by the size of the group population of interest and include only those metros with at least 1,000 members of the group of interest. Sources: 1980–2010 numbers from Iceland and Sharp 2013; 1970 numbers from Iceland et al. 2010.

trations of that group, such as Altoona, Pennsylvania, and Parkersburg, West Virginia, for whites; Detroit and Mcmphis for blacks; Laredo and McAllen, Texas, for Hispanics (both of these metropolitan areas are located along the U.S.-Mexico border); and Honolulu and San Jose for Asians.[24]

Economic Residential Segregation

Economic segregation in modern America can be traced in part to increases in suburbanization through the twentieth century, described above. In the nineteenth century the urban poor generally lived in areas and alleyways near the homes of the affluent, as people of all classes typically lived in the central city, where jobs were located.[25] Class segregation in northern cities began increasing in the first decades of the twentieth century with the growth in black population and with improvements in transportation and the rise of the automobile industry, which allowed the construction and growth of accessible suburban neighborhoods. Suburbanization surged dramatically after World War II, and suburbanites were overwhelming white and middle class.[26]

By the 1960s and 1970s there was growing discussion about the increase in "ghetto" poverty, which referred specifically to black poverty in inner cities and to "concentrated" poverty (a racially more neutral term), commonly defined as neighborhoods with poverty rates of 40 percent or more. Research indicated a rapid increase in concentrated poverty during this time period and lasting until about 1990.[27] The popular press also described the growth of the urban "underclass," referring to the nonnormative behaviors of those living in high-poverty dysfunctional neighborhoods, such as dropping out of school, having children out of wedlock, receiving welfare, having low attachment to the labor force, and abusing drugs and alcohol.[28]

Interest and research on concentrated poverty waned somewhat after the mid-1990s, in part because the number of people living in high-poverty neighborhoods declined substantially in the 1990s. The 1990s were a decade of declining poverty more generally, as well as the depopulation of inner cities and the growing suburbanization of blacks and other minority groups of all income levels.[29] Nevertheless, in the wake of growing income inequality and the economic downturn in the 2000s, concentrated poverty once again appears to have increased in the 2000s. Those living in high-poverty neighborhoods were more racially diverse than in the past, suggesting that concentrated poverty is less of an inner-city black phenomenon than it used to be.[30]

While the studies above focused on concentrated poverty—the proportion of people living in neighborhoods with very high poverty rates— others have focused on income segregation more generally. In one study, researchers Sean Reardon and Kendra Bischoff divided families along the income distribution into six groups. They then measured how segregated they were from one another using the information theory index, which, like the dissimilarity index, measures how evenly different groups are distributed across neighborhoods. It varies from 0 to 100, with 100 indicating the highest level of segregation.[31] Figure 46 shows income segregation averaged over 117 metropolitan areas from 1970 to 2005–9 for all groups together and also for the poor and the affluent families in particular (i.e., those in the bottom and top deciles of the income distribution, respectively). It indicates that income segregation generally increased over the period, with the largest increases occurring in the 1980s but with some stability since. Residential segregation by income was particularly pronounced among African American families in both the 1980s and the

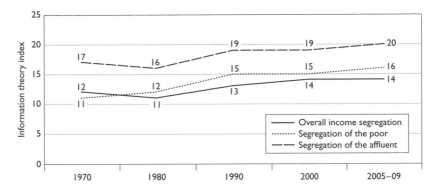

Figure 46. Average family income segregation and segregation of poverty and affluence, 1970–2009. Note: The analysis includes 117 metro areas with populations greater than 500,000. Income segregation is based on a six-category income variable. The poor are defined as families with incomes in the lowest income decile, and the affluent are families in the highest income decile. Source: Reardon and Bischoff 2011, 28.

2000s and among Hispanic families in the 2000s (not shown in the figure). Among the most segregated metropolitan areas by income are Bridgeport, Connecticut, New York City, Philadelphia, Newark, and Dallas—all metro areas with large affluent populations who often live in expensive housing enclaves that poorer families cannot afford.[32]

In conclusion, in recent decades we have witnessed the regional redistribution of the American population from Rust Belt to Sun Belt areas, increasing suburbanization, declines in racial residential segregation, but increases in economic residential segregation. What factors explain these patterns? I have touched on some of the explanations above, but in the next section I turn to a more systematic discussion of why people move and directly link these different theoretical perspectives to migration patterns and the spatial distribution of the population during the past few decades.

WHY PEOPLE MOVE

People move for a variety of reasons, though here I highlight economic factors, social networks, and the role of structural constraints, such as racial discrimination, in shaping broad patterns. Classic economic theories of migration (which are often used to explain international immigration) highlight the factors that "push" people out of certain places and "pull" them into new ones. Push factors can include low living standards, lack of jobs, or political repression. Pull factors often include economic opportunities, availability of land or cheap housing or both, political freedom, and good climate. This economic theory assumes that people make rational decisions based on sound information about different places, coupled with the resources they have available to fulfill their preferences.[33] These preferences, however, can vary across people; married couples with children, for example, might look for amenities (good schools and parks) that are different from those that young singles might look for (vibrant night life and a social scene). The stories at the beginning of the chapter illustrate this rational decision making at work, as the women weighed factors such job opportunities, climate, and social environment of different places, and these are the factors that helped draw them to Austin.

Likewise, when we think of the black Great Migration to the North in the early and middle decades of the twentieth century, we can easily see the role of oppressive conditions in the South in pushing African Americans out of that region and bustling northern factories pulling them there. Today, the social and economic context has changed substantially. People are leaving Rust Belt cities of the North to look for greater economic opportunities elsewhere. The Sun Belt grew because of lower land and home prices, lower labor costs, and the development of effective and economical air-conditioning, which made hot places more habitable during the summer.[34] For blacks in recent years, moving to the Sun Belt has also often meant moving away from poor inner-city ghettos to more racially and economically mixed areas. Similarly, suburbanization through the twentieth century, facilitated by technological advances and improved infrastructure (cars and highways), allowed people to act on their preferences to live in cleaner, less dense, lower-crime areas with other desirable qualities (such as parks and good schools) at an affordable price. Today, the calculus in some metropolitan areas might be changing, as some people may be trading in long commutes from quiet suburbs for city living if they see the city neighborhoods as relatively clean, crime free, and vibrant.

California serves as a case study of how push-full factors can affect broad migration flows. As one report documenting California's changing fortunes notes:

> For decades after World War II, California was a destination for Americans in search of a better life. In many people's minds, it was the state with more jobs, more space, more sunlight, and more opportunity. They voted with their feet, and California grew spectacularly (its population increased by 137 percent between 1960 and 2010). However, this golden age of migration into the state is over. For the past two decades, California has been sending more people to other American states than it receives from them. Since 1990, the state has lost nearly 3.4 million residents through this migration.... What has caused California's transformation from a "pull in" to a "push out" state? The data have revealed several crucial drivers. One is chronic economic adversity (in most years, California unemployment is above the national average). Another is density: the Los Angeles and Orange County region now has a population density of 6,999.3 per square mile—well ahead of New York or Chicago.... A third factor is state and local governments' constant fiscal instability, which sends at least two discouraging messages to businesses and individuals.[35]

At a finer geographic level, economics can also play a role in explaining why different groups of people live in different neighborhoods within metropolitan areas if there are socioeconomic differences among those groups. In terms of racial residential segregation, for example, blacks' and Hispanics' lower incomes and possession of less wealth on average than whites might help explain why the former groups are more concentrated in low-income inner-city neighborhoods: they can't afford to live in middle- and upper-class suburbs where many whites and Asians are likely to reside. In an ethnographic study of people's residential choices, one low-income respondent described her rationale for living in an environment she did not enjoy as being rooted in economic concerns:

> I'm here because it's really what I can afford even though I'm working three jobs. It's convenient because we don't have to pay no gas and no electric.... I plan on leaving, but I can't just up and run out there. Might lose my job and then I'll be having to live with somebody else. I got to think about that, you know. But I love my little place, but I don't like the environment and I tell my children. They all be hollering, "When we going to move?" It's not where you live, it's how you live. You know, we don't live outside, we live in

here. . . . People raise their children different from the way I raise mine, you know. 'Cause we live in the project, that don't mean we have to act like the project and stuff like that.[36]

Nobody doubts that economic theory has considerable explanatory power. It makes intuitive sense that people weigh the pros and cons of alternatives when making important life choices, such as in deciding where to live. They use the resources they have to purchase (or rent) the best house or apartment they feel they can afford. Purely economic theories, however, have limitations. They do not fully explain why members of different groups often congregate in different places in a way that can't be explained by socioeconomic differentials across groups. Why did Scandinavian immigrants to the United States in the nineteenth century settle in states in the upper Midwest, or Puerto Ricans in New York between the 1950s and 1980s, or Vietnamese in Orange County and San Jose since the 1970s? These cases vividly display the role of social networks in shaping migration streams.

Social networks are a form of *social capital*. Social capital refers to the benefits people receive through cooperation with the people they know. The underlying idea is that social networks have value. Among potential immigrants, for example, ties to current or former U.S. migrants are a valuable social asset, because these connections can be used to obtain information and assistance that reduce the costs and risks of entering the United States and increase the probability of getting a good job.[37] In a study of Mexican immigrants to St. Paul's west side, for example, one fifty-five-year-old respondent described why he wanted to live in an ethnic enclave: "I like the people, I like being familiar with my community, and my community being familiar with me. . . . I like to know who runs the business, and when I go in there they'll call me by name, um, I like being around people that look like me, that act like me, and uh, and, come from a basic fundamental value system, of what I come from."[38]

These networks have also worked in a variety of ways for different groups over time. Networks likely reinforced white suburbanization in the twentieth century, black suburbanization by the end of the century (often in inner suburbs adjacent to existing black inner-city neighborhoods), and immigrant communities growing rapidly in new metropolitan destinations and in suburbs (following in the footsteps of successful pioneers) rather than in traditional inner-city locations. Recall again that the one of the women introduced at the beginning of the chapter went to Austin for the first time for a national meeting of Las Comadres, a social and professional networking organization for Latinas. Networks also help explain the rise of wealthy enclaves in certain parts of Manhattan, Los Angeles, Connecticut, and northern Virginia, among other places.

Social networks can be a valuable resource to individuals, but they can also contribute to residential segregation (racial/ethnic or socioeconomic), because networks both reflect and reinforce preexisting group ties. Because networks often funnel group members in a particular direction, people often have "blind spots" when it comes to considering neighborhoods to which to move. Whites, blacks, and Latinos in Chicago, for example, are much less knowledgeable about neighborhoods with few of their own group members; thus, members of each group tend to target different neighborhoods (often in geographic proximity to their current neighborhood) in their housing searches. This serves to reproduce racially segregated neighborhoods.[39] Interestingly, people who make a move to a different metropolitan area altogether tend to choose neighborhoods with more of a racial mix than the one they grew up in than people making an intrametropolitan move, which may help explain lower levels of racial and ethnic residential segregation in newer and growing Sun Belt metropolitan areas.[40]

Last but not least, people of some groups have historically been constrained in their choices. Many hold that some of these structural constraints still impede people's abilities to realize their preferences and that they also contribute to racial and economic segregation. Certainly, given that not all neighborhoods are created equal, some areas are more desirable to live in than others. The attraction of neighborhoods could stem from their physical attributes (e.g., ocean view), the built environment (parks), the strength of local institutions (schools), or the sociodemographic composition of the existing residents, among other attributes. To the extent that the price of housing varies across neighborhoods, we should expect to see some level of economic and racial/ethnic segregation.

However, even if we take group differences in income into account, we still see racial and ethnic neighborhood sorting. Some of this may be a function of social networking and preferences to live with coethnics, but a significant number of studies indicate that other factors are at work, including discrimination against minorities. Historically, such discrimination was easy to document. In the South, residential segregation was paradoxically modest in the early twentieth century, with traditional grids of white avenues and black alleys, mainly because the Jim Crow system so thoroughly subordinated blacks in southern life.[41] Many northern whites reacted with alarm to the Great Migration of southern blacks to northern cities. Sometimes violence was directed toward blacks who entered formerly white neighborhoods. For example, between 1900 and 1920 a series of race riots occurred in a number of cities, such as in New York City in 1900, East St. Louis, Illinois, in 1917, and Chicago in 1919, where many African Americans living outside black neighborhoods had their houses destroyed. As the century wore on violence became less common, but white neighborhood "improvement associations" used a variety of tools to keep African Americans out, such as by boycotting real estate agents who sold homes to blacks in white neighborhoods. They sometimes also implemented restrictive covenants, which were contractual agreements among property owners whereby they would not sell or lease their houses to black home seekers. Local real estate boards also sometimes took the lead in establishing their own restrictive covenants.[42] The Supreme Court ruled that these covenants were unconstitutional in *Shelley v. Kraemer* in 1948. Twenty years later the Fair Housing Act of 1968 went further by prohibiting discrimination in most housing market transactions.

Nevertheless, studies since then have shown that African American home seekers are still generally showed fewer properties, are steered toward certain neighborhoods with more African Americans, and have more trouble arranging financing for a home purchase than whites. There is some indication that Hispanics and Asians face some of these barriers as well.[43] During the housing boom of the late 1990s and early 2000s, credit denial became less a problem than predatory lending: many low-income and minority home buyers (as well as whites) were offered credit with deceptive or hard-to-understand terms they could not possibly meet. This contributed to the foreclosure crisis that helped precipitate the Great Recession.[44] Many whites also avoid multiracial, especially black, neighborhoods, sometimes believing them to be worse (such as in terms of school quality and levels of crime) than they actually are or because of racial prejudice.[45]

The interaction between discrimination and residential preferences can also contribute to segregation. That is, minorities are not necessarily prevented from buying a home in an all-white neighborhood, but they may nevertheless be leery of being a pioneer and "standing out."[46] As one of the Mexican respondents in the St. Paul, Minnesota, study put it when queried about the possibility of living in a neighborhood outside the Mexican enclave: "Well, we would like to live in an area with not so much traffic and less noise, you know . . . in the kind of areas where the Americans are. They are cleaner and quieter. . . . But then we would not like to live there because the people there treat you as the 'bad Latino' or they look at you with a strange face, you know."[47]

In these ways economic factors, social networks, and structural constraints help explain recent residential patterns. There are signs that discrimination in the housing market has declined, as have blatantly racist white attitudes. Together, these forces have likely helped produce the declines in black-white segregation since the 1960s highlighted earlier. They also explain the stability of Hispanic and Asian segregation, even with the rapid increase of immigration from Asia and Latin America since the 1960s.[48] However, demographic and economic trends also help us understand the growing influence of economic factors, including increasing income inequality, in determining where people live today.

INTERNATIONAL COMPARISONS

The United States has a reputation as a nation with sprawling, decentralized metropolitan areas. In many American suburban neighborhoods, the population density is low enough that people are often not in walking distance to shops, jobs, or public transit. In contrast, western European cities are known for their high density and well-developed public transportation systems. The sprawl of U.S. cities is thought to be reflective of its car-centered, individualistic culture, which, according to critics, contributes to an array of problems ranging from environmental stress (excessive energy consumption and accompanying greenhouse emissions), lower quality of life (traffic congestion), and poorer health (obesity arising from lack of exercise).[49] U.S. policies have facilitated suburbanization through public investments in highways, tax policies that encourage homeowner-ship, relatively low taxes on gas, considerable single-family home zoning, and the poor quality of many urban schools that are locally funded.[50] All of these make living in the suburbs more economical and attractive.

Conducting empirical comparisons of the extent of suburbanization across countries can be tricky because of the lack of standard definitions of cities and metropolitan areas. However, considerable evidence indi-cates that Americans rely on cars more than people in other countries. One study indicates that 89 percent of commuting trips in the United States are by car, compared with 76 percent in Canada, 65 percent in Great Britain, 56 percent in France, and less than half in Germany (49 percent), Sweden (46 percent), Switzerland (46 percent), the Netherlands (45 percent), and Denmark (42 percent).[51] These are, of course, indirect measures of suburbanization, as people can still commute from the sub-urbs to the city center by train in cities with good public transportation. However, American cities are also less dense than European ones, also indicative of more suburbanization in the former.[52]

Nevertheless, suburbanization does appear to have generally increased in Europe, as indicated by declining population densities and the faster growth of outlying areas in many European cities. Suburbanization is like-wise occurring in a wide range of other countries around the world with growing affluent populations.[53] Until recently, in the United States ethnic minorities were mainly concentrated in central cities as whites fled to the suburbs, while at least in some European cities, such as Paris, minorities often lived in low-income suburbs, sometimes in subsidized housing.[54]

A growing number of countries have different kinds of suburban settle-ments, ranging from poor fringe shantytowns and favelas to middle- and upper-class suburbs and gated communities, thus making it difficult to gen-eralize about the sociodemographic profiles of suburbs versus central cit-ies.[55] This pattern suggests a significant amount of segregation by income, though we know relatively little about how this varies across countries or about trends over time in a wide variety of contexts. We can plausibly hypothesize that to the extent that income inequality has increased in many developed countries in recent years, neighborhood income inequality may have increased as well. As noted above, this occurred in many American cities, and evidence suggests that it has occurred in Canada too.[56]

Ethnic residential segregation across neighborhoods is also a common feature of cities with multiethnic and immigrant populations worldwide. Black-white residential segregation in the United States generally has been higher than ethnic segregation in other developed countries, though the difference has likely narrowed in recent years as black segregation in the United States has declined.[57] The historical oppression of blacks by whites, its legacy, especially in Rust Belt cities, and continued discrimination help explain the relatively high segregation levels in the United States, as does the fragmented and sprawling nature of many American cities.[58]

Ethnic residential segregation in a number of cities in Europe and other Western countries has its roots in immigration, which prompts immigrants to settle in ethnic enclaves, as they do in the United States. However, animosity by the native population, especially against immigrants who are "visible minorities," also contributes to segregation. In many European countries, segregation is highest among Muslim groups, such as Pakistanis and Bangladeshis in Great Britain, Moroccans in Barcelona, and Turks and Moroccans in The Hague.[59] One study comparing segregation in the United States and Great Britain found that while black segregation in U.S. metropolitan areas was considerably higher than black segregation in British cities (with information theory indexes of 46 and 19, respectively), Asian segregation was a little lower in the United States (20) than in Great Britain (23). This greater disadvantage of blacks in the United States and South Asians in Great Britain indicates that patterns of ethnic inequality vary across contexts.[60]

The 2011 census in Great Britain also indicates that, for the first time, white Britons were a minority in London ("white British" is an ethnic category in the British census), constituting 45 percent of its residents, and that there were 600,000 fewer white British Londoners in 2011 than in 2001. Some dubbed this "white flight," akin to the process of white suburbanization that occurred in many U.S. metropolitan areas in the past. One news story reporting on this demographic change included the following interview in trying to explain it:

> Ralph Baldwin, a Tory councillor in Barking and Dagenham, said: "I think people left for a variety of reasons. If you look back to the early 2000s many people were able to retire to Clacton-on-Sea and they saw their friends going and followed. But people also watched all this demographic change

going on between 2000 and 2010 and they thought, 'We don't know where we are living any more.' One day they are in a place that they think is Essex and then they are living in another place. It has never been an issue of race. It's about the inability of people to affect change. The world was changing around them and they couldn't do anything about it."[61]

This story of the decline in the white British population indicates the importance of ethnic divisions (notwithstanding the protestations by the councillor that race had nothing to do with it), though it does not necessarily mean that such divisions are growing. The general trend observed in London and other areas of Great Britain is due to the growth of immigration and ethnic enclaves, the increasing share of the minority population in the country as a whole, some avoidance by whites of minority neighborhoods, and minority fears of discrimination in white ones. Some studies have suggested that when measured by the dissimilarity index—a measure of evenness—segregation has declined in Great Britain. Second-generation immigrants also tend to live in more ethnically mixed neighborhoods than the first generation in many European countries, indicative of some measure of immigrant residential integration.[62] How high levels of immigration will change internal migration patterns and the distribution of different groups will continue to be of interest in multicultural societies around the globe.

CONCLUSION

Economic factors, social networks, and structural constraints faced by different groups have shaped patterns and trends in migration and residential segregation in the United States. The rapid growth of industrializing northeastern and midwestern cities in the first half of the twentieth century slowed, and then in many cases reversed, by the century's end. In postindustrial America, growth has occurred particularly in the Sun Belt—in economically vibrant southern and western cities that drew immigrants and internal migrants alike. Suburbanization transformed the organization of the American city during the twentieth century. At first suburbs attracted mainly middle-class whites, but the last few decades have seen the rapid growth of minorities and immigrants living in suburban areas. There are also signals of central city revival in many metropolitan areas. As a result of these trends, the economic and demographic divide between cities and suburbs has diminished considerably in recent years.

Black-white neighborhood segregation was universally high in American metropolitan areas in the middle of the twentieth century, driven by white racism and discrimination. Since the 1960s segregation has been declining and is only moderate in growing Sun Belt cities. Segregation remains most prominent in Rust Belt cities of the Northeast and Midwest that have historically entrenched black ghettos. Hispanic and Asian segregation is moderate, with new immigrants often settling in ethnic enclaves and the second generation tending to live in more integrated settings. The role of income in shaping residential patterns has increased in the last few decades even as the effect of race and ethnicity has declined. Increasing income inequality as a whole has likely contributed to this kind of neighborhood sorting. Notably, many countries around the globe have also experienced increasing suburbanization, and those with large immigrant populations are also grappling with ethnic divisions that have accompanied the growth of ethnic enclaves. While immigrants and their children often fare reasonably well in these new multicultural societies, the demographic, social, and residential changes that immigration brings are still being followed with great interest, and often concern, in these countries.

8   Health and Mortality

Few issues have been more contentious than the state of our nation's health and health care system. People differ in their views on how to best deliver quality care while containing health care costs that threaten to overwhelm federal and state budgets. As a way of providing a firm factual footing for these discussions, the National Academies convened an expert panel of researchers to report on the health of Americans in comparison with people in a number of peer countries. The report, released in 2013, was ominously titled *U.S. Health in International Perspective: Shorter Lives, Poorer Health.* Indeed, the panel concluded: "The United States is among the wealthiest nations in the world, but it is far from the healthiest. Although life expectancy and survival rates in the United States have improved dramatically over the past century, Americans live shorter lives and experience more injuries and illnesses than people in other high-income countries."[1]

The findings were widely reported in the press, and naturally the public weighed in with their opinions on why the United States fares so poorly. Some pointed to the health care system. One tweet sent in to CNN read: "America has made healthcare most difficult to access even for the middle class. Imagine the poor. That's what greed does!" Others pointed to obesity and the environment: "We invented the term #supersize" and "I moved from Europe to the U.S. about six months ago. First observation after a visit to the supermarket: fruits and vegetables way too expensive; cheap products stuffed with fats and sugars. In short, if you want to kill off a whole population, slow but sure, I couldn't come up with a better strategy." CNN commentator Steve Cray added, "They [the National Academies panel] needed 18 months to determine the problem! It will take me less than a minute: obesity, sedentary lifestyle, a for-profit healthcare system controlled by insurance and pill-pushing pharmaceutical companies that try to limit preventative healthcare."[2]

Many of these observations hold at least some truth. There is no single reason why health in the United States is worse than in other countries; rather, it is a confluence of factors, including disparities in people's access to health care, individual health behaviors, and the physical and social environment.[3] The rest of this chapter provides an in-depth discussion of these and related issues. First, I document recent patterns and trends in health and mortality in the United States. I review evidence on health disparities by gender, race, and socioeconomic status and describe their origins. I discuss the aging of the American population and the strains this puts on the health care system and the U.S. budget. I end by systematically describing why the health of Americans lags behind their peers in other developed countries.

PATTERNS AND TRENDS IN HEALTH AND MORTALITY

Let's start with the good news. In many important respects the health of Americans has improved. Figure 47 shows that life expectancy at birth grew from 66 years in 1950 to 76 in 2010 for men and from 71 to 81 for women. This kind of gradual health improvement shows up in other ways. In 1970, the infant mortality rate was 20 (indicating that 20 infants out of 1,000 died before their first birthday). By 2011, this figure was less than a third as large, at 6.[4] As a National Center for Health Statistics reported in an examination of mortality patterns over the 1935 to 2010 period, "Although there were year to year exceptions, the last 75 years witnessed sustained declines in the risk of dying in the United States."[5] Decreases in death rates occurred for men and women, all age groups, and for all racial

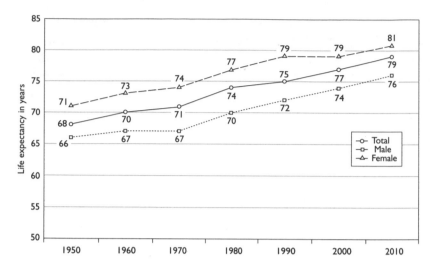

Figure 47. Life expectancy at birth, by sex, 1970–2010. Source: Centers for Disease Control and Prevention 2011.

and ethnic groups. The number of Americans living to see their hundredth birthday has risen from 32,000 to 53,000 from 1980 to 2010. The centenarian population increased by a greater percentage (66 percent) than the increase in the population as a whole (36 percent).[6]

Why women live longer than men is not fully understood, but part of the reason may be biological (the female advantage in life expectancy is found among a majority of animals), and part is due to environmental and behavioral factors. Men consume more tobacco, alcohol, and drugs than women, and they are more likely to die from accidents and intentional injuries (homicides, suicides, and in war). The slight narrowing of the gender gap in life expectancy in the United States and other developed countries since the 1970s is likely a function of a reduction in lifestyle differences. Women, for example, are more likely to smoke than they used to be, and this has contributed to a decline in the gender mortality gap.[7]

Health outcomes vary considerably by race and Hispanic origin. The life expectancy among whites was 79 in 2010, four years more than the life expectancy among blacks (75). This gap, however, is narrower than in the past, especially since 1990 (see figure 48).[8] This trend applies to both men

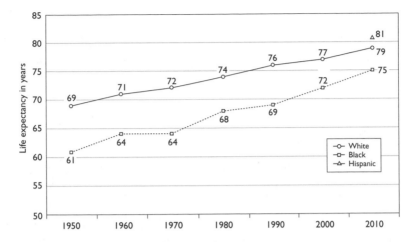

Figure 48. Life expectancy at birth, by race and Hispanic origin, 1950–2010. Note: The Centers for Disease Control and Prevention time series for Hispanic life expectancy does not begin until 2006. Source: Centers for Disease Control and Prevention 2011.

and women, though the black-white gap among women (3 years) is narrower than among men (5 years).[9] The persistence of significant health disparities between blacks and whites—but the narrowing of the gap in recent years—shows up in other ways, including age-adjusted death rates, cause-specific death rates, infant mortality, and disability.[10] The higher rates of disease and death among blacks compared with whites reflect the earlier onset of illness, the greater severity of diseases, and lower rates of survival.[11] A final finding of note in the figure is that, contrary to what one might expect given socioeconomic differentials across groups described in chapter 6, Hispanics have a higher life expectancy (81) than both blacks and whites. This "Hispanic health paradox" is discussed in more detail shortly. The Centers for Disease Control do not publish life expectancy figures for Asians, but other data indicate that Asians are not disadvantaged when it comes to health outcomes and in fact often fare better than whites.[12] For example, the infant mortality rate for babies born to Asian mothers (4.5 per 1,000 live births) is lower than among non-Hispanic whites (5.5). Finally, it should be noted that statistics for pan-ethnic groups mask some variation across origins within a given group. For

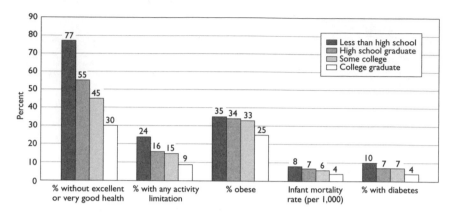

Figure 49. Health, by educational attainment, 2000s. Note: The percentage of those without excellent or very good health refers to self-reported health among respondents ages 25 to 74; activity limitation refers to respondents age 25 and over; the percentage of obese respondents refers to those age 20 and over with a body mass index greater than or equal to 30 kg. Source: Braveman et al. 2010, table 2.

example, regarding Hispanics, the infant mortality rate among Puerto Ricans (7.3) is higher than among Mexicans (5.6) and Cubans (4.9).[13]

Health and mortality are strongly associated with socioeconomic status. Figure 49 shows the differences in health outcomes by levels of education. (These patterns are also observed across income groups.) Only 30 percent of people who graduated from college report that their health is not excellent or very good, compared with 77 percent of those who did not finish high school. Disability is likewise less prevalent among those with a college degree, as are obesity, diabetes, and infant mortality.[14] Socioeconomic status has also been linked to an even wider array of health problems, including low birth weight, cardiovascular disease, hypertension, arthritis, cancer, and depression.[15] Contrary to the narrowing of the racial health gap, the strength of the relationship between socioeconomic status and health has increased in recent decades, with growing gaps in mortality, life expectancies, and the prevalence of disabilities by educational attainment.[16]

What explains these socioeconomic health disparities? Education, income, and occupational status can all affect one's health. Better-educated people tend to have greater access to information and resources that promote health—no small matter when considering the complexity of diagnosing and treating health problems and navigating through our health care system. People with higher levels of education also tend to have a greater sense of control over their lives, are more likely to plan ahead, and are better able to draw upon useful social networks that can provide advice and assistance during difficult times.[17] Obtaining a higher level of education also increases one's earning power and probability of landing a high-status, stable job, which in turn also lead to better health and lower mortality.

With regard to income, people with fewer resources may not have the means to purchase health care insurance that provides access to better health services. More than 60 percent of the uninsured are in low-income families. Although many poor individuals may be eligible for Medicaid, many do not end up enrolling. As a result, low-income individuals are less likely to see a physician and get preventative screening.[18] In addition, lower-income families may not have the resources to access quality housing, schooling, recreation, and nutrition that can enhance health. For example, poorer neighborhoods are more likely to be located near highways, industrial areas, and toxic waste sites, since land is cheaper in those areas. Families of low socioeconomic status (SES) are more likely to live in crowded and noisy environments, which can lead to, among other conditions, hypertension. The struggle to get by can be stressful, and this can affect both physical and mental health.

Similarly, people employed in lower-status occupations often have jobs that expose them to greater physical risk. For example, some blue-collar jobs involve exposure to toxic substances or to physical activity that can lead to injury and disability.[19] In contrast, people in higher-status professions have more control over their own working environment and are generally less likely to lose their job.[20]

In addition to the direct ways in which SES may contribute to poorer health, a number of indirect pathways have also been identified, including behavior and lifestyle, which might account for half of the earlier mortality among lower-SES individuals. Those with less education and income are more likely to smoke and drink heavily, are less likely to exercise and eat nutritiously, and are thus more likely to be overweight. Low-income individuals and their children have less access to safe, well-lit places to walk, bike, and play, and these all contribute to less healthy living.[21]

The following story on the growing poverty in the United States in the wake of the Great Recession illustrates the health challenges faced by poor individuals:

> Millions of workers and their families are similarly vulnerable to such mundane changes as a slight decline in the number of hours per workweek or an extra few cents per gallon in the cost of gasoline. . . . One such person is 67-year-old Mary Vasquez, whose Social Security check is $600 and whose rent is $500. A tiny woman, her health broken by cancer, heart attacks, diabetes, high blood pressure and a multitude of other ailments, Vasquez works as a phone operator at a Walmart on the outskirts of Dallas. . . . A large part of her salary went for medical expenses not covered by Medicare or her Walmart healthcare plan; much of the rest went to pay down usurious payday loans she'd accumulated in recent years as her health declined. Sitting in a union hall in the suburb of Grapevine, Vasquez (one of a handful of employees working to unionize her workplace) explains that she skips "mostly breakfast and sometimes lunch." As a diabetic, she is supposed to eat fresh produce. Instead, she says, "a lot of times I buy a TV dinner; we have them on sale for 88 cents. A lot of times, food, I can't pay for."
>
> Another American who struggles to put food on the table is Jorge, a 57-year-old who migrated to the United States from Mexico in 1982. Jorge (who doesn't want his last name used) lives with his wife in the large Chaparral *colonia,* an informal settlement of trailers, small houses and shanties near Las Cruces, New Mexico. . . . "There's a lot of deterioration of the trailers," Jorge says in Spanish. "In winter, pipes explode because of the freeze. I don't have water right now. Heating is so expensive, with propane gas. Those who have little children, they have to use it, but it's so expensive." A volunteer firefighter, he adds, "We see a lot of accidents with water heaters and explosions with the propane tanks."[22]

These stories illustrate the many factors contributing to the poor health of low-income Americans, including the challenge of paying for health care, the propensity to purchase low-cost and often high-caloric food of dubious nutritional value, and problems with housing conditions that can lead to accidents and poor health.

Regarding racial disparities, the health disadvantage among blacks stems not only from their disadvantaged socioeconomic position but also from racism and residential segregation. Differences in their health outcomes cannot be attributed entirely to SES, because blacks are more disadvantaged than whites even when compared with those in the same income brackets and at the same educational levels. Simple comparisons overlook the multiple SES disadvantages that blacks often face. Blacks have less income and wealth than whites of the same educational backgrounds, and they also live in worse neighborhoods with higher poverty. The differences in the residential circumstances of blacks and whites, rooted in residential segregation, ensure that blacks are more likely to live in neighborhoods with greater social disorder and isolation. These differences reflect the historical legacy of institutional discrimination as well as contemporary racism. Experiences of discrimination can increase stress and hypertension and are predictive of an increased risk of substance abuse to cope with the extra stress.[23]

Given what we know about the association among socioeconomic status, race, and health, why do Hispanics have a higher life expectancy and lower levels of fatal chronic diseases, such as heart disease, cancer, lung disease, and stroke, than both blacks and whites?[24] This unexpected finding has been termed the *Hispanic paradox*. Further deepening the puzzle, immigrants' risk of disability and chronic disease increases with increasing length of residence in the United States, and native-born Hispanics have worse health and lower life expectancies than Hispanic immigrants. A number of explanations have been offered to explain these patterns. Some believe that cultural factors, such as better health habits and strong networks of social support in Hispanic communities help explain it. Thus, according to this view, as Hispanic immigrants and their children acculturate to the poor eating habits of the native population, their health outcomes worsen and their life expectancy declines.[25] Certainly, anecdotal evidence supports the view that Hispanic health behaviors become unhealthier in the United States. As one story in the news described it:

> Becoming an American can be bad for your health. . . . For the recently arrived, the quantity and accessibility of food speaks to the boundless promise of the United States. Esther Angeles remembers being amazed at the size of hamburgers—as big as dinner plates—when she first came to the United States from Mexico 15 years ago. "I thought, this is really a country of opportunity," she said. "Look at the size of the food!"
>
> Fast-food fare not only tasted good, but was also a sign of success, a family treat that new earnings put in reach. "The crispiness was delicious," said

Juan Muniz, 62, recalling his first visit to Church's Chicken with his family in the late 1970s. "I was proud and excited to eat out. I'd tell them: 'Let's go eat. We can afford it now.'"

For others, supersize deals appealed. "You work so hard, you want to use your money in a smart way," said Aris Ramirez, a community health worker in Brownsville, explaining the thinking. "So when they hear 'twice the fries for an extra 49 cents,' people think, 'That's economical.'"

For Ms. Angeles, the excitement of big food eventually wore off, and the frantic pace of the modern American workplace took over. She found herself eating hamburgers more because they were convenient and she was busy in her 78-hour-a-week job as a housekeeper. What is more, she lost control over her daughter's diet because, as a single mother, she was rarely with her at mealtimes.[26]

While these stories seem compelling, there is danger in relying too much on anecdotes, as the evidence supporting the notion that migration to the United States is wholly responsible for causing increasing obesity is actually not overwhelming. Notably, important shifts in nutritional patterns and trends toward inactivity have occurred in countries around the globe in recent years. Barry Popkin, who has written extensively about this *nutritional transition,* notes: "The diet of poor people in rural or urban settings in Asia during the 1960s was simple and rather monotonous: rice with a small amount of vegetables, beans or fish. Today, their eating is transformed. It is common for people in these settings to regularly consume complex meals at any number of away-from-home food outlets— western or indigenous. The overall composition of diets in the developing world is shifting rapidly, particularly with respect to fat, caloric sweeteners, and animal-source foods."[27]

The prevalence of obesity has increased so rapidly in Mexico that the obesity rate there now surpasses the rate in the United States—making Mexico the most obese country in the hemisphere.[28] This suggests that immigrants and their children who are eating less nutritional foods now in the United States would be doing so regardless of whether they had migrated to the United States or not. As one commentator on growing obesity in Mexico put it, "The speed at which Mexicans have made the change from a diet dominated by maize and beans to one that bursts at the seams with processed fats and sugars poses one of the greatest challenges to public health officials."[29]

Factors that have contributed to growing obesity in Mexico and other developing countries include globalization and lifestyle changes. Some of these changes are cultural, in that patterns of food consumption associated with Western countries (the United States in particular) are being diffused throughout the world. Migration networks may have helped diffuse these eating patterns to Mexican communities,[30] but they may have occurred eventually anyway given their rise in countries around the globe. International food trade, commercialization, and marketing have made many new high-calorie foods and beverages with little nutritional value widely available at a relatively low cost. Such foods were initially mainly accessible to wealthier families in urban areas in developing countries, but they are increasingly available to poor families in rural areas as well.[31] Lifestyle changes stem from urbanization and the decline in physical activity in many occupations, both in the United States and abroad. Mechanization at work and in the household has reduced the need for strenuous labor. Many fewer people are employed in physically intensive activities such as farming, mining, and forestry, and an increasing number in the service sector are employed to perform sedentary activities, such as sitting in front of a computer terminal (much as I am as I write this).[32]

A growing consensus suggests that the issue of the Hispanic advantage in life expectancy in the United States is primarily related to *migration*. Specifically, Hispanics who migrate to the United States tend to be healthier than those who stay behind (in other words, immigrants are positively selected for their good health), and immigrants who leave the United States to return to home often do so when their health worsens. Indeed, studies have found that foreign-born Hispanics who left the United States had higher mortality levels than those who remained, and returnees to Mexico were more than three times more likely to rate their health as fair or poor than those who remained in the United States.[33] The Hispanic paradox has thus sometime been referred to as the immigrant paradox, as immigrants from a wide range of countries have longer life expectancies than do native-born Americans, and much of this has been attributed to the selectivity of immigrants more generally.[34] This issue is not fully settled, as it is not clear if migration fully explains the Hispanic health advantage. Research continues on the potentially protective roles that immigrant communities and health behaviors play.[35]

THE AGING OF THE AMERICAN POPULATION AND
HEALTH CARE COSTS

Like the population of most developed countries around the world, the U.S. population is gradually aging. This is a function of declining fertility rates, the aging of the relatively large baby boom generation, and declining mortality. Figure 50 shows that the median age of the U.S. population dipped slightly from 30 to 28 between 1960 and 1970 because of the lingering effects of the baby boom, before increasing to 37 by 2010. Likewise, the percentage of the population over the age of 65 increased from 9 percent in 1960 to 13 percent in 2010. This is expected to rise to 20 percent by the year 2050. The percentage of the population that is over the age of 65 is lower in the United States than in other countries with low fertility, such as Japan, Germany, and Italy (all of whose percentage over the age of 65 already exceeds 20 percent), but considerably higher than the corresponding percentages in rapidly growing developing countries such as Uganda and Egypt, where 2 percent and 5 percent of the population are over the age of 65, respectively.[36]

The composition of the older population varies by gender and race/ethnicity. Because of women's longer life expectancies, women made up well over half of the elderly population (57 percent) in 2010, though the narrowing of the male-female life expectancy gap in recent years has reduced the percentage of the older population that is female. (Women made up 59 percent of the elderly population in 2000.)[37] Whites currently constitute about 80 percent of the elderly population, but they make up just 63 percent of the total population. Moreover, only about 54 percent of all births in 2011 were to white women, indicative of the very different racial and ethnic composition of the American population by age. By 2030, the projection is that about a third of the elderly population will be ethnic minority group members.[38]

The leading causes of death vary across the life course. Chapter 1 described how the five leading causes of death for the population as a whole in 2010 were heart disease, cancer, chronic lower respiratory disease, stroke, and accidents. However, as shown in figure 51, among children and young adults of ages 1 to 24, the leading causes of death were accidents (unintentional injuries), homicides, and suicides, followed by

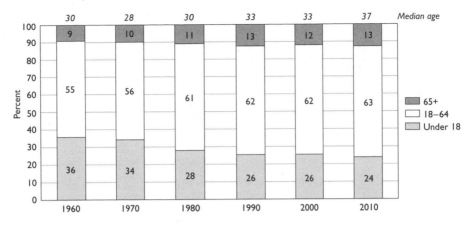

Figure 50. Age distribution and median age of the U.S. population, 1960–2010.
Source: Howden and Meyer 2011, figure 4.

cancer and heart disease, while among those age 65 and over, the leading causes nearly mirrored the totals for the population as a whole (reflecting the concentration of deaths in this age group): heart disease, cancer, chronic lower respiratory diseases, stroke, and Alzheimer's. Accidents top the list for those age 25 to 44, while cancer was the top killer among people age 45 to 64.[39] Health and mortality vary across states. Life expectancy is longer and health is better in states such as Hawaii, Florida, and Connecticut, and worse in many states of the South, such as Mississippi, Kentucky, and West Virginia, where rates of obesity, diabetes, heart disease, and smoking are relatively high.[40]

One general concern about an aging population is that it can strain government budgets. While the elderly often amass savings during their lifetime in the form of pension plans, savings accounts, mutual funds, and equity in their homes—and they often continue to work even after the age of 65—they are nevertheless often economically dependent on the working-age population. The two main programs that serve the elderly—and whose growth has been met with alarm—are Social Security and Medicare. These two programs cost the federal government $1.3 trillion in 2012, accounting for about 37 percent of federal spending.[41] As many understand it, people contribute payroll taxes during their working years and then, when they retire, receive in benefits what they paid in. However, the way the program

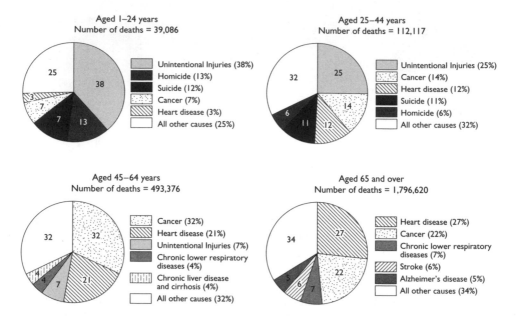

Figure 51. Percentage distribution of five leading causes of death, by age group, in the United States, 2010. Source: Minino and Murphy 2012, 4.

is structured, people who are currently employed pay for current retirees. While a Social Security trust fund was set up to cover future needs, some of these funds have been used to help finance other government programs. In short, because the U.S. population is aging and the number of elderly is swelling compared with the size of the working-age population, the Social Security trust fund is projected to run out of revenue at some point in the next couple of decades (in 2033, according to a recent estimate).[42]

Likewise, the elderly require, on average, much more medical attention than younger people, and health care costs have been soaring well beyond inflation in recent years. The hospital component of Medicare, which accounts for about half of Medicare spending, is financed much like Social Security, through payroll taxes. This trust fund is expected to be depleted by about 2026.[43] Making structural changes to these programs is difficult because they are generally popular and actually quite effective, as Social Security significantly reduces poverty, and Medicare helps provide access to much-needed health care services. Medicare is in fact often better at controlling costs than other kinds of health insurance, as it is able to bargain with doctors and hospitals for lower prices because of the number of people it represents.[44]

While an aging population has put some stress on health care spending, it is important to note that the problem is considerably broader. Our health care system is not well designed to provide efficient care to either young or old Americans. In just the ten years between 1999 and 2009, the average annual premium for employer-sponsored family insurance coverage rose from $5,800 to $13,400, and the average cost per Medicare beneficiary went from $5,500 to $11,900.[45] Our medical spending is high and increasing for many reasons. Part of it has to do with the fact that doctors and hospitals are paid for the tests and procedures they conduct rather than for results (health outcomes). Thus, the incentive is to prescribe many such tests and procedures. Moreover, prices are often vastly inflated and arbitrary. *Time* magazine ran a series of articles on health care costs run amok in the United States:

> When Sean Recchi, a 42-year-old from Lancaster, Ohio, was told last March that he had non-Hodgkin's lymphoma, his wife Stephanie knew she had to get him to MD Anderson Cancer Center in Houston. Stephanie's father had been treated there 10 years earlier, and she and her family credited the doctors and nurses at MD Anderson with extending his life by at least eight years.
>
> Because Stephanie and her husband had recently started their own small technology business, they were unable to buy comprehensive health insurance. For $469 a month, or about 20% of their income, they had been able to get only a policy that covered just $2,000 per day of any hospital costs. "We don't take that kind of discount insurance," said the woman at MD Anderson when Stephanie called to make an appointment for Sean. . . . The total cost, in advance, for Sean to get his treatment plan and initial doses of chemotherapy was $83,900.
>
> Why? The first of the 344 lines printed out across eight pages of his hospital bill—filled with indecipherable numerical codes and acronyms—seemed innocuous. But it set the tone for all that followed. It read, "1 ACETAMINOPHEN TABS 325 mg." The charge was only $1.50, but it was for a generic version of a Tylenol pill. You can buy 100 of them on Amazon for $1.49 even without a hospital's purchasing power.
>
> Dozens of midpriced items were embedded with similarly aggressive markups, like $283.00 for a "CHEST, PA AND LAT 71020." That's a simple

chest X-ray, for which MD Anderson is routinely paid $20.44 when it treats a patient on Medicare, the government health care program for the elderly. Every time a nurse drew blood, a "ROUTINE VENIPUNCTURE" charge of $36.00 appeared, accompanied by charges of $23 to $78 for each of a dozen or more lab analyses performed on the blood sample. In all, the charges for blood and other lab tests done on Recchi amounted to more than $15,000. Had Recchi been old enough for Medicare, MD Anderson would have been paid a few hundred dollars for all those tests. By law, Medicare's payments approximate a hospital's cost of providing a service, including overhead, equipment and salaries.[46]

This story helps provide an inkling as to why the health of Americans compares poorly with that of people in other rich countries—the topic to which I now turn.

INTERNATIONAL COMPARISONS

Among the many indicators of relatively poor health in the United States is life expectancy at birth. As shown in figure 52, the U.S. life expectancy, at 79, is slightly below the OECD average (80), and below that of all western European countries, such as France, Sweden, the United Kingdom, and Germany. The United States fares slightly better than OECD countries that have considerably lower GDPs than that of the United States, such as the Czech Republic, Poland, Turkey, and Mexico. Granted, all of these countries fare well compared with truly poor or war-torn developing nations, such as Zimbabwe, Somalia, and Afghanistan, where the life expectancy for women at birth ranges from 49 to 53. Nevertheless, the United States surprisingly falls behind other non-OECD countries not shown in figure 52, including Cuba and Costa Rica, and not far ahead of others, such as Albania and Uruguay.[47] As a result, the life expectancy gap between Mexico and the United States (a 1.8-year U.S. advantage) is smaller than the gap between the United States and Canada (a 2.5-year Canadian advantage).[48]

Unfortunately, the United States has become more disadvantaged relative to other developed countries over time. For example, while female life expectancy had been near the median among sixteen of its peers in 1979,

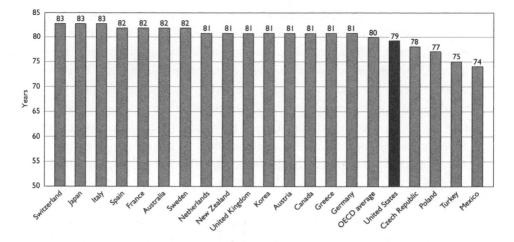

Figure 52. Life expectancy at birth in selected OECD countries, 2011. Source: OECD 2013c.

by 2006 it ranked last among these countries, according the National Academies report mentioned at the beginning of this chapter. The United States also fares poorly across a number of indicators, including age-specific death rates and infant mortality. The infant mortality rate in the United States in the 2005–9 period was 6.7, well above the rates in the other sixteen countries. Sweden and Japan had the lowest infant mortality rates, at 2.5 and 2.6, respectively. The three most important reasons for extra years of life lost in the United States among men under the age of 50 (accounting for 57 percent of the deficit) include homicides, motor vehicle accidents, and accidents and injuries due to other causes. Noncommunicable diseases also play an important role, especially among women. The U.S. mortality disadvantage is accompanied by worse health along a number of indicators, including relatively high levels of child and adult obesity, diabetes, heart disease, and disability. The adolescent birthrate is also relatively high in the United States, as are sexually transmitted infections, HIV and AIDS, and drug-related mortality.[49]

The disparities in health and mortality are likely caused by differences in access to health care, individual behaviors, social factors, physical and environmental factors, and political and social values. Regarding the first, access to health care, the National Academies panel was careful to note that definitively assessing the magnitude of the impact of health care systems on health is difficult. It does note, however, that access to health care in the United States is more dependent on family resources than in other rich countries. For example, a higher percentage of Americans report having difficulty paying for medical bills (27 percent) than in ten other countries in the study, which ranged from a low of 1 percent in the United Kingdom to 14 percent in the Netherlands. Similarly, 29 percent of Americans reported not visiting a doctor when having a medical problem because of cost issues, compared with 6 to 18 percent of respondents in the other countries.[50]

Individual behaviors might help explain some of the cross-national differences, though again better data and more research are needed to definitively show how individual behaviors vary across countries. While Americans are currently less likely to smoke than people in many other countries, they used to have the highest rates of tobacco consumption. These previously high rates, combined with the lagged effect between smoking and disease, may contribute to some of the relatively high mortality among Americans today.[51] In addition, the diets of Americans are less healthy and the U.S. population tends to be more sedentary than its peers in many other countries. This would help explain higher rates of obesity and diabetes in the United States—conditions that can later contribute to heart disease. Likewise, the greater incidence of accidents and homicides in the United States is likely a function of the greater prevalence of drug abuse and firearms, as well riskier behaviors more generally.[52] For example, the proportion of drivers wearing seatbelts is lower in the United States than all but one of fifteen peer countries in one study; in addition, the percentage of road traffic deaths attributable to alcohol is higher in the United States than in all of the other countries. There are 89 firearms per 100 people in the United States—about double the number in the country with the second highest level of gun ownership (Switzerland, at 46 per 100) among the fifteen countries compared, not to mention many orders of magnitude greater than the country with the lowest level (Japan, at fewer than 1 per 100).[53]

In terms of social conditions, the rise in income inequality, child poverty, single-parent households, and incarceration—problems that are worse in the United States than in other countries—may also contribute to the American health disadvantage. Similarly, environmental factors, in the form of low-density housing and dependence on cars, the wide availability of unhealthy foods, and racial and economic segregation, may all contribute to poor health and mortality in the United States. Finally, political and social values can affect health disparities, as there is relatively less public support for policies that redistribute income and resources to alleviate poverty, health, and other inequalities in the United States than in many other welfare states.[54] These factors collectively help explain worse health outcomes among Americans than among people in other rich countries.

CONCLUSION

Life expectancies in the United States have continued to increase over the last several decades. Infant mortality is down, other age-specific death rates arc also down, and mortality from curable diseases has also declined. Nevertheless, significant disparities in health and mortality by ethnicity and socioeconomic status remain. Blacks live shorter lives on average and are more likely to suffer from a number of health conditions than whites. People with relatively low levels of education and income and those who work in low-status occupations likewise suffer from health deficits. However, ethnic disparities have slowly declined in recent years, and socioeconomic ones have significantly increased—consistent with broader trends in ethnic and socioeconomic inequality in the United States.

Those with higher levels of education have more information about healthy living and the ability to navigate through our complex health care system, those with higher income have greater access to health care services and healthy homes and neighborhood environments, and those in high-status occupations are less exposed to risky working conditions. Some of the ethnic disparity in health is explained by socioeconomic disparities associated with ethnicity, but minority—especially black—individuals also contend with residential segregation that exacerbates social and health inequality and with discrimination that increases stress and hypertension. Notably, Hispanics have higher life expectancies than both blacks and whites, though at least a significant portion of this health advantage is a function of the selectivity of relatively healthy immigrants who come to the United States (compared with those who stay behind), as well as the selective migration back home of immigrants with worsening health.

With relatively low fertility, declining mortality, and the aging of the relatively large baby boom generation, a growing proportion of the American population is over the age of sixty-five. This has led to greater expenditures on popular and effective programs such as Social Security and Medicare, which has in turn put a greater stress on government budgets. Health expenditures are very high in the United States for a variety of reasons, including the absence of incentives to reduce the number of tests and procedures prescribed by doctors as well as the high cost of these procedures.

Despite the large amount of money spent on health care, Americans suffer from high mortality and worse health than people in other rich countries. The U.S. life expectancy, for example, is below the OECD average even though the United States has a higher GDP per capita than nearly all of the other countries. While the causes of this health deficit are difficult to pinpoint, they are likely rooted in differences in health care accessibility, individual behaviors, social factors, physical and environmental factors, and political and social values across countries.

The National Academies report on these issues offers recommendations for improving health outcomes in the United States, such as setting specific national health objectives. The report provides a concrete list of such objectives, ranging from improving the quality of air, land, and water to expanding community-based preventative services. It also recommends alerting the public about the U.S. health disadvantage to spark a national discussion on these issues, which might help promote a broader campaign on healthy living.[55] Thus, even though the health of Americans currently lags behind that of their peers, many positive steps can be taken to improve health and well-being in the future.

Conclusion

My goal in this book has been to provide a detailed account of the changing population of the United States. Gaining a deeper insight into who we are as a country is facilitated by recognizing where we've been and comparing our situation to that of our peer countries. Understanding our history helps us gauge where we are going, and looking at our peers gives us a sense of the alternative paths we could have taken and the forces that have made us different.

A demographic lens helps provide a connection between various social and economic phenomena in American society. Sometimes these phenomena are publicly discussed in isolation—each as a distinct problem or trend—when in fact they are intrinsically tied to other processes. To provide just a couple of examples:

- Life course transitions and family formation patterns have become more varied over time. How is this related to other patterns? This variation has been facilitated by long-term economic growth, which has provided the means for self-actualization among a growing number of people in affluent societies. In contrast, in subsistence societies, living alone or without familial or community support or both is hardly an option.

- Immigration has swelled the population of the United States, and many groups have experienced upward mobility across generations. How does this relate to other population processes? Immigrants continue to be drawn by economic opportunities and high standards of living in the United States. Declines in racial/ethnic bias have facilitated the integration of immigrants into U.S. society. Immigration may have even helped soften the historically rigid black-white divide. Finally, immigrants in turn have contributed to American economic growth and prosperity over the years.

Many of the same demographic changes occurring in the United States have been experienced by countries in western Europe and elsewhere. The *first demographic transition*—consisting of a long-term decline in fertility and mortality—occurred many decades ago in all developed countries. In more recent years, the *second demographic transition,* which involves increases in age at marriage, cohabitation, and nonmarital childbearing, has also occurred in most of the same countries. In fact, most countries across the globe have experience the first demographic transition, and an increasing number are also seeing more diverse family formation patterns.

Despite the similarities that the United States has to many of its peers, it still differs in some important respects, such as in its higher level of income inequality and poorer health outcomes alongside its high per capita income. Research has not arrived at a definitive answer to the reasons for these differences, but commentators have pointed to some peculiarities of the United States. While improving living standards and the spread of individualism have facilitated the first and especially the second demographic transitions in many countries, the individualism streak may burn brighter in the United States than in many other places. As discussed in chapter 1, Alexis de Tocqueville described American exceptionalism in the 1830s, noting its national ideology based on liberty, egalitarianism, individualism, populism, and laissez-faire. Most Americans today would continue to affirm these values. However, some argue that an excessive emphasis on individualism can contribute to some social problems that are best addressed collectively, and by governments in particular, especially in large, modern, and heterogeneous societies. The stronger safety net in western Europe, for example, does more to curb the pernicious effects of income inequality than the American safety net—as measured by outcomes ranging from poverty to health and mortality.

THE DEMOGRAPHIC FUTURE

Predicting the demographic future is dangerous. There have been many wildly misguided populations predictions and projections over the years, and I am not altogether eager to add to them. One of the most respected forefathers in the field of demography, Thomas Robert Malthus (1766–1834), famously argued that population growth would be curbed by catastrophic famine and disease. His argument rested on the assumption that the food supply grows arithmetically, whereas populations grow geometrically (that is, populations grow at a much faster pace than food supplies). He did not foresee the tremendous technological improvements in agriculture that allowed the growth of the food supply to match rapid population growth in Europe and then later around the world.

Nevertheless, I will offer some modest predictions. Perhaps the safest is that the United States' population will continue to grow in the coming decades. Fertility is slightly below replacement level in the United States, but it is still higher than in most peer countries. Also of importance, the United States continues to attract many immigrants from around the world. These immigrants and their children are helping to reshape American society, its economy, and its culture—much as immigrants have done throughout the nation's history.

As a result, racial and ethnic diversity has increased in communities across the country. This diversity will almost certainly continue, as diversity is more pronounced among younger cohorts than older ones. As noted in chapter 8, whites make up about 80 percent of the elderly population but just 63 percent of the total population; moreover, in 2011 only 54 percent of all births were to white women.

In contrast to traditional family formation patterns characterized by early and near universal marriage and childbearing, the more varied life course transitions and family formation patterns in contemporary society will likely continue for the foreseeable future. The forces that helped produce them (relatively high standards of living and the high value placed on individualism) are not currently in retreat.

Moving on to more contested ground, I venture that racial/ethnic and gender gaps will continue to narrow. No controversy exists about whether such gaps are narrower than they were, say, fifty years ago, but we have less agreement on how much progress the country has made in the last twenty years or so in both areas. With regard to race/ethnicity, younger cohorts are much comfortable with diversity than older cohorts and thus are probably less likely to be prejudiced and discriminate against members of other groups. Racial/ethnic segregation has declined, the black middle class is growing, and Hispanics are experiencing some measure of upward mobility. Prominent race gaps remain, however, especially with regard to poverty. But on the whole I see progress as more likely than not in the future.

While a male-female earnings gap likewise remains and is narrowing only slowly, the increasing educational attainment of women—and their growing advantage over men in this respect—will likely translate into important future gains in the economic standing of women. Additional reductions in the earnings gap may also occur if traditional gender care-giving norms continue to change—eventually making women no longer the expected sole or primary caretakers of children and dependent elderly parents.

It is important to note that changes in the economy in recent decades—such as continued deindustrialization—have tended to hit men harder than women, and this is probably reducing gender inequality. However, these same changes have tended to hit African Americans harder than whites, and this has slowed the pace of change in racial inequality in recent years. Thus, continuing to track the impact of economic changes on patterns of racial and gender inequality is important.

Speaking of the economy, this is where prediction making becomes harder yet. The U.S. economy has been in the doldrums since about 2000, with relatively modest economic growth in most years—and a spectacular crash during 2007–9. Income inequality has also grown, and the path toward upward mobility has become more uncertain. One traditional route to the middle class—a higher education—has become more costly over time and sometimes involves soul-crunching debt. Disparities in residential environments and health outcomes by socioeconomic status have also widened. In fact, socioeconomic disparities are now often larger than racial ones—such as when looking at life expectancy at birth and children's reading gaps. Changes in family structure, including the increasing prevalence of single-parent families, are both caused and reinforced by economic inequalities. Deindustrialization and globalization have also contributed to these inequalities by reducing the number of relatively well-paying jobs for less-educated workers. Policies that redistribute wealth in the United States seem to have little domestic support. Thus, I do not see any change soon in patterns of high economic inequality. Now, whether the U.S. economy can resume higher levels of economic growth is a different question. Average living standards will likely continue to grow over the long run, consistent with long-term patterns of growth and the continued strength and innovation in important sectors of the U.S. economy (e.g., high-tech industries), though such gains won't be shared equally among Americans.

The regional variation in economic changes and migration patterns that have led to a relative decline of the Rust Belt and growth in the Sun Belt shows no sign of abating. However, there are signs that suburban growth may be peaking and that many central cities are experiencing a renaissance of sorts. It should be interesting to track whether these patterns continue. As a result of the declining racial and ethnic divisions described above, I would expect that ethnic residential segregation will continue to decline gradually, even as income segregation—bolstered by increasing income inequality—will increase. Finally, we should expect to see some continued improvement in morbidity, mortality, and life expectancy patterns among Americans, given continued improvements in medicine. However, even as racial and ethnic disparities in health will continue to decline, health disparities by income may increase. Some of this increase is based on differential access to resources and to different lifestyle choices associated with socioeconomic status.

If one is keeping a balance sheet, among the positive social and demographic changes we may see in the years ahead: the bolstering of demographic and economic growth through immigration, general increases in standards of living, and declines in gender and racial inequality. Negative changes may include economic growth that is slower than in the past;

growing, or at least continuing, income inequality; and the accompanying growth in disparities by socioeconomic status in other outcomes, such as family formation, residential attainment, and health. In addition, the fiscal pressures that accompany an aging population may dampen initiatives that could foster investment in future economic growth or provide greater security in a time of growing income inequality.

One of the more troubling developments in recent years is the weakness in our political process, as manifested by congressional inaction on a wide array of problems confronting the nation. Political polarization and ideological rigidity are hampering efforts to address issues ranging from immigration to budget deficits to education. As in the realm of demographics, it is difficult to predict the future political atmosphere and what policy decisions might be implemented to address this myriad of problems. The ultimate answer lies in the actions of our changing population and the political leaders they elect.

Notes

INTRODUCTION

1. The information on the population size of the United States is from U.S. Census Bureau 2012e, table 1.

2. Ventura and Bachrach 2000; Martin et al. 2011.

3. Migration Policy Institute 2012a.

4. Data from 1960 come from U.S. Census Bureau 2010b; data from 2010 come from U.S. Census Bureau 2010a.

5. U.S. Census Bureau 2011d, 2011i.

6. U.S. Census Bureau 2012m.

7. Life expectancy comparisons across Organisation for Economic Co-operation and Development nations are in OECD 2011b. Life expectancy in the United States from Centers for Disease Control and Prevention 2011.

8. Dewan and Gebeloff 2012.

9. CBSNEWS 2011.

10. Fischer and Hout 2006, 66.

11. DeParle and Tavernise 2012.

12. Smock and Greenland 2010.

13. Smock and Greenland 2010.

14. McLanahan and Sandefur 1997.

15. Blau, Ferber, and Winkler 1998.

16. U.S. Bureau of Labor Statistics 2010a.

17. U.S. Census Bureau 2011h.

18. Looney and Greenstone 2011.

19. Buchmann, DiPrete, and McDaniel 2008, 319–37.

20. Congressional Budget Office 2011, 64–68.

21. U.S. Bureau of Labor Statistics 2011a, 7.

22. Blank 2009, 76.

23. Iceland 2009; Kasinitz et al. 2008.

24. Holzer 2011; Martin and Midgley 2006, 17–23; Bolin 2004.

25. Massey and Denton 1993.

26. Schuman et al. 2001.

27. Lee and Bean 2012.

28. Tolnay 2003.

29. Lemann 1991.

30. Frey 2005.

31. Mather, Pollard, and Jacobsen 2011.

32. Frey 2012a, 2012b.

33. Iceland 2009; Iceland, Sharp, and Timberlake 2013.

34. Life expectancy in 1900 from Arias 2011; in 2010 from Centers for Disease Control and Prevention 2011.

35. Hoyert 2012.

CHAPTER 1

1. Smith cited in Daniels 2002, 31–32.

2. de Tocqueville 1840; Wood 2011; Lipset 1996.

3. Lipset 1996, 22, 26, 31.

4. Lipset 1996, 26.

5. The 1820 U.S. population estimate is from U.S. Census Bureau 2012e, table 1; all of the 2012 population figures are from Population Reference Bureau 2012; the rest of the 1820 population figures are from Maddison 2001, table B-10.

6. Gill, Glazer, and Thernstrom 1992, 23.

7. Population Reference Bureau 2012.

8. Population Reference Bureau 2012.

9. Klein 2012, 89–93.

10. Gill, Glazer, and Thernstrom 1992, 22.

11. Life expectancy comparisons across OECD nations are in OECD 2011b.

12. Fischer and Hout 2006, 63.

13. Gill, Glazer, and Thernstrom 1992, 29.

14. Cutler and Miller 2004; Gill, Glazer, and Thernstrom 1992, 25–26.

15. Easterlin 2000.

16. Lee 2003, 131; Byrne 2008, 99.

17. Wikipedia 2012a.

18. Cutler and Miller 2004.

19. Klein 2012, 129.

20. Cutler and Meara 2001.

21. Wikipedia 2012c.

22. Cutler and Meara 2001; Gill, Glazer, and Thernstrom 1992, 25–26.

23. Westoff 1986, 554–59.

24. Malthus 1998.

25. Franklin (1751), as cited in Kennedy and Bailey 2010, 87.

26. Klein 2012, 68.

27. Gill, Glazer, and Thernstrom 1992, 41–44.

28. Klein 2012, 73.

29. Hacker 2003.

30. Klein 2012, 108.

31. See Gill, Glazer, and Thernstrom 1992, table 3–2, for 1800–1980 data; see Martin et al. 2012, table 4, for 1990–2010 data.

32. Fischer and Hout 2006, 65–67.

33. Klein 2012, 69.

34. Gill, Glazer, and Thernstrom 1992, 44.

35. Gill, Glazer, and Thernstrom 1992, 44–45.

36. Klein 2012, 70.

37. Gill, Glazer, and Thernstrom 1992, 44–45.

38. Guest and Tolnay 1983.

39. Jones and Tertilt 2006; Gill, Glazer, and Thernstrom 1992, 44–45.

40. Gill, Glazer, and Thernstrom 1992, 45–46.

41. Klein 2012, 111.

42. Doepke, Hazan, and Maoz 2007.

43. Fischer and Hout 2006, 68.

44. Gill, Glazer, and Thernstrom 1992, 42–43.

45. Martin and Midgley 2006, 8.

46. Daniels 2002, 20.

47. Martin and Midgley 2003, 12.

48. Gill, Glazer, and Thernstrom 1992, 56.

49. Gill, Glazer, and Thernstrom 1992, 55.

50. Daniels 2002, 267–69.

51. Martin and Midgley 2006, 9–10.

52. Martin and Midgley 2006, 12.

53. Martin and Midgley 2003, 16.

54. Daniels 2002, 329.

55. U.S. Department of Homeland Security 2012.

56. U.S. Immigration and Naturalization Service 2002, 19–21; U.S. Department of Homeland Security 2012.

57. Pew Research Center 2013.

58. Gill, Glazer, and Thernstrom 1992, 64.

59. Pierson 1972, 7, as cited in Gill, Glazer, and Thernstrom 1992, 57.

60. Glaeser and Tobio 2007; Frey 2002.

61. Gill, Glazer, and Thernstrom 1992, 64; Ren 2011; see also Kelly Hall and Ruggles 2004.

62. Klein 2012, 80.

63. Gill, Glazer, and Thernstrom 1992, 66–67; Tolnay 2003.

64. Klein 2012, 82–83; Gibson 1998.

65. Riis 1997, 23–24.

66. Wikipedia 2012e.

67. U.S. Census Bureau 2012e, table 20.

68. Wikipedia 2012b, 2012d.

69. United Nations 2011.

70. Mather, Pollard, and Jacobsen 2011, 15.

71. Gill, Glazer, and Thernstrom 1992, 67.

72. Gill, Glazer, and Thernstrom 1992, 68.

73. Frey 2001, 1–7.

CHAPTER 2

1. DeParle 2012c.

2. Gill, Glazer, and Thernstrom 1992, 147.

3. Gill, Glazer, and Thernstrom 1992, 148.

4. Gill, Glazer, and Thernstrom 1992, 149–50.

5. U.S. Census Bureau 2012l.

6. Fitch and Ruggles 2000, 63–65.

7. Elliott et al. 2012.

8. Jacobsen, Mather, and Dupuis 2012, 9.

9. Cherlin 1981, 2010; Stevenson and Wolfers 2011, 96–108.

10. Martin 2006.

11. Isen and Stevenson 2010.

12. England and Bearak 2012.

13. Manning 2013, 2–3.

14. Kennedy and Bumpass 2008.

15. Manning and Smock 2005, 998.

16. Manning and Smock 2005, 995.

17. OECD 2011a.

18. O'Connell and Feliz 2011, 31.

19. Krivickas 2010.

20. Burgoyne 2012.

21. Ventura and Bachrach 2000; Martin et al. 2011; see also Wildsmith, Steward-Streng, and Manlove 2011; DeParle and Tavernise 2012.

22. Smock and Greenland 2010.

23. U.S. Census Bureau 2011e.

24. Kennedy and Bumpass 2008.

25. Child Trends 2012.

26. Lesthaeghe 1995.

27. OECD 2011a, table 1.1.

28. OECD 2011a, table 1.1.

29. Kennedy and Fitch 2012, 1494.

30. Findings reported in Lesthaeghe 2010. Other sources for the figures include Raymo, Iwasawa, and Bumpass 2008; and Jones 2005.

31. Much of the discussion below also appears in Iceland 2013, ch. 6.

32. See Murray 1984; Rector 1993.

33. Cherlin 2009, 25–26.

34. Becker 1981.

35. Ruggles 1997.

36. For one example of this argument, see Krugman 2012.

37. England and Bearak 2012.

38. Kristof 2012.

39. Smock and Greenland 2010; see also Gibson-Davis, Edin, and McLanahan 2005.

40. See Edin and Kefalas 2005.

41. See Lareau 2003.

42. DeParle and Tavernise 2012.

43. Lesthaeghe 2010, 33–34.

44. Cherlin 2009, 189.

45. A. Williams 2012.

46. A. Williams 2012.

47. Kotkin 2012, 6; Klineberg 2012; the 2010 figure for the United States is from U.S. Census Bureau 2012e, table 61.

48. Brooks 2012a.

49. Brooks 2012a.

50. Cherlin 2009, 190.

51. Amato 2000, 1282.

52. Amato 2005, 75.

53. McLanahan 2004, 608.

54. McLanahan 2004, 616.

55. Frazier 1932, 1939; Myrdal 1996; Moynihan 1965; Bianchi 1990; Hogan and Lichter 1995, 93–139; Lichter 1997.

56. Murray 2012.

57. U.S. Census Bureau 2012h.

58. Bianchi 1999; O'Hare 1996; CONSAD Research Corp. 2009.
59. Gornick and Jantti 2012, 564.
60. Gornick and Jantti 2012, 564.
61. See Rainwater and Smeeding 2003.

CHAPTER 3

1. Quote from Rosin 2012b; see also Rosin 2012a.
2. Coontz 2012.
3. Lorber 2009, 111–12.
4. Newman 2007, 90.
5. Blau, Ferber, and Winkler 1998, 16.
6. Marger 2011, 336.
7. Blau, Ferber, and Winkler 1998, 19; Nodi 2008, 268–69.
8. Kerbo 2009, 307.
9. Kerbo 2009, 308.
10. May 1982.
11. Blau, Ferber, and Winkler 1998, 20–25.
12. Coontz 1992.
13. Gill, Glazer, and Thernstrom 1992, 184–86.
14. Blau, Ferber, and Winkler 1998, 25; Reskin and Roos 1990.
15. Gill, Glazer, and Thernstrom 1992, 186–88.
16. U.S. Census Bureau 2012f.
17. Siebens and Ryan 2012, table 2.
18. Ryan 2012, 2.
19. Correll 2001; Jacobs 1989.
20. U.S. Bureau of Labor Statistics 2010a.
21. U.S. Bureau of Labor Statistics 2011c, table 2.
22. Blau, Brummund, and Yung-Hsu Liu 2012, 19–22.
23. England 2010; Reskin and Maroto 2011.
24. England 2010, 150; C. L. Williams 1995.
25. An extended discussion of these issues can be found in Damaske 2011; Gerson 2009; Stone 2007; and J. C. Williams 2000.
26. U.S. Census Bureau 2012m, table P-40.
27. Kerbo 2009, 313.
28. England 2005.
29. Institute for Women's Policy Research 2012, table 2.
30. Kreider and Elliott 2010; Frech and Damaske, 2012.
31. CONSAD Research Corp. 2009.
32. Budig and Hodges 2010.
33. Roth 2006.

34. Kerbo 2009, 317.

35. Sandberg quoted in Kristoff 2013.

36. P. Stone 2007.

37. U.S. Bureau of Labor Statistics 2011a, 62–76.

38. See Bianchi 1995, 107–54; Damaske 2011.

39. Lareau 2003.

40. Bianchi et al. 2012, 56–58.

41. Hausman, Tyson, and Zahidi 2012, table 3a.

42. Hausman, Tyson, and Zahidi 2012, appendix D.

43. Misra, Budig, and Bockmann 2010.

44. Misra, Budig, and Bockmann 2011, 139.

45. Looney and Greenstone 2011.

46. Buchmann, DiPrete, and McDaniel 2008.

47. U.S. Bureau of Labor Statistics 2012b.

48. Brooks 2012b.

49. Rosin 2012b.

50. Rosin 2012b.

51. Dwyer 2013.

52. Coontz 2012.

53. Rosin 2012b.

54. J. C. Williams and Segal 2003, 77–78; Glauber 2008.

55. J. C. Williams 2013; see also Galinsky, Aumann, and Bond 2011.

56. England 2010.

57. Polachek and Siebert 1994, 83–89.

CHAPTER 4

1. Kennedy 1999, 214–19.

2. National Bureau of Economic Research 2010; U.S. Bureau of Labor Statistics 2010b.

3. Condon and Wiseman 2013.

4. Markoff 2012.

5. Fischer and Hout 2006, 154–56; U.S. Census Bureau 2011a.

6. Klein 2012, 89–93; Gill, Glazer, and Thernstrom 1992, 22; OECD 2011b.

7. U.S. Census Bureau 2012f.

8. Auerbach and Kellermann 2011.

9. These poverty statistics rely on the official U.S. poverty measure. Specifically, this measure has two components: poverty thresholds and the definition of family income that is compared with these thresholds. The measure was originally devised by Mollie Orshansky, a researcher at the Social Security Administration, in the early 1960s. She constructed poverty thresholds by calculating

what it cost to feed a family on a low-cost food plan and then multiplying this amount by three, since families at the time spent close to a third of their incomes on food. Thresholds have been updated yearly for inflation using the consumer price index (CPI). The poverty threshold for a four-person family in 2011 was $22,811. The definition of family resources used to compare with the thresholds is gross annual cash income. A family and its members are considered poor if their income falls below the poverty threshold for a family of that size and composition. This poverty measure is not without its critics, as many think the threshold is too low, and others point out that it imperfectly measures people's incomes, because it leaves out near-cash government transfers like housing subsidies and food assistance vouchers. See Iceland 2013 for a fuller discussion of poverty measurement issues.

10. Blank 1997, 2009.

11. Congressional Budget Office, 2012.

12. Piketty and Saez 2003, 29; Piketty and Saez 2013.

13. Levine 2012, summary page.

14. Wolff 2013, 1.

15. Iceland 2013 also has an extended discussion of these issues.

16. Blank 2009, 76.

17. Blank 2009, 64–68.

18. U.S. Bureau of Labor Statistics 2011a, 7.

19. Grusky and Weeden 2011.

20. Bluestone and Harrison 2000, 190–97; Harrison and Bluestone 1990.

21. Duhigg and Bradsher 2012.

22. Stangler 2012.

23. Richtel 2005.

24. Danziger and Gottschalk 1995, 130–31.

25. Bernstein et al. 2000, table 1.

26. See Osterman 1999; Blank 2009, 77–78.

27. Duncan and Trejo 2011a.

28. Lindsey 2009, 48.

29. Congressional Budget Office 2011, xii.

30. Grusky and Weeden 2011, 95.

31. Congressional Budget Office 2011, 18–19.

32. Freeland 2011.

33. Levine 2012, 12; Smeeding 2008.

34. OECD 2011c.

35. D'Addio 2007, table 1.

36. OECD 2010a, 17.

37. OECD 2010a, 10; see also Beller and Hout 2006, 30.

38. DeParle 2012b; see also Chetty et al. 2013 for a discussion of the variation in economic mobility across regions and metropolitan areas within the United States.

39. National Bureau of Economic Research 2010; U.S. Bureau of Labor Statistics 2010b.

40. Bosworth 2012; U.S. Bureau of Labor Statistics 2012a.

41. A discussion of these issues is also included in Iceland 2013.

42. Rajan 2010.

43. Sherman 2011.

44. Wolff, Owens, and Burak 2011, 134 and 150–51; Food Research Action Center 2012, 3.

45. Schoen 2012.

46. Rampell 2012.

47. Kenworthy 2004, 2011; Scholz, Moffitt, and Cowan 2009.

48. Frank 2007, 2.

49. Frank 2007, 40.

50. Financial Crisis Inquiry Commission 2011, 5.

51. Frank 2007, 44–45.

52. Ehrenreich 2001, 199–200.

53. Stiglitz 2013; see also Stiglitz 2012; and Berg and Ostry 2011.

54. Bailey and Dynarski 2011, figure 3.

55. DeParle 2012a.

CHAPTER 5

1. Daniels 2002, 266.

2. Daniels 2002, 275–76.

3. Brimelow 1995, 9 and 232.

4. Daniels 2002, 267–69.

5. Martin and Midgley 2006, 12. See also Daniels 2002, 271.

6. Martin and Midgley 2006, 12.

7. Daniels 2002, 287.

8. Daniels 2002, 329.

9. Daniels 2002, 310–11.

10. Brimelow 1995, 76–77.

11. Martin and Midgley 2010, 2.

12. Daniels 2002, 311.

13. Passel and Cohn 2012.

14. Daniels 2002, tables 6.4 and 16.2; Migration Policy Institute 2012b.

15. Pew Research Center 2013.

16. U.S. Department of Homeland Security 2012.

17. U.S. Census Bureau 2012i.

18. Parrado 2011; Parrado and Flippen 2012; Duncan and Trejo 2011b.

19. Branigin 1998.

20. Alba and Nee 2003, 11.

21. Alba and Nee 2003, 38.

22. Daniels 2002, 159.

23. Daniels 2002, 189.

24. Daniels 2002, 195–98.

25. See Alba and Nee 2003 for a detailed discussion of these issues.

26. Daniels 2002, 276.

27. Alba and Nee 2003, 131–32.

28. Portes and Zhou 1993; Zhou 1999, 196–211.

29. Reitz, Zhang, and Hawkins 2011, 1064.

30. Park and Myers 2010; White and Glick 2009; Bean and Stevens 2003. For a careful and fascinating study of immigrant assimilation in New York, see Kasinitz et al. 2008; and Kasinitz, Mollenkopf, and Waters 2004.

31. Bean et al. 2013; Brown 2007.

32. White and Glick 2009, 111.

33. Specifically, individual-equivalent household income is calculated by dividing household income by the square root of the number of persons in the household. For more details, see Reitz, Zhang, and Hawkins 2011, 1054.

34. Reitz, Zhang, and Hawkins 2011, table 5.

35. White and Glick 2009, 148.

36. J. Lee and Bean 2007, 2012; Golash-Boza and Darity 2008; Frank, Akresh, and Lu 2010.

37. Note that the bar for All Blacks is below that of both Native-born and Foreign-born blacks. While the average segregation for the group as a whole is typically between the segregation experienced by the two component groups, it does not have to be. Each of the component groups could live in different segregated neighborhoods, but if combined into one group, they may be spread across a broader array of neighborhoods.

38. Iceland and Scopilliti 2008.

39. Iceland, Sharp, and Timberlake 2013.

40. Lippard and Gallagher 2011, 1–23.

41. Telles and Ortiz 2008.

42. Perlmann 2005, 117.

43. See also Brown 2007.

44. Smith and Edmonston 1997, 6.

45. Holzer 2011.

46. Smith and Edmonston 1997; Holzer 2011.

47. Holzer 2011, 10.

48. Smith and Edmonston 1997.

49. Immigrant Learning Center 2013.

50. Fiscal Policy Institute 2012.

51. Salkever and Wadhwa 2012.
52. Salkever and Wadhwa 2012.
53. Sullivan 2012.
54. Smith and Edmonston 1997.
55. Singer et al. 2008, 29.
56. Jackson 2011.
57. Smith and Edmonston 1997, 4.
58. Johnson, Farrell, and Guinn 1997, 1055–56.
59. Johnson, Farrell, and Guinn 1997, 1074–75.
60. Gabriel 2013.
61. Putnam 2007, 137.
62. Alba and Nee 2003, 32.
63. Putnam 2007, 137.
64. Portes and Vickstrom 2011.
65. M. T. Lee and Martinez 2009; Sampson 2008; Martinez, Stowell, and Lee 2010; Stowell et al. 2009; Wadsworth 2010.
66. Sampson 2008, 28–33.
67. Central Intelligence Agency 2013.
68. Hansen 2003.
69. OECD 2013d.
70. Hansen 2003.
71. Modood 2003; BBC News 2011.
72. Simon 2012, 1.
73. See Caldwell 2006; Modood 2003.
74. Modood 2003; Simon 2012.
75. Heath, Rothon, and Kilpi 2008, 218.
76. Reitz, Zhang, and Hawkins 2011, 1063–64.
77. Alba, Sloan, and Sperling 2011.
78. Passel 2005.

CHAPTER 6

1. Diggins 1976, 216.
2. Lipscomb and Bergh 1903–4, 14: 183–84.
3. Ambrose 2003, 4.
4. Peterson 1984, 1343–46.
5. National Public Radio 2013.
6. Arthur 2007, 3731–32.
7. Brodkin 2009, 58.
8. Alba 2009, 30.

9. Waters 2009, 31.

10. Alba 2009, 81–89.

11. Dulitzky 2001, 85; Marger 2011, 282.

12. Omi and Winant 2009, 21.

13. Hirschman, Alba, and Farely 2000, 381–93.

14. Compton et al. 2012.

15. Hirschman, Alba, and Farley 2000, 390–91.

16. U.S. Census Bureau 2013d.

17. Wolff 2013, 15.

18. Weber 1994, 128.

19. See Alba 2009.

20. Gill, Glazer, and Thernstrom 1992, 221.

21. See Foner 1988.

22. Myrdal 1996, 485.

23. Tolnay 2003.

24. Pager 2008, 24–25, from Schuman et al. 2001.

25. W.J. Wilson 1996, 29–30.

26. W.J. Wilson 1978.

27. W.J. Wilson 1987.

28. Hout 1994, 531–42; Sakamoto, Wu, and Tzeng 2000; Farkas and Vicknair 1996.

29. Fryer 2011, 856.

30. See Pager 2009; Cross et al. 1990; Turner, Fix, and Struyk 1991.

31. Charles and Guryan 2008.

32. Loury 2000, 60.

33. Massey and Denton 1993, 141–42.

34. Iceland 2009; Iceland, Sharp, and Timberlake 2013.

35. Western and Wildeman 2009, 221–42; Wakefield and Uggen 2010.

36. Ventura and Bachrach 2000; J.A. Martin et al. 2011; see also Wildsmith, Steward-Streng, and Manlove 2011; and DeParle and Tavernise 2012.

37. U.S. Census Bureau 2012h.

38. Wenger 2013, 1.

39. Lin and Harris 2008, 1–17; Fryer 2011.

40. Reardon 2011.

41. Landry and Marsh 2011.

42. Gill, Glazer, and Thernstrom 1992, 349.

43. Marger 2011, 293.

44. Rodriguez 1989.

45. Portes and Rumbaut 2006.

46. Daniels 2002, 239–43; Gill, Glazer, and Thernstrom 1992, 33.

47. Daniels 2002, 245.

48. Daniels 2002, 250–55; Gill, Glazer, and Thernstrom 1992, 333–34.

49. Bulosan 1946, as quoted in Daniels 2002, 357.

50. San Juan 1995, 9.

51. Iceland, Weinberg, and Hughes 2013 (from decennial censuses).

52. Grieco 2010, 6–8.

53. Camarota 2007, 23.

54. Chiswick and Sullivan 1995, 211–70.

55. Camarota 2007, 18.

56. Logan and Turner 2013, 11.

57. Camarota 2007, 18.

58. White and Glick 2009, 111; see also Bean and Stevens 2003.

59. Takei and Sakamoto 2011.

60. Duncan, Hotz, and Trejo 2006.

61. White and Glick 2009, 148.

62. Healey 2012, 123; Gill, Glazer, and Thernstrom 1992, 30.

63. Gill, Glazer, and Thernstrom 1992, 31.

64. Shoemaker 1999.

65. Norris, Vines, and Hoeffel 2012, 4.

66. U.S. Census Bureau 2010c. Note that the statistics cited here for Native Americans and those cited for other groups come from different surveys (the American Community Survey for Native Americans; and for the other groups see U.S. Census Bureau 2012k). The CPS is too small a survey to provide reliable annual data on Native Americans. Since the data come from different sources, the two sets are not perfectly comparable, but they still provide an accurate general picture of Native American socioeconomic disadvantage in American society.

67. Sakamoto, Wu, and Tzeng 2000; Sandefur and Scott 1983.

68. Huyser, Sakamoto, and Takei 2010.

69. Saulny 2011; see also Humes, Jones, and Ramirez 2011.

70. Qian and Licther 2007.

71. Wang 2012, 8 and 19.

72. Wang 2012, 7.

73. Yen 2009.

74. Woodhouse 2012.

75. Alba 2009, 90–135.

76. Woodhouse 2012.

77. Mamdani 2001, 45.

78. Heath, Rothon, and Kilpi 2008, 218.

79. Fisher 2013.

80. Higgins 2013a.

81. Higgins 2013b.

CHAPTER 7

1. U.S. Census Bureau 1998, 2012d.

2. The population of Austin more than doubled from a little over 300,000 in 1980 to over 800,000 in 2012 (U.S. Census Bureau 1998, 2013c).

3. Castillo 2013.

4. In 2010 African Americans lived in neighborhoods that were, on average, 65 percent black, and whites lived in neighborhoods that were 73 percent white (diversitydata.org 2011). Income segregation information comes from Reardon and Bischoff 2011.

5. U.S. Census Bureau 2013b.

6. CNNMoney 2013.

7. W.J. Wilson 1996, 29–30.

8. Frey 2012b, 1.

9. Singer 2004; J.H. Wilson and Singer 2011.

10. Frey 2011, 1–9.

11. Kneebone 2009.

12. Frey 2012b, 11–12.

13. Frey 2012a.

14. Ehrenhalt 2012, 38.

15. Lambrecht 2012.

16. U.S. Census Bureau 2012j.

17. Burgess 1925.

18. Burgess 1928; Massey and Denton 1993; Taeuber and Taeuber 1965; Myrdal 1996.

19. Logan and Stults 2011; Iceland, Sharp, and Timberlake 2013.

20. Iceland and Wilkes 2006.

21. Iceland 2009; Iceland and Scopilliti 2008.

22. Isolation is a little lower for non-Hispanic whites than for whites in general because of the relative size of the two white groups. (Holding other factors constant, larger groups tend to be more isolated.)

23. Logan and Stults 2011.

24. Sharp et al. 2010; Marsh et al. 2010; Sanchez et al. 2010; Hall et al. 2010.

25. Sugrue 1993, 92–93.

26. Massey and Denton 1993, 26–59.

27. Jargowsky 1997, 38–43.

28. Auletta 1982.

29. Frey 2011, 1.

30. Kneebone, Nadeau, and Berube 2011, 1–16.

31. It should be noted that a score of 50 when using dissimilarity is not indicative of the same level of segregation as a score of 50 when using the information theory index.

32. Reardon and Bischoff 2011, 14–18.

33. Castles and Miller 2003, 21–32.

34. Gill, Glazer, and Thernstrom 1992, 69–70.

35. Gray and Scardamalia 2012, 1.

36. Rosenblatt and DeLuca 2012, 273–74.

37. Massey and Espinosa 1997.

38. Dick 2008, 7.

39. Krysan and Bader 2009, 677; Chen and Lin 2012.

40. Marsh, Crowder, and Polimis 2011.

41. Massey and Denton 1993, 40–41.

42. Massey and Denton 1993, 30–37.

43. Massey and Denton 1993; Ross and Turner 2005; Lacey 2007, 100–110.

44. Engel and McCoy 2008; Fligstein and Goldstein 2011, 24; Rugh and Massey 2010.

45. Krysan and Bader 2007.

46. Krysan and Farley 2002.

47. Dick 2008, 7.

48. Cutler, Glaeser, and Vigdor 1999; Iceland 2009; Ross and Turner 2005; Turner et al. 2013.

49. Lewyn 2009, 86–87.

50. Gordon and Cox 2012, 566.

51. Lewyn 2009, 91.

52. Gordon and Cox 2012; Richardson and Bae 2004.

53. Patacchini et al. 2009, 131–33; OECD 2010b, 31–33; Gordon and Cox 2012, 567.

54. Patacchini et al. 2009, 131–33.

55. Clapson and Hutchison 2010, 1–14.

56. Chen, Myles, and Picot 2012, 877.

57. Musterd 2005.

58. Van Kempen and Murie 2009.

59. Musterd and Van Kempen 2009; Glikman and Semyonov 2012.

60. Iceland, Mateos, and Sharp 2011.

61. Doyle 2013.

62. Peach 2009; Glikman and Semyonov 2012, 198–213.

CHAPTER 8

1. National Research Council and Institute of Medicine 2013, 1.

2. J. Wilson 2013.

3. National Research Council and Institute of Medicine 2013, 4–6.

4. World Bank 2012.

5. Hoyert 2012, 2.

6. Meyer 2012.

7. Thorslund et al. 2013, 2–3; Preston and Wang 2006, 631.

8. Race and Hispanic origin information is collected from two separate questions. Hispanics can be of any race.

9. Centers for Disease Control and Prevention 2011.

10. Hoyert 2012, 5; MacDorman, Hoyert, and Mathews 2013; Schoeni, Freedman, and Martin 2009.

11. D. R. Williams et al. 2010.

12. Centers for Disease Control and Prevention 2012b, 5–6.

13. Centers for Disease Control and Prevention 2012c.

14. Braveman et al. 2010, table 2.

15. Adler and Newman 2002; Gallup 2012.

16. Hummer and Lariscy 2011, 254; Masters, Hummer, and Powers 2012; Miech et al. 2011; Montez et al. 2011; Olshansky et al. 2012, 1806; Schoeni, Freedman, and Martin 2009.

17. Hummer and Lariscy 2011, 243–45.

18. Peckham and Wyn 2009.

19. Adler and Newman 2002, 61–68; Williams and Mohammed 2008, 136.

20. Hummer and Lariscy 2011, 245.

21. Adler and Newman 2002, 68–69; Hummer and Lariscy 2011, 243.

22. Abramsky 2012.

23. D. R. Williams and Sternthal 2010, S20–S21.

24. Zhang, Hayward, and Lu 2012.

25. Singh and Miller 2004; Osypuk et al. 2009; see also Population Reference Bureau 2013 for a concise discussion of the Hispanic paradox.

26. Tavernise 2013.

27. Popkin 2004, 38.

28. Food and Agriculture Organization of the United Nations 2013, annex table.

29. Lakhani 2013.

30. Riosmena et al. 2012.

31. Popkin, Adair, and Ng 2012.

32. Popkin 2004, 39.

33. Palloni and Arias 2004; Turra and Elo 2008; Riosmena, Wong, and Palloni 2013.

34. Markides and Eschbach 2011, 227; Singh and Miller 2004.

35. Markides and Eschbach 2011, 237.

36. Jacobsen et al. 2011, 3.

37. Werner 2011, 2.

38. Jacobsen et al. 2011, 4–5; Motel and Patten 2013, tables 1 and 11.

39. Minino and Murphy 2012, 2–4.

40. Centers for Disease Control and Prevention 2013.

41. Holzer and Sawhill 2013.

42. Board of Trustees, Federal Old-Age and Survivors Insurance and Federal Disability Trust Funds 2013.

43. Board of Trustees, Federal Old-Age and Survivors Insurance and Federal Disability Trust Funds 2013.

44. Isaacs et al. 2012.

45. Gawande 2009.

46. Brill 2013.

47. United Nations 2012.

48. Caselli et al. 2013, 5.

49. National Research Council and Institute of Medicine 2013, 27–88.

50. Schoen et al. 2011, exhibit 1.

51. National Research Council and Institute of Medicine 2013, 190–238; Preston and Wang 2006; Pampel 2005.

52. National Research Council and Institute of Medicine 2013, 190–238.

53. National Research Council and Institute of Medicine 2013, 155–58.

54. National Research Council and Institute of Medicine 2013, 159.

55. National Research Council and Institute of Medicine 2013, 347–74.

References

Abramsky, Sasha. 2012. "The Other America, 2012: Confronting the Poverty Epidemic." *The Nation*, April 25.

Adler, Nancy E., and Katherine Newman. 2002. "Socioeconomic Disparities in Health: Pathways and Policies." *Health Affairs* 21 (2): 60–76.

Alba, Richard. 2009. *Blurring the Color Line: The New Chance for a More Integrated America*. Cambridge, MA: Harvard University Press.

Alba, Richard, and Victor Nee. 2003. *Remaking the American Mainstream: Assimilation and Contemporary Immigration*. Cambridge, MA: Harvard University Press.

Alba, Richard, Jennifer Sloan, and Jessica Sperling. 2011. "The Integration Imperative: The Children of Low-Status Immigrants in the Schools of Wealthy Societies." *Annual Review of Sociology* 37: 395–415.

Amato, Paul R. 2000. "The Consequences of Divorce for Adults and Children." *Journal of Marriage and the Family* 62: 1269–87.

———. 2005. "The Impact of Family Formation Change on the Cognitive, Social, and Emotional Well-Being of the Next Generation." *Future of Children* 15 (2): 75–96.

Ambrose, Stephen E. 2003. *To America: Personal Reflections of an Historian*. New York: Simon & Schuster.

Arias, Elizabeth. 2011. "United States Life Tables, 2007." *CDC National Vital Statistics Reports* 59 (9) (September 28).

Arthur, Mikaila Mariel Lemonik. 2007. "Race." In *The Blackwell Encyclopedia of Sociology*, vol. 8, edited by George Ritzer. Malden, MA: Blackwell Publishing.

Atkinson, A. B. 1999. *The Economic Consequences of Rolling Back the Welfare State*. Cambridge, MA: MIT Press.

Auerbach, David I., and Arthur L. Kellermann. 2011. "A Decade of Health Care Cost Growth Has Wiped Out Real Income Gains for an Average US Family." *Health Affairs* 30 (9): 1–7.

Auletta, Ken. 1982. *The Underclass*. New York: Random House.

Bailey, Martha J., and Susan M. Dynarski. 2011. *Gains and Gaps: Changing Inequality in U.S. College Entry and Completion*. National Bureau of Economic Research Working Paper no. 17633, December.

BBC News. 2011. "State of Multiculturalism Has Failed, Says David Cameron." Online article, February 5. Available at www.bbc.co.uk/news/uk-politics-12371994 (accessed March 13, 2013).

Bean, Frank D., and Gillian Stevens. 2003. *America's Newcomers and the Dynamics of Diversity*. New York: Russell Sage Foundation.

Bean, Frank D., James D. Bachmeier, Susan K. Brown, Jennifer Van Hook, and Mark A. Leach. 2013. *Unauthorized Mexican Migration and the Socioeconomic Integration of Mexican Americans*. Research Report, US2010: Discover America in a New Century, Russell Sage Foundation, May.

Becker, Gary S. 1981. *A Treatise on the Family*. Cambridge, MA: Harvard University Press.

Beller, Emily, and Michael Hout. 2006. "Intergenerational Social Mobility: The United States in Comparative Perspective." *Future of Children* 16 (2): 19–36.

Berg, Andrew G., and Jonathan D. Ostry. 2011. *Inequality and Unsustainable Growth: Two Sides of the Same Coin?* International Monetary Fund Staff Discussion Note, SDN/11/08, April 8.

Bernstein, Jared, Elizabeth C. McNichol, Lawrence Mishel, and Robert Zahradnik. 2000. *Pulling Apart: A State-by-State Analysis of Income Trends*. Center on Budget and Policy Priorities and Economic Policy Institute Report, Washington, D.C., January.

Bianchi, Suzanne M. 1990. "America's Children: Mixed Prospects." *Population Bulletin* 45: 1–43.

———. 1995. "Changing Economic Roles of Women and Men." In *State of the Union: America in the 1990s*, vol. 1, edited by Reynolds Farley. New York: Russell Sage Foundation.

———. 1999. "Feminization and Juvenilization of Poverty: Trends, Relative Risks, Causes, and Consequences." *Annual Review of Sociology* 25: 307–33.

Bianchi, Suzanne M., Liana C. Sayer, Melissa A. Milkie, and John P. Robinson. 2012. "Housework: Who Did, Does or Will Do It, and How Much Does It Matter?" *Social Forces* 91 (1): 55–63.

Blank, Rebecca. 1997. "Why Has Economic Growth Been Such an Ineffective Tool against Poverty in Recent Years?" In *Poverty and Inequality: The Political Economy of Redistribution,* edited by Jon Neil. Kalamazoo, MI: W. E. Upjohn Institute for Employment Research.

———. 2009. "Economic Change and the Structure of Opportunity for Less-Skilled Workers." In *Changing Poverty, Changing Policies,* edited by Maria Cancian and Sheldon Danziger. New York: Russell Sage Foundation.

Blau, Francine D., Peter Brummund, and Albert Yung-Hsu Liu. 2012. *Trends in Occupational Segregation by Gender 1970–2009: Adjusting for the Impact of Changes in the Occupational Coding System.* National Bureau of Economic Research Working Paper 17993. Available at www.nber.org/papers/w17993.pdf (accessed January 22, 2013).

Blau, Francine D., Marianne A. Ferber, and Anne E. Winkler. 1998. *The Economics of Women, Men, and Work.* 3rd ed. Saddle River, NJ: Prentice Hall.

Bluestone, Barry, and Bennett Harrison. 2000. *Growing Prosperity: The Battle for Growth with Equity in the Twenty-First Century.* Boston: Houghton Mifflin.

Board of Trustees, Federal Old-Age and Survivors Insurance and Federal Disability Trust Funds. 2013. *The 2013 Annual Report of the Board of Trustees, Federal Old-Age and Survivors Insurance and Federal Disability Trust Funds.* Washington, DC: Social Security Administration.

Bolin, Tim. 2004. *The Economic and Fiscal Impacts of Immigration.* Institute for Research on Labor and Employment Research Report, University of California, Berkeley.

Bosworth, Barry. 2012. *Economic Consequences of the Great Recession: Evidence from the Panel Study of Income Dynamics.* Center for Retirement Research at Boston College Working Paper, CRR WP 2012-4.

Branigin, William. 1998. "Immigrants Shunning Idea of Assimilation." *Washington Post,* May 25, A1.

Braveman, Paula A., Catherine Cubbin, Susan Egerter, David R. Williams, and Elsie Pamuk. 2010. "Socioeconomic Disparities in Health in the United States: What the Patterns Tell Us." *American Journal of Public Health* 100, S1: S186–96.

Brill, Steven. 2013. "Bitter Pill: Why Medical Bills Are Killing Us." *Time* 181 (8), March 4: 16–55.

Brimelow, Peter. 1995. *Alien Nation: Common Sense about America's Immigration Disaster.* New York: Random House.

Britton, Marcus L., and Pat Rubio Goldsmith. 2013. "Keeping People in Their Place? Young-Adult Mobility and the Persistence of Residential Segregation in US Metropolitan Areas." *Urban Studies,* DOI 10.1177/0042098013482506.

Brodkin, Karen. 2009. "How Did Jews Become White Folks?" In *The Social*

Construction of Difference and Inequality: Race, Class, Gender, and Sexuality, 4th ed., edited by Tracy E. Ore. Boston: McGraw-Hill.

Brooks, David. 2012a. "The Age of Possibility." *New York Times*, November 15.

———. 2012b. "Why Men Fail." *New York Times*, September 10.

Brown, Susan K. 2007. "Delayed Spatial Assimilation: Multigenerational Incorporation of the Mexican-Origin Population in Los Angeles." *City and Community* 6 (3): 193–209.

Buchmann, Claudia, Thomas A. DiPrete, and Anne McDaniel. 2008. "Gender Inequalities in Education." *Annual Review of Sociology* 34: 319–37.

Budig, Michelle J., and Melissa J. Hodges. 2010. "Differences in Disadvantage: Variation in the Motherhood Penalty across White Women's Earnings Distribution." *American Sociological Review* 75 (5): 705–28.

Bulosan, Carlos. 1946. *America Is in the Heart*. Seattle: University of Washington Press.

Burgess, Ernest W. 1925. "The Growth of the City: An Introduction to a Research Project." In *The City*, edited by Robert E. Park, Ernest W. Burgess, and Robert D. McKensize, 47–62. Chicago: University of Chicago Press.

———. 1928. "Residential Segregation in American Cities." *Annals of the American Academy of Political and Social Science* 140: 105–15.

Burgoyne, S. 2012. *Demographic Profile of Same-Sex Parents*. National Center for Family & Marriage Research, FP-12–15. Available at ncfmr.bgsu.edu/pdf /family_profiles/file115683.pdf (accessed November 2, 2012).

Byrne, Joseph Patrick. 2008. *Encyclopedia of Pestilence, Pandemics, and Plagues: A-M*. Westport, CT: Greenwood Publishing Group.

Caldwell, Christopher. 2006. "Islam on the Outskirts of the Welfare State." *New York Times Magazine*, February 5.

Camarota, Steven A. 2007. *Immigrants in the United States, 2007*. Center for Immigration Studies Backgrounder, November.

Caselli, Graziella, Sven Drefahl, Marc Luy, and Christian Wegner-Siegmundt. 2013. "Future Mortality in Low Mortality Countries." In *World Population and Human Capital in the 21st Century*, edited by Wolfgang Lutz, William Butz, and Samir KC. New York: Oxford University Press.

Castillo, Juan. 2013. "For People on the Move, Austin Is a Place to Stop and Live." *Austin Statesman*, March 30. Available at www.statesman.com/news /news/local/for-people-on-the-move-austin-is-a-place-to-stop-a/nW75T / (accessed June 3, 2013).

Castles, Stephen, and Mark J. Miller. 2003. *The Age of Migration*. 3rd ed. New York: Guilford Press.

CBSNEWS. 2011. "Poverty in America: Faces behind the Figures." CBSNEWS web story, September 19. Available at www.cbsnews.com/2100–201_162–20108085.html (accessed August 1, 2012).

Centers for Disease Control and Prevention. 2011. "Table 22. Life Expectancy at Birth, at Age 65, and at Age 75, by Sex, Race, and Hispanic Origin: United States, Selected Years 1900–2010." National Vital Statistics System. Available at www.cdc.gov/nchs/data/hus/2011/022.pdf (accessed June 30, 2013).

———. 2012a. *Deaths: Preliminary Data for 2010.* National Vital Statistics Reports, January 11.

———. 2012b. "Summary Health Statistics for the U.S. Population: National Health Interview Survey, 2011." *Vital and Health Statistics* 10 (255) (December).

———. 2012c. "Table 11. Infant, Neonatal, and Postneonatal Mortality Rates, by Detailed Race and Hispanic Origin of Mother: United States, Selected Years 1983–2008." Health, United States, 2012: Infant Mortality. Available at www.cdc.gov/nchs/hus/asian.htm (accessed August 15, 2013).

———. 2013. "State-Specific Health Life Expectancy at Age 65 Years—United States, 2007–2009." *Morbidity and Mortality Weekly Report (MMWR)* 62 (28) (July 19): 561–66.

Central Intelligence Agency. 2013. "The World Factbook: Net Migration Rate." Internet datatables. Available at www.cia.gov/library/publications/the-world-factbook/rankorder/2112rank.html (accessed March 13, 2013).

Charles, Kerwin Kofi, and Jonathan Guryan. 2008. "Prejudice and Wages: An Empirical Assessment of Becker's *The Economics of Discrimination.*" *Journal of Political Economy* 116 (5): 773–809.

Chen, Cynthia, and Haiyun Lin. 2012. "How Far Do People Search for Housing? Analyzing the Roles of Housing Supply, Intra-Household Dynamics, and the Use of Information Channels." *Housing Studies* 27 (7): 898–914.

Chen, Wen-Hao, John Myles, and Garnett Picot. 2012. "Why Have Poorer Neighborhoods Stagnated Economically while the Richer Have Flourished? Neighborhood Income Inequality in Canadian Cities." *Urban Studies* 49 (4): 877–96.

Cherlin, Andrew J. 1981. *Marriage, Divorce, Remarriage.* Cambridge, MA: Harvard University Press.

———. 2004. "The Deinstitutionalization of American Marriage." *Journal of Marriage and Family* 66: 848–61.

———. 2009. *The Marriage-Go-Round: The State of Marriage and the Family in America Today.* New York: Vintage Books.

———. 2010. "Demographic Trends in the United States: A Review of Research in the 2000s." *Journal of Marriage and Family* 72 (3): 403–19.

Chetty, Raj, Nathaniel Hendren, Patrick Kline, and Emmanuel Saez. 2013. *The Economic Impacts of Tax Expenditures: Evidence from the Spatial Variation Across the United States.* Harvard University Working Paper. Available at http://scholar.harvard.edu/hendren/publications/economic-impacts-tax-expenditures-evidence-spatial-variation-across-us (accessed July 22, 2013).

Child Trends. 2012. "Nonmarital Births: Educational Differences." Nonmarital Birth Data, table 4, 2012. Available at www.childtrends.org/_docdisp_page.cfm?LID = 8082B78A-929B-422A-B6C94F31702B9CCB (accessed November 2, 2012).

Chiswick, Barry R., and Teresa A. Sullivan. 1995. "The New Immigrants." In *State of the Union America in the 1990s,* vol. 2, edited by Reynolds Farley. New York: Russell Sage Foundation.

Clapson, Mark, and Ray Hutchison. 2010. "Introduction: Suburbanization in Global Society." In *Suburbanization in Global Society,* edited by Mark Clapson and Ray Hutchison. Research in Urban Sociology Series, vol. 10. Bingley, UK: Emerald Group Publishing.

CNNMoney. 2013. "7 Fastest Shrinking Cities: Pine Bluff, Ark." CNNMoney report, April 5. Available at http://money.cnn.com/gallery/real_estate/2013/04/05/shrinking-cities/index.html (accessed June 5, 2013).

Compton, Elizabeth, Michael Bentley, Sharon Ennis, and Sonya Rastogi. 2012. *2010 Census Race and Hispanic Origin Alternative Questionnaire Experiment.* U.S. Census Bureau, Decennial Statistical Studies Division and Population Division, Final Report, 2010 Census Planning Memoranda Series, no. 211 (reissue), August 8.

Condon, Bernard, and Paul Wiseman. 2013. "Millions of Middle-Class Jobs Killed by Machines in Great Recession's Wake." Associated Press, as reported in *Huffington Post,* January 23. Available at www.huffingtonpost.com/2013/01/23/middle-class-jobs-machines_n_2532639.html (accessed January 30, 2013).

Congressional Budget Office. 2011. *Trends in the Distribution of Household Income between 1979 and 2007.* October report.

———. 2012. "Trends in the Distribution of Household Income between 1979 and 2009." Presentation to the NBER Conference on Research in Income and Wealth, August 6. Available at www.cbo.gov/sites/default/files/cbofiles/attachments/Trends_in_household_income_forposting.pdf (accessed February 6, 2013).

CONSAD Research Corp. 2009. *An Analysis of Reasons for the Disparity in Wages between Men and Women.* Report prepared for the U.S. Department of Labor, January 12.

Coontz, Stephanie. 1992. *The Way We Never Were: American Families and the Nostalgia Trap.* New York: Basic Books.

———. 2012. "The Myth of Male Decline." *New York Times Sunday Review.* September 29.

Correll, S.J. 2001. "Gender and the Career Choice Process: The Role of Biased Self-Assessments." *American Journal of Sociology* 106: 1691–730.

Cross, Harry, Genevieve Kenney, Jane Mell, and Wendy Zimmermann. 1990. *Employer Hiring Practices.* Washington, DC: Urban Institute Press.

Cutler, David M., Edward L. Glaeser, and Jacob L. Vigdor. 1999. "The Rise and Decline of the American Ghetto." *Journal of Political Economy* 107 (3): 455–506.

Cutler, David, and Ellen Meara. 2001. *Changes in the Age Distribution of Mortality over the 20th Century.* National Bureau of Economic Research Working Paper 8556, October.

Cutler, David, and Grant Miller. 2004. *The Role of Public Health Improvements in Health Advances: The 20th Century United States.* Harvard University Working Paper, February. Available at scholar.harvard.edu/cutler/files /cutler_miller_cities.pdf (accessed September 1, 2012).

D'Addio, Anna Cristina. 2007. *Intergenerational Transmission of Disadvantage: Mobility or Immobility across Generations? A Review of the Evidence for OECD Countries.* Organisation for Economic Co-operation and Development, Social, Employment and Migration Working Paper no. 52.

Damaske, Sarah. 2011. *For the Family? How Class and Gender Shape Women's Work.* New York: Oxford University Press.

Daniels, Roger. 2002. *Coming to America.* 2nd ed. New York: Perennial.

Danziger, Sheldon H., and Peter Gottschalk. 1995. *America Unequal.* Cambridge, MA: Harvard University Press.

DeNavas-Walt, Carmen, Bernadette D. Proctor, and Jessica C. Smith. 2012. *Income, Poverty, and Health Insurance Coverage in the United States: 2011.* U.S. Census Bureau Current Population Reports, P60–243, U.S. Government Printing Office, Washington, DC.

DeParle, Jason. 2012a. "For Poor, Leap to College Often Ends in a Hard Fall." *New York Times,* December 22.

———. 2012b. "Harder for Americans to Rise from Lower Rungs." *New York Times,* January 4.

———. 2012c. "Two Classes, Divided by 'I Do.'" *New York Times,* July 14.

DeParle, Jason, and Sabrina Tavernise. 2012. "For Women under 30, Most Births Occur outside of Marriage." *New York Times,* February 17.

de Tocqueville, Alexis. 1840. *Democracy in America.* New York: Langley.

Dewan, Shaila, and Robert Gebeloff. 2012. "Among the Wealthiest 1 Percent, Many Variations." *New York Times,* January 14. Available at www.nytimes. com/2012/01/15/business/the-1-percent-paint-a-more-nuanced-portrait-of-the-rich.html?pagewanted = all (accessed July 31, 2012).

Dick, Eva. 2008. *Residential Segregation of Immigrants: A Case Study of the Mexican Population on St. Paul's West Side.* University of Minnesota Center for Urban and Regional Affairs report. Available at www.cura.umn.edu /publications/catalog/reporter-38–1–5 (accessed June 12, 2013).

Diggins, John P. 1976. "Slavery, Race, and Equality: Jefferson and the Pathos of the Enlightenment." *American Quarterly* 28 (2): 206–28.

DiPrete, Thomas A., and Claudia Buchmann. 2013. *Gender Disparities in Educational Attainment in the New Century: Trends, Causes, and Consequences.* Census Brief prepared for the Projection US2010. Available at www .s4.brown.edu/us2010/Projects/Reports.htm (accessed July 22, 2013).

Diversitydata.org. 2011. "Segregation of the Population: Isolation by Race /Ethnicity." Diversitdata.org in the Harvard School of Public Health. Available at diversitydata.sph.harvard.edu (accessed June 3, 2013).

Doepke, Matthias, Moshe Hazan, and Yishay D. Maoz. 2007. *The Baby Boom and World War II: A Macroeconomic Analysis.* California Center for Population Research Working Paper, CCPR-039-07, December.

Doyle, Jack. 2013. "600,000 Move Out in a Decade of 'White Flight' from London: White Britons Are Now in Minority in the Capital." *Daily Mail Online,* February 20. Available at www.dailymail.co.uk/news/article-2281941/600-000-decade-white-flight-London-White-Britons-minority-capital.html (accessed June 19, 2013).

DuBois, W. E. B. 1996. *The Philadelphia Negro: A Social Study.* Reprint. Philadelphia: University of Pennsylvania Press. First published in 1899.

Duhigg, Charles, and Keith Bradsher. 2012. "How U.S. Lost Out on iPhone Work." *New York Times,* Business Day, January 22.

Dulitzky, Ariel E. 2001. "A Region in Denial: Racial Discrimination and Racism in Latin America." *Beyond Law* 8 (24): 85–107.

Duncan, Brian, V. Joseph Hotz, and Stephen J. Trejo. 2006. "Hispanics in the U.S. Labor Market." In *Hispanics and the Future of America,* edited by Marta Tienda and Faith Mitchell. Washington, DC: National Academies Press.

Duncan, Brian, and Stephen J. Trejo. 2011a. *Low-Skilled Immigrants and the U.S. Labor Market.* IZA Discussion Paper no. 5964, September.

———. 2011b. "Tracking Intergenerational Progress for Immigrant Groups: The Problem of Ethnic Attrition." *American Economic Review* 101 (3): 603–8.

Dwyer, Rachel E. 2013. "The Care Economy? Gender, Economic Restructuring, and Job Polarization in the U.S. Labor Market." *American Sociological Review* 78 (3): 390–416.

Easterlin, Richard A. 2000. "The Worldwide Standard of Living since 1800." *Journal of Economic Perspectives* 14 (1): 7–26.

Edin, Kathryn, and Maria Kefalas. 2005. *Promises I Can Keep: Why Poor Women Put Motherhood before Marriage* Berkeley: University of California Press.

Ehrenreich, Barbara. 2001. *Nickel and Dimed: On (Not) Getting By in America.* New York: Metropolitan Books.

Elliott, Diana B., Kristy Krivickas, Matthew W. Brault, and Rose M. Kreider. 2012. *Historical Marriage Trends from 1890–2010: A Focus on Race Differences.* U.S. Census Bureau, SEHSD Working Paper no. 2012-12.

Engel, Kathleen C., and Patricia A. McCoy. 2008. "From Credit Denial to Predatory Lending: The Challenge of Sustaining Minority Homeownership." In *Segregation: The Rising Costs for America*, edited by James H. Carr and Nandinee K. Kutty. New York: Routledge.

England, Paula. 2005. "Emerging Theories of Care Work." *Annual Review of Sociology* 31 (1): 381–99.

———. 2010. "The Gender Revolution: Uneven and Stalled." *Gender and Society* 24 (2): 149–66.

England, Paula, and Jonathan Bearak. 2012. "Women's Education and Their Likelihood of Marriage: A Historical Reversal." Council on Contemporary Families Fact Sheet on Marriage and Education, April 11. Available at www.contemporaryfamilies.org/womens-education-likelihood-marriage-historic-reversal/ (accessed March 5, 2014).

Farkas, G., and K. Vicknair. 1996. "Appropriate Tests of Racial Wage Discrimination Require Controls for Cognitive Skill: Comment on Cancio, Evans, and Maume." *American Sociological Review* 1: 557–60.

Fausto-Sterling, Ann. 2009. "The Five Sexes, Revisited." In *The Social Construction of Difference and Inequality: Race, Class, Gender, and Sexuality*, 4th ed., edited by Tracy E. Ore. Boston: McGraw-Hill.

Financial Crisis Inquiry Commission. 2011. *The Financial Crisis Inquiry Report: Final Report of the National Commission on the Causes of the Financial and Economic Crisis in the United States*. Official Government Edition. Washington, DC: U.S. Government Printing Office.

Fiscal Policy Institute. 2012. *Immigrant Small Business Owners: A Significant and Growing Part of the Economy*. Fiscal Policy Institute Immigration Research Initiative Report, June. Available at fiscalpolicy.org/wp-content/uploads/2012/06/immigrant-small-business-owners-FPI-20120614.pdf (accessed March 12, 2013).

Fischer, Claude S., and Michael Hout. 2006. *Century of Difference: How America Changed in the Last One Hundred Years*. New York: Russell Sage Foundation.

Fisher, Max. 2013. "A Fascinating Map of the World's Most and Least Tolerant Countries." *Washington Post*, May 15.

Fitch, Catherine, and Steven Ruggles. 2000. "Historical Trends in Marriage Formation." In *Ties That Bind: Perspectives on Marriage and Cohabitation*, ed. Linda Waite, Christine Bachrach, Michelle Hindin, Elizabeth Thomson, and Arland Thornton. New York: Aldine de Gruyter.

Fligstein, Neil, and Adam Goldstein. 2011. "The Roots of the Great Recession." In *The Great Recession*, edited by David B. Grusky, Bruce Western, and Christopher Wimer. New York: Russell Sage Foundation.

Florida, Richard. 2002. *The Rise of the Creative Class: And How It's Transforming Work, Leisure, and Everyday Life*. New York: Basic Books.

Foner, Eric. 1988. *Reconstruction: America's Unfinished Revolution, 1863-1877.* New York: Harper & Row.

Food and Agriculture Organization of the United Nations. 2013. *The State of Food and Agriculture.* Rome: FAO.

Food Research and Action Center. 2012. *Food Hardship in America 2011.* FRAC Research Report, February.

Frank, Reanne, Ilana Redstone Akresh, and Bo Lu. 2010. "Latino Immigrants and the U.S. Racial Order: How and Where Do They Fit?" *American Sociological Review* 75 (3): 378–401.

Frank, Robert H. 2007. *Falling Behind: How Rising Inequality Harms the Middle Class.* Berkeley: University of California Press.

Franklin, Benjamin. 1755. *Observations concerning the Increase of Mankind, Peopling of Countries, etc.* Boston: Printed and sold by S. Kneeland in Queenstreet.

Frazier, E. Franklin. 1932. *The Negro Family in Chicago.* Chicago: University of Chicago Press.

———. 1939. *The Negro Family in the United States.* Chicago: University of Chicago Press.

Frech, Adrianne, and Sarah Damaske. 2012. "The Relationships between Mothers' Work Pathways and Physical and Mental Health." *Journal of Health and Social Behavior* 53 (4): 396–412.

Freeland, Chrystia. 2011. "The Rise of the New Global Elite." *Atlantic,* January /February. Available at www.theatlantic.com/magazine/archive/2011/01 /the-rise-of-the-new-global-elite/308343/?single_page = true (accessed February 11, 2013).

Frey, William H. 2001. *Melting Pot Suburbs: A Census 2000 Study of Suburban Diversity.* Brookings Institution Center on Urban and Metropolitan Policy, Census 2000 Series, June.

———. 2002. "Three Americas: The Rising Significance of Regions." *Journal of the American Planning Association* 68 (4): 349–55.

———. 2005. *The New Great Migration: Black Americans' Return to the South, 1965-2000.* Brookings Institution Center on Urban and Metropolitan Policy, Living Cities Census Series, May.

———. 2011. *Melting Pot Cities and Suburbs: Racial and Ethnic Change in Metro America in the 2000s.* Brookings Institution, State of Metropolitan America Report, May.

———. 2012a. *Demographic Reversal: Cities Thrive, Suburbs Sputter.* Brookings Institution, State of Metropolitan America, Opinion, June 29.

———. 2012b. *Population Growth in Metro America since 1980: Putting the Volatile 2000s in Perspective.* Brookings Institution Metropolitan Policy Program, March.

Fryer, Roland. 2011. "Racial Inequality in the 21st Century: The Declining Significance of Discrimination." *Handbook of Labor Economics* 4b: 855–971.

Gabriel, Trip. 2013. "New Attitude on Immigration Skips an Old Coal Town." *New York Times*, March 31.

Galinsky, Ellen, Kerstin Aumann, and James T. Bond. 2011. *Times Are Changing: Gender and Generation at Work and at Home*. Families and Work Institute, 2008 National Study of the Changing Workforce.

Gallup. 2012. *With Poverty Comes Depression, More Than Other Illnesses*. Gallup Well-Being Report, October 30. Available at www.gallup.com /poll/158417/poverty-comes-depression-illness.aspx (accessed July 10, 2013).

Garrett, Aaron. 2000. "Hume's Revised Racism Revisited." *Hume Studies* 26 (1): 171–78.

Gawande, Atul. 2009. "Testing, Testing." *New Yorker*, December 14.

Gerson, Kathleen. 2009. *The Unfinished Revolution: How a New Generation Is Reshaping Family, Work and Gender in America*. New York: Oxford University Press.

Gibson, Campbell. 1998. *Population of the 100 Largest Cities and Other Urban Places in the United States: 1790 to 1990*. U.S. Census Bureau Population Division Working Paper no. 27, June.

Gibson-Davis, C. M., K. Edin, and S. McLanahan. 2005. "High Hopes but Even Higher Expectations: The Retreat from Marriage among Low-Income Couples." *Journal of Marriage and Family* 67: 1301–12.

Gill, Richard T., Nathan Glazer, and Stephan A. Thernstrom. 1992. *Our Changing Population*. Englewood Cliffs, NJ: Prentice-Hall.

Glaeser, Edward L., and Kristina Tobio. 2007. *The Rise of the Sunbelt*. NBER Working Paper Series, no. 13071, April.

Glauber, Rebecca. 2008. "Race and Gender in Families and at Work." *Gender & Society* 22 (1): 8–30.

Glikman, Anya, and Moshe Semyonov. 2012. "Ethnic Origin and Residential Attainment of Immigrants in European Countries." *City and Community* 11 (2): 198–219.

Golash-Boza, Tanya, and William Darity. 2008. "Latino Racial Choices: The Effects of Skin Colour and Discrimination on Latinos' and Latinas' Racial Self-Identifications." *Ethnic & Racial Studies* 31: 899–934.

Goldin, Claudia, and Cecilia Rouse. 2000. "Orchestrating Impartiality: The Impact of 'Blind' Auditions on Female Musicians." *American Economic Review* 90 (4): 715–41.

Gordon, Peter, and Wendell Cox. 2012. "Cities in Western Europe and the United States: Do Policy Differences Matter?" *Annals of Regional Science* 48: 565–94.

Gornick, Janet C., and Markus Jantti. 2012. "Child Poverty in Cross-National Perspective: Lessons from the Luxembourg Income Study." *Children and Youth Services Review* 34: 558–68.

Gray, Tom, and Robert Scardamalia. 2012. *The Great California Exodus: A Closer Look*. Manhattan Institute for Policy Research, Civic Report no. 71 (September). Available at www.manhattan-institute.org/html/cr_71.htm#.Ubne07ahAel (accessed June 13, 2013).

Grieco, Elizabeth M. 2010. *Race and Hispanic Origin of the Foreign-Born Population in the United States: 2007*. U.S. Census Bureau, American Community Survey Report ACS-11, January.

Grusky, David B., and Kim A. Weeden. 2011. "Is Market Failure behind the Takeoff in Inequality?" In *The Inequality Reader: Contemporary and Foundational Readings in Race, Class, and Gender*. 2nd ed., edited by David B. Grusky and Szonja Szelényi. Boulder, CO: Westview Press.

Guest, Avery M., and Stewart E. Tolnay. 1983. "Children's Roles and Fertility: Late Nineteenth-Century United States." *Social Science History* 7 (4): 355–80.

Hacker, J. David. 2003. "Rethinking the 'Early' Decline of Marital Fertility in the United States." *Demography* 40 (4): 605–20.

Hall, Matthew, John Iceland, Gregory Sharp, Luis Sanchez, and Kris Marsh. 2010. *Racial and Ethnic Residential Segregation in the United States: Residential Patterns of Asians, 1980–2009*. Changing American Neighborhoods and Communities Report Series, Population Research Institute, Penn State University, Report no. 4. Available at http://projects.pop.psu.edu/canc/segregation (accessed June 10, 2013).

Hansen, Randall. 2003. "Migration to Europe since 1945: Its History and Its Lessons." *Political Quarterly* 74, S1: 25–38.

Harrison, Bennett, and Barry Bluestone. 1990. *The Great U-Turn: Corporate Restructuring and the Polarizing of America*. New York: Basic Books.

Hausmann, Ricardo, Laura D. Tyson, and Saadia Zahidi. 2012. *The Global Gender Gap Report: 2012*. World Economic Forum Insight Report. Available at www3.weforum.org/docs/WEF_GenderGap_Report_2012.pdf (accessed January 24, 2013).

Healey, Joseph F. 2012. *Diversity and Society Race, Ethnicity, and Gender*. 3rd ed. Los Angeles: Russell Sage.

Heath, Anthony F., Catherine Rothon, and Elina Kilpi. 2008. "The Second Generation in Western Europe: Education, Unemployment, and Occupational Attainment." *Annual Review of Sociology* 34: 211–35.

Higgins, Andrew. 2013a. "In Its Efforts to Integrate Roma, Slovakia Recalls U.S. Struggles." *New York Times,* May 9.

———. 2013b. "In Sweden, Riots Put an Identity in Question." *New York Times,* May 26.

Hirschman, Charles, Richard Alba, and Reynolds Farely. 2000. "The Meaning and Measurement of Race in the U.S. Census: Glimpses into the Future." *Demography* 37 (3): 381–93.

Hogan, Dennis, and Daniel Lichter. 1995. "Children and Youth: Living Arrange-ments and Welfare." In *State of the Union: America in the 1990s,* vol. 2, edited by Reynolds Farley. New York: Russell Sage Foundation.

Holzer, Harry J. 2011. *Immigration Policy and Less-Skilled Workers in the United States: Reflection on Future Directions for Reform.* National Poverty Center Working Paper Series no. 11–01, January. Available at npc.umich.edu /publications/u/working_paper11-01.pdf (accessed January 22, 2013).

Holzer, Harry J., and Isabel V. Sawhill. 2013. *Payments to Elders Are Harming Our Future.* Brookings Institution report, March 8. Available at www. brookings.edu/research/opinions/2013/03/08-entitlements-holzer-sawhill (accessed July 11, 2013).

Hout, Michael. 1994. "Occupational Mobility of Black Men: 1962 to 1973." In *Social Stratification in Sociological Perspective,* edited by David B. Grusky. Boulder, CO: Westview Press.

Howden, Lindsay M., and Julie A. Meyer. 2011. *Age and Sex Composition.* U.S. Census Bureau 2010 Census Briefs, C2010BR-03, May.

Hoyert, Donna L. 2012. *75 Years of Mortality in the United States, 1935–2010.* National Center for Health Statistics Data Brief 88, March.

Humes, Karen R., Nicholas A. Jones, and Roberto R. Ramirez. 2011. *Overview of Race and Hispanic Origin: 2010.* U.S. Census Bureau, 2010 Census Briefs, C2010BR-02, March.

Hummer, Robert A., and Joseph T. Lariscy. 2011. "Educational Attainment and Adult Mortality." In *International Handbook of Adult Mortality,* edited by Richard G. Rogers and Eileen M. Crimmins. New York: Springer.

Huyser, Kimberly R., Arthur Sakamoto, and Isao Takei. 2010. "The Persistence of Racial Disadvantage: The Socioeconomic Attainments of Single-Race and Multi-Race Native Americans." *Population Research and Policy Review* 29: 541–68.

Iceland, John. 2009. *Where We Live Now: Immigration and Race in the United States.* Berkeley: University of California Press.

———. 2013. *Poverty in America.* 3rd ed. Berkeley: University of California Press.

Iceland, John, Pablo Mateos, and Gregory Sharp. 2011. "Ethnic Residential Segregation by Nativity in Great Britain and the United States." *Journal of Urban Affairs* 33 (4): 409–29.

Iceland, John, and Melissa Scopilliti. 2008. "Immigrant Residential Segregation in U.S. Metropolitan Areas, 1990–2000." *Demography* 45: 79–94.

Iceland, John, and Gregory Sharp. 2013. "White Residential Segregation in U.S. Metropolitan Areas: Conceptual Issues, Patterns, and Trends from the U.S. Census, 1980 to 2010." *Population Research and Policy Review* 32 (5): 663–86.

Iceland, John, Gregory Sharp, Luis Sanchez, Matthew Hall, and Kris Marsh. 2010. *Racial and Ethnic Residential Segregation in the United States:*

Comparisons across Racial and Ethnic Groups, 1970–2009. Changing American Neighborhoods and Communities Report Series, Population Research Institute, Penn State University, Report no. 3, December. Available at http://projects.pop.psu.edu/canc/segregation (accessed June 10, 2013).

Iceland, John, Gregory Sharp, and Jeffrey M. Timberlake. 2013. "Sun Belt Rising: Regional Population Change and the Decline in Black Residential Segregation, 1970–2009." *Demography* 50 (1): 97–123.

Iceland, John, Daniel H. Weinberg, and Lauren Hughes. 2013. "The Residential Segregation of Hispanic and Asian Ethnic Groups." Unpublished paper.

Iceland, John, and Rima Wilkes. 2006. "Does Socioeconomic Status Matter? Race, Class, and Residential Segregation." *Social Problems* 52 (2): 248–73.

Immigrant Learning Center. 2013. "Immigrant Entrepreneur Hall of Fame." Online list. Available at www.ilctr.org/promoting-immigrants/immigrant-entrepreneur-hof/ (accessed March 14, 2013).

Institute for Women's Policy Research. 2010. *Separate and Not Equal? Gender Segregation in the Labor Market and the Gender Wage Gap.* IWPR Briefing Paper C377, September.

———. 2012. *The Gender Wage Gap by Occupation.* IWPR Fact Sheet C350a, April.

Isaacs, Julia, Katherine Toran, Heather Hahn, Karina Fortuny, and C. Eugene Steuerle. 2012. *Kids' Share 2012: Report on Federal Expenditures on Children through 2011.* Urban Institute report, July 19. Available at www.urban.org/publications/412600.html (accessed July 11, 2013).

Isen, Adam, and Betsey Stevenson. 2010. *Women's Education and Family Behavior: Trends in Marriage, Divorce and Fertility.* CESifo Working Paper, no. 2940. Available at hdl.handle.net/10419/30703 (accessed October 31, 2012).

Jackson, Geena. 2011. *Declining Cities Look to Immigrants to Revitalize Economies and Increase University Enrollment.* Immigration Impact report. Available at http://immigrationimpact.com/2011/10/03/declining-cities-look-to-immigrants-to-revitalize-economies-and-increase-university-enrollment/ (accessed March 12, 2013).

Jacobs, Jerry A. 1989. *Revolving Doors: Sex Segregation and Women's Careers.* Stanford, CA: Stanford University Press.

Jacobsen, Linda A., Mary Kent, Marlene Lee, and Mark Mather. 2011. "America's Aging Population." Population Reference Bureau, *Population Bulletin* 66 (1): 1–16.

Jacobsen, Linda A., Mark Mather, and Genevieve Dupuis. 2012. "Household Change in the United States." Population Reference Bureau, *Population Bulletin* 67 (1): 1–13.

Jantti, Markus, Bernt Bratsberg, Knut Roed, Oddbjorn Raaum, Robin Naylor, Eva Osterbacka, Anders Bjorklund, and Tor Eriksson. 2006. *American*

Exceptionalism in a New Light: A Comparison of Intergenerational Earnings Mobility in the Nordic Countries, the United Kingdom and the United States. IZA Discussion Paper no. 1938, January.

Jargowsky, Paul A. 1997. *Poverty and Place: Ghettos, Barrios, and the American City.* New York: Russell Sage Foundation.

Jefferson, Thomas. 1984. *Writings.* Edited by Merrill Peterson. New York: Library of America.

Johnson, James H., Walter C. Farrell, and Chandra Guinn. 1997. "Immigration Reform and the Browning of America: Tensions, Conflicts and Community Instability in Metropolitan Los Angeles." *International Migration Review* 31 (4): 1055–95.

Johnston, Louis, and Samuel H. Williamson. 2012. "What Was the U.S. GDP Then?" MeasuringWorth website. Available at www.measuringworth.com /index.php (accessed January 31, 2013).

Jones, G. W. 2005. "The Flight from Marriage in South-East and East Asia." *Journal of Comparative Family Studies* 36 (1): 93–119.

Jones, Larry E., and Michele Tertilt. 2006. *An Economic History of Fertility in the U.S.: 1826–1960.* NBER Working Paper Series no. 12796, December.

Kasinitz, Philip, John II. Mollenkopf, and Mary C. Waters. 2004. "Worlds of the Second Generation." In *Becoming New Yorkers: Ethnographies of the New Second Generation,* edited by Philip Kasinitz, John II. Mollenkopf, and Mary C. Waters. New York: Russell Sage Foundation.

Kasinitz, Philip, John H. Mollenkopf, Mary C. Waters, and Jennifer Holdaway. 2008. *Inheriting the City: The Children of Immigrants Come of Age.* Cambridge, MA: Harvard University Press.

Kelly Hall, Patricia, and Steven Ruggles. 2004. "'Restless in the Midst of Their Prosperity': New Evidence on the Internal Migration of Americans, 1850–2000." *Journal of American History* 91 (3): 829–46.

Kennedy, David M. 1999. *Freedom from Fear: The American People in the Depression and War, 1929–1945.* New York: Oxford University Press.

Kennedy, David M., and Thomas A. Bailey. 2010. *The American Spirit: United States History as Seen by Contemporaries,* vol. 1: *To 1877,* 12th ed. Boston: Wadsworth.

Kennedy, Sheila, and Larry Bumpass. 2008. "Cohabitation and Children's Living Arrangements: New Estimates from the United States." *Demographic Research* 19: 1663–92.

Kennedy, Sheila, and Catherine A. Fitch. 2012. "Measuring Cohabitation and Family Structure in the United States: Assessing the Impact of New Data from the Current Population Survey." *Demography* 49 (4): 1479–98.

Kenworthy, Lane. 2004. *Egalitarian Capitalism: Jobs, Incomes, and Growth in Affluent Countries.* New York: Russell Sage Foundation.

———. 2011. *Progress for the Poor.* Oxford: Oxford University Press.

Kerbo, Harold R. 2009. *Social Stratification and Inequality: Class Conflict in Historical, Comparative, and Global Perspective.* 7th ed. New York: McGraw-Hill.

Klein, Herbert S. 2012. *A Population History of the United States.* 2nd ed. New York: Cambridge University Press.

Klineberg, Eric. 2012. *Going Solo: The Extraordinary Rise and Surprising Appeal of Living Alone.* New York: Penguin Press.

Kneebone, Elizabeth. 2009. *The Suburbanization of American Poverty.* Brookings Institution Spotlight on Poverty and Opportunity Opinion, October 19. Available at www.brookings.edu/research/opinions/2009/10/19-poverty-kneebone (accessed June 7, 2013).

Kneebone, Elizabeth, Carey Nadeau, and Alan Berube. 2011. *The Re-emergence of Concentrated Poverty: Metropolitan Trends in the 2000s.* Brookings Institution, Metropolitan Opportunity Series no. 26, November.

Kotkin, Joel. 2012. *The Rise of Post-Familialism: Humanity's Future?* Research Report for the Seminar on the Rise of Post-Familialism. Available at www.joelkotkin.com/sites/default/files/The%20Rise%20of%20Post-Familial-ism%20(ISBN9789810738976).pdf (accessed January 3, 2013).

Kreider, Rose M., and Diana B. Elliott. 2010. "Historical Changes in Stay-at-Home Mothers: 1969 to 2009." Paper presented at the annual American Sociological Association meetings, Atlanta, GA.

Kristof, Nicholas. 2012. "The White Underclass." Op-ed piece. *New York Times,* February 8.

———. 2013. "She's (Rarely) the Boss." Op-ed piece. *New York Times,* January 26.

Krivickas, K. 2010. *Same-Sex Couple Households in the U.S., 2009.* National Center for Family & Marriage Research, FP-10–08. Available at ncfmr.bgsu.edu/pdf/family_profiles/file87414.pdf (accessed November 2, 2012).

Krugman, Paul R. 2012. "Money and Morals." Op-ed piece. *New York Times,* February 10.

Krysan, Maria, and Michael D. M. Bader. 2007. "Perceiving the Metropolis: Seeing the City through a Prism of Race." *Social Forces* 86: 699–733.

———. 2009. "Racial Blind Spots: Black-White-Latino Differences in Community Knowledge." *Social Problems* 56 (4): 677–701.

Krysan, Maria, and Reynolds Farley. 2002. "The Residential Preferences of Blacks: Do They Explain Persistent Segregation?" *Social Forces* 80 (2): 937–80.

Lacy, Karyn. 2007. *Blue-Chip Black: Race, Class, and Status in the New Black Middle Class.* Berkeley: University of California Press.

Lakhani, Nina. 2013. "Mexico Obesity Bulges on Diet Concerns." *Al Jazeera,* April 26.

Lambrecht, Claire. 2012. "Q&A: Urbanist Alan Ehrenhalt on the 'The Great Inversion.'" Solving Cities blog, April 25. Available at www.smartplanet.com

/blog/cities/q-a-urbanist-alan-ehrenhalt-on-the-8220the-great-inversion-8221
/2910 (accessed June 7, 2013).

Landry, Bart, and Kris Marsh. 2011. "The Evolution of the New Black Middle
Class." *Annual Review of Sociology* 37: 373–94.

Lareau, Annette. 2003. *Unequal Childhoods: Race, Class, and Family Life.*
Berkeley: University of California Press.

Lee, Jennifer, and Frank D. Bean. 2007. "Reinventing the Color Line: Immigration and America's New Racial/Ethnic Divide." *Social Forces* 86 (2): 561–86.

———. 2012. *The Diversity Paradox: Immigration and the Color Line in
Twenty-First Century America.* New York: Russell Sage Foundation.

Lee, Kelley 2003. *Health Impacts of Globalization: Towards Global Governance.* New York: Palgrave Macmillan.

Lee, Mathew T., and Ramiro Martinez. 2009. "Immigration Reduces Crime: An
Emerging Scholarly Consensus." *Sociology of Crime Law and Deviance* 13:
3–16.

Lemann, Nicholas. 1991. *The Promised Land: The Great Black Migration and
How It Changed America.* New York: Vintage Books.

Lesthaeghe, Ron. 1995. "The Second Demographic Transition in Western
Countries: An Interpretation." In *Gender and Family Change in Industrial-
ized Countries,* edited by Karen O. Masen and A. M. Jensen, 17–62. Oxford:
Clarendon Press.

———. 2010. *The Unfolding Story of the Second Demographic Transition.*
University of Michigan, Population Studies Center Research Report no.
10–696, January. Available at www.psc.isr.umich.edu/pubs/pdf/rr10–696
.pdf (accessed December 10, 2012).

Levine, Linda. 2012. *The U.S. Income Distribution and Mobility: Trends and
International Comparisons.* Congressional Research Service Report 7–5700,
November 29.

Lewyn, Michael. 2009. "Sprawl in Europe and America." *San Diego Law
Review* 85: 85–112.

Lichter, Daniel T. 1997. "Poverty and Inequality among Children." *Annual
Review of Sociology* 23: 121–45.

Lin, Ann Chih, and David R. Harris. 2008. "Why Is American Poverty Still
Colored in the Twenty-First Century?" In *The Colors of Poverty: Why Racial
and Ethnic Disparities Persist,* edited by Ann Chih Lin and David R. Harris.
New York: Russell Sage Foundation.

Lindsey, Duncan. 2009. *Child Poverty and Inequality: Securing a Better Future
for America's Children.* New York: Oxford University Press.

Lippard, Cameron D., and Charles A. Gallagher. 2011. "Introduction: Immigration, the New South, and the Color of Backlash." In *Being Brown in Dixie:
Race, Ethnicity, and Latino Immigration in the New South,* edited by Cameron D. Lippard and Charles A. Gallagher. Boulder, CO: First Forum Press.

Lipscomb, Andrew A., and Albert E. Bergh, eds. 1903–4. *The Writings of Thomas Jefferson.* 20 vols. Washington, DC: Thomas Jefferson Memorial Association of the United States.

Lipset, Seymour Martin. 1996. *American Exceptionalism: A Double-Edged Sword.* New York: W. W. Norton.

Logan, John R., and Brian J. Stults. 2011. *The Persistence of Segregation in the Metropolis: New Findings from the 2010 Census.* Census Brief prepared for the Projection US2010. Available at www.s4.brown.edu/us2010/Data /Report/report2.pdf (accessed June 10, 2013).

Logan, John R., and Richard N. Turner. 2013. *Hispanics in the United States: Not Only Mexicans.* Census Brief prepared for the Projection US2010. Available at www.s4.brown.edu/us2010/Data/Report/report03202013.pdf (accessed May 29, 2013).

Looney, Adam, and Michael Greenstone. 2011. *Trends: Reduced Earnings for Men in America.* Hamilton Project research report, July 2011.

Lorber, Judith. 2009. "The Social Construction of Gender." In *The Social Construction of Difference and Inequality: Race, Class, Gender, and Sexuality,* 4th ed., edited by Tracy E. Ore. Boston: McGraw-Hill. First published in 1994.

Loury, Glenn C. 2000. "What's Next? Some Reflections on the Poverty Conference." *Focus* 21 (2) (Fall): 58–60.

MacDorman, Marian F., Donna L. Hoyert, and T. J. Mathews. 2013. *Recent Declines in Infant Mortality in the United States, 2005–2011.* National Center for Health Statistics Data Brief no. 120, April.

Maddison, Angus. 2001. *The World Economy: A Millennial Perspective.* Organisation of Economic Co-operation and Development Centre Studies Report.

Malthus, Thomas. 1998. *An Essay on the Principle of Population.* Electronic Scholarly Publishing Project. Available at 129.237.201.53/books/malthus /population/malthus.pdf (accessed September 6, 2012). First published in 1798.

Mamdani, Mahmood. 2001. "A Brief History of Genocide." *Transition* 87: 26–47.

Manning, Wendy D. 2013. "Trends in Cohabitation: Over Twenty Years of Change, 1987–2010." National Center for Family and Research, Family Profile 13–12. Available at http://ncfmr.bgsu.edu/pdf/family_profiles /file130944.pdf (accessed November 4, 2013).

Manning, Wendy D., and Pamela J. Smock. 2005. "Measuring and Modeling Cohabitation: New Perspectives from Qualitative Data." *Journal of Marriage and Family* 67: 989–1002.

Marger, Martin N. 2011. *Social Inequality: Patterns and Processes.* 5th ed. New York: McGraw-Hill.

Markides, Kyriakos S., and Karl Eschbach. 2011. "Hispanic Paradox in Adult Mortality in the United States." In *International Handbook of Adult*

Mortality, edited by Richard G. Rogers and Eileen M. Crimmins. New York: Springer.

Markoff, John. 2012. "The iEconomy, Part 5: Artificial Competence: Skilled Work, without the Worker." *New York Times,* August 18.

Marsh, Kris, Kyle Crowder, and Kivan Polimis. 2011. "Adolescent Experiences and Adult Neighborhood Attainment." Paper presented at the annual meetings of the Population Association of America, Washington, DC, March 31–April 2.

Marsh, Kris, John Iceland, Gregory Sharp, Luis Sanchez, and Matthew Hall. 2010. *Racial and Ethnic Residential Segregation in the United States: Residential Patterns of Blacks, 1970–2009.* Changing American Neighborhoods and Communities Report Series, Population Research Institute, Penn State University, Report no. 6. Available at http://projects.pop.psu.edu/canc/segregation (accessed June 10, 2013).

Martin, Joyce A., Brady E. Hamiliton, Stephanie J. Ventura, M.A. Michelle, J.K. Osterman, Elizabeth C. Wilson, and T.J. Mathews. 2012. "Births: Final Data for 2010." In *National Vital Statistics Reports* 61 (1) (August). Hyattsville, MD: National Center for Health Statistics.

Martin, J.A., B.E. Hamilton, S.J. Ventura, M.J.K. Osterman, S. Kirmeyer, T.J. Mathews, E.C. Wilson. 2011. "Births: Final Data for 2009." In *National Vital Statistics Reports* 60 (1). Hyattsville, MD: National Center for Health Statistics.

Martin, Philip, and Elizabeth Midgley. 2003. "Immigration: Shaping and Reshaping America." Population Reference Bureau, *Population Bulletin* 58 (2) (June): 1–44.

———. 2006. "Immigration: Shaping and Reshaping America." Population Reference Bureau, *Population Bulletin* 61 (4) (December).

———. 2010. "Immigration in America 2010." Population Reference Bureau, *Population Bulletin Update* (June).

Martin, Steven P. 2006. "Trends in Marital Dissolution by Women's Education in the United States." *Demographic Research* 15: 537–60.

Martinez, Ramiro, Jacob I. Stowell, and Matthew T. Lee. 2010. "Immigration and Crime in an Era of Transformation: A Longitudinal Analysis of Homicides in San Diego Neighborhoods, 1980–2000." *Criminology* 48 (3): 797–829.

Massey, Douglas S., and Nancy Denton. 1993. *American Apartheid: Segregation and the Making of the Underclass.* Cambridge, MA: Harvard University Press.

Massey, Douglas S., and Kristin E. Espinosa. 1997. "What's Driving Mexico-U.S. Migration? A Theoretical, Empirical, and Policy Analysis." *American Journal of Sociology* 102 (4): 939–99.

Masters, Ryan K., Robert A. Hummer, and Daniel A. Powers. 2012. "Educational Differences in U.S. Adult Mortality: A Cohort Perspective." *American Sociological Review* 77 (4): 548–72.

Mather, Mark, Kelvin Pollard, and Linda A. Jacobsen. 2011. *First Results from the 2010 Census.* Population Reference Bureau, Reports on America Series, July.

May, Martha. 1982. "The Historical Problem of the Family Wage: The Ford Motor Company and the Five Dollar Day." *Feminist Studies* 8 (2): 399–424.

McLanahan, Sara. 2004. "Diverging Destinies: How Children Are Faring under the Second Demographic Transition." *Demography* 41 (4): 607–27.

McLanahan, Sara, and Gary Sandefur. 1997. *Growing Up with a Single Parent: What Hurts, What Helps.* Cambridge, MA: Harvard University Press.

Meyer, Julie. 2012. *Centenarians: 2010.* U.S. Census Bureau, 2010 Census Special Reports C2010SR-03, December.

Miech, Richard, Fred Pampel, Jinyoung Kim, and Richard G. Rogers. 2011. "The Enduring Association between Education and Mortality: The Role of Widening and Narrowing Disparities." *American Sociological Review* 76 (6): 913–34.

Migration Policy Institute. 2012a. "Immigrant Population by Country of Birth Residing in the United States, 1960 to 2010." MPI Immigration to the United States: A Historical Perspective Table Series. Available at www.migrationinformation.org/datahub/historicaltrends.cfm (accessed July 31, 2012).

———. 2012b. "2010 American Community Survey and Census Data on the Foreign Born by State." Data Hub information. Available at www.migration-information.org/datahub/acscensus.cfm (accessed September 18, 2012).

Minino, Arialdi M., and Sherry L. Murphy. 2012. *Death in the United States, 2010.* National Center for Health Statistics Data Brief no. 99, July.

Misra, Joya, Michelle Budig, and Irene Bockmann. 2010. *Cross-National Patterns in Individual and Household Employment and Work Hours by Gender and Parenthood.* Luxembourg Income Study Working Paper Series no. 544, July.

———. 2011. "Work-Family Policies and the Effects of Children on Women's Employment Hours and Wages." *Community, Work & Family* 14 (2): 139–57.

Modood, Tariq. 2003. "Muslims and the Politics of Difference." *Political Quarterly* 74, S1: 100–115.

Montez, Jennifer Karas, Robert A. Hummer, Mark D. Hayward, Hyeyoung Woo, and Richard G. Rogers. 2011. "Trends in the Educational Gradient of U.S. Adult Mortality from 1986 through 2006 by Race, Gender, and Age Group." *Research on Aging* 33 (2): 145–71.

Motel, Seth, and Eileen Patten. 2013. *Statistical Portrait of Hispanics in the United States, 2011.* Pew Research Hispanic Center Report, February 15. Available at www.pewhispanic.org/2013/02/15/statistical-portrait-of-hispanics-in-the-united-states-2011/ (accessed February 15, 2013).

Moynihan, Daniel Patrick. 1965. *The Negro Family: The Case for National Action.* Washington, DC: U.S. Department of Labor.

Murray, Charles. 1984. *Losing Ground: American Social Policy, 1950–1980.* New York: Basic Books.

———. 2012. *Coming Apart: The State of White America, 1960–2010.* New York: Crown Forum.

Musterd, Sako. 2005. "Social and Ethnic Desegregation in Europe: Levels, Causes, and Effects." *Journal of Urban Affairs* 27 (3): 331–48.

Musterd, Sako, and Ronald Van Kempen. 2009. "Segregation and Housing of Minority Ethnic Groups in Western European Cities." *Tijdschrift voor economische en sociale geografie* 100 (4): 559–66.

Myrdal, Gunnar. 1996. *An American Dilemma: The Negro Problem and Modern Democracy.* Reprint. New Brunswick, NJ: Transaction Publishers. First published in 1944.

National Bureau of Economic Research. 2010. *Business Cycle Dating Committee Report, September 20, 2010.* NBER, Cambridge, MA. Available at www .nber.org/cycles/sept2010.pdf (accessed January 30, 2013).

National Public Radio. 2013. *When You're Mixed Race, Just One Box Is Not Enough.* The Race Card Project, April 2. Available at www.npr. org/2013/04/02/175292625/when-youre-mixed-race-just-one-box-is-not-enough (accessed April 5, 2013).

National Research Council and Institute of Medicine. 2013. *U.S. Health in International Perspective: Shorter Lives, Poorer Health.* Edited by Steven H. Woolf and Laudan Aron. Panel on Understanding Cross-National Health Differences among High-Income Countries. Washington, DC: National Academies Press.

Newman, David M. 2007. *Identities and Inequality: Exploring the Intersections of Race, Class, Gender, and Sexuality.* Boston: McGraw-Hill.

Nodi, Syeda Reswana. 2008. "Proud to Wear My Hijab." In *The Meaning of Difference: American Constructions of Race, Sex and Gender, Social Class, Sexual Orientation, and Disability,* edited by Karen E. Rosenblum and Toni-Michelle C. Travis. 5th ed. New York: McGraw-Hill.

Norris, Tina, Paula L. Vines, and Elizabeth M. Hoeffel. 2012. *The American Indian and Alaska Native Population: 2010.* U.S. Census Bureau 2010 Census Brief, C2010BR-10, January.

O'Connell, Martin, and Sarah Feliz. 2011. *Same-Sex Couple Household Statistics from the 2010 Census.* U.S. Census Bureau SEHSD Working Paper no. 2011–26, released September 27.

O'Connor, Alice. 2001. *Poverty Knowledge: Social Science, Social Policy, and the Poor in Twentieth-Century U.S. History.* Princeton, NJ: Princeton University Press.

OECD (Organisation for Economic Co-operation and Development). 2010a. "A Family Affair: Intergenerational Social Mobility across OECD Countries." Economic Policy Reforms, Going for Growth Report.

———. 2010b. "Trends in Urbanisation and Urban Policies in OECD Countries: What Lessons for China?" Research Report.

———. 2011a. *Doing Better for Families.* Available at www.oecd.org/els /familiesandchildren/doingbetterforfamilies.htm (accessed November 15, 2012).

———. 2011b. "Health at a Glance 2011: OECD Indicators." Health Status Figure 1.1.1. Available at www.oecd.org/els/healthpoliciesanddata/healthataglance2011 .htm#B5 (accessed July 30, 2012).

———. 2011c. "An Overview of Growing Income Inequalities in OECD Countries: Main Findings." In *Divided We Stand: Why Inequality Keeps Rising.* Available at www.oecd.org/els/socialpoliciesanddata/49499779.pdf (accessed February 7, 2013).

———. 2012. *OECD Family Database.* Available at www.oecd.org/social/family /database (accessed January 28, 2013).

———. 2013a. "Breakdown of Gross Domestic Product Per Capita in Its Components." OECD StatExtracts, Productivity Levels and GDP Per Capita Data (Find by Theme). Available at stats.oecd.org (accessed February 7, 2013).

———. 2013b. "Income Distribution—Inequality." OECD StatExtracts, Social and Welfare Statistics, Social Protection Measures (Find by Theme). Available at stats.oecd.org (accessed February 7, 2013).

———. 2013c. "OECD Health Data 2013—Frequently Requested Data—Health Status (Mortality), Life Expectancy, Total Population at Birth." OECD Health Policies and Data. Available at http://stats.oecd.org/Index. aspx?DataSetCode = HEALTH_STAT (accessed July 12, 2013).

———. 2013d. "Stock of Foreign-Born Population by Country of Origin." OECD StatExtracts, International Migration Database. Available at stats.oecd.org (accessed March 13, 2013).

O'Hare, William P. 1996. "A New Look at Poverty in America." *Population Bulletin* 51 (2): 1–48.

Olshansky, S. Jay, Toni Antonucci, Lisa Berkman, Robert H. Binstock, Axel Boersch-Supan, John T. Cacioppo, Bruce A. Carnes, Laura L. Carstensen, Linda P. Fried, Dana P. Goldman, James Jackson, Martin Kohli, John Rother, Yuhui Zheng, and John Rowe. 2012. "Differences in Life Expectancy Due to Race and Educational Differences Are Widening, and Many May Not Catch Up." *Health Affairs* 31 (8): 1803–13.

Omi, Michael, and Howard Winant. 2009. "Racial Formations." In *The Social Construction of Difference and Inequality: Race, Class, Gender, and Sexuality,* 4th ed., edited by Tracy E. Ore. Boston: McGraw-Hill.

Osterman, Paul. 1999. *Securing Prosperity.* Princeton, NJ: Princeton University Press.

Osypuk, Theresa L., Ana V. Diez Roux, Craig Hadley, and Namratha R. Kandula. 2009. "Are Immigrant Enclaves Healthy Places to Live? The

Multi-ethnic Study of Atherosclerosis." *Social Science & Medicine* 69 (1): 110–20.

Pager, Devah. 2008. "The Dynamics of Discrimination." In *The Colors of Poverty: Why Racial and Ethnic Disparities Persist,* edited by Ann Chih Lin and David R. Harris, 21–51. New York: Russell Sage Foundation.

————. 2009. "Discrimination in a Low-Wage Labor Market: A Field Experiment." *American Sociological Review* 74 (5): 777–99.

Palloni, Alberto, and Elizabeth Arias. 2004. "Paradox Lost: Explaining the Hispanic Adult Mortality Advantage." *Demography* 41 (3): 385–415.

Pampel, Fred. 2005. "Forecasting Sex Differences in Mortality in High Income Nations: The Contribution of Smoking." *Demographic Research* 13 (18): 455–84.

Park, Julie, and Dowell Myers. 2010. "Intergenerational Mobility in the Post-1965 Immigration Era: Estimates by an Immigrant Generation Cohort Method." *Demography* 47 (2): 369–92.

Parrado, Emilio A. 2011. "How High Is Hispanic/Mexican Fertility in the United States? Immigration and Tempo Considerations." *Demography* 48: 1059–80.

Parrado, Emilio A., and Chenoa A. Flippen. 2012. "Hispanic Fertility, Immigration, and Race in the Twenty-First Century." *Race and Social Problems* 4 (1): 18–30.

Passel, Jeffrey S. 2005. *Unauthorized Migrants: Numbers and Characteristics.* Pew Hispanic Center Research Report, June 14. Available at pewhispanic. org/files/reports/46.pdf (accessed March 13, 2013).

Passel, Jeffrey, and d'Vera Cohn. 2012. *Unauthorized Immigrants: 11.1 Million in 2011.* Pew Research Hispanic Trends Project Brief. Available at www .pewhispanic.org/2012/12/06/unauthorized-immigrants-11-1-million-in-2011/ (accessed August 19, 2013).

Patacchini, Eleonora, Yves Zenou, J. Vernon Henderson, and Dennis Epple. 2009. "Urban Sprawl in Europe." *Brookings-Wharton Papers in Urban Affairs* 1: 125–49.

Peach, Ceri. 2009. "Slipper Segregation: Discovering or Manufacturing Ghettos?" *Journal of Ethnic and Migration Studies* 35 (9): 1381–95.

Peckham, Erin, and Roberta Wyn. 2009. *Health Disparities among California's Nearly Four Million Low-Income Nonelderly Adult Women.* UCLA Center for Health Policy Research, Policy Brief, November 1.

Perlmann, Joel. 2005. *Italians Then, Mexicans Now: Immigrant Origins and Second-Generation Progress, 1980 to 2000.* New York: Russell Sage Foundation.

Pew Research Center. 2013. *The Rise of Asian Americans.* Pew Research, Social and Demographic Trends Report, June 19, 2012, updated on April 4, 2013. Available at www.pewsocialtrends.org/2012/06/19/the-rise-of-asian-americans/ (accessed August 20, 2013).

Pierson, George W. 1972. *The Moving American*. New York: Knopf.

Piketty, Thomas, and Emmanuel Saez. 2003. "Income Inequality in the United States, 1913–1998." *Quarterly Journal of Economics* 118 (1): 1–39.

———. 2013. "Income Inequality in the United States, 1913–2011." Updated tables and figures. Available at elsa.berkeley.edu/~saez/ (accessed February 7, 2013).

Polachek, Solomon W., and W. Stanley Siebert. 1994. "Gender in the Labour Market." In *Social Stratification in Sociological Perspective*, edited by David B. Grusky. Boulder, CO: Westview Press.

Popkin, Barry M. 2004. "The Global Shift towards Obesity." *Diabetes Voice* 49 (3): 38–40.

Popkin, Barry M., Linda S. Adair, and Shu Wen Ng. 2012. "Global Nutrition Transition and the Pandemic of Obesity in Developing Countries." *Nutrition Reviews* 70 (1): 3–21.

Population Reference Bureau. 2012. *2012 World Population Data Sheet*. Washington, DC: PRB.

———. 2013. *The Health and Life Expectancy of Older Blacks and Hispanics in the United States*. Today's Research on Aging Report 28, June.

Portes, Alejandro, and Ruben G. Rumbaut. 2006. *Immigrant America: A Portrait*. 3rd ed. Berkeley: University of California Press.

Portes, Alejandro, and Erik Vickstrom. 2011. "Diversity, Social Capital, and Cohesion." *Annual Review of Sociology* 37: 461–79.

Portes, Alejandro, and Min Zhou. 1993. "The New Second Generation: Segmented Assimilation and Its Variants among Post-1965 Immigrant Youth." *Annals of the American Academy of Political and Social Science* 530 (November): 74–96.

Preston, Samuel H., and Haidong Wang. 2006. "Sex Mortality Differences in the United States: The Role of Cohort Smoking Patterns." *Demography* 43 (4): 631–46.

Putnam, Robert D. 2007. "*E Pluribus Unum:* Diversity and Community in the Twenty-First Century: The 2006 Johan Skytte Prize Lecture." *Scandinavian Political Studies* 30 (2): 137–74.

Qian, Zhenchao, and Daniel Lichter. 2007. "Social Boundaries and Marital Assimilation: Interpreting Trends in Racial and Ethnic Intermarriage." *American Sociological Review* 72: 68–94.

Quadagno, Jill. 1994. *The Color of Welfare: How Racism Undermined the War on Poverty*. New York: Oxford University Press.

Rainwater, Lee, and Timothy M. Smeeding. 2003. *Poor Kids in a Rich Country: America's Children in Comparative Perspective*. New York: Russell Sage Foundation.

Rajan, Raghuram G. 2010. *Fault Lines: How Hidden Fractures Still Threaten the World Economy*. Princeton, NJ: Princeton University Press.

Rampell, Catherine. 2012. "Majority of New Jobs Pay Low Wages, Study Finds." *New York Times*, August 30. Available at www.nytimes.com/2012/08/31 /business/majority-of-new-jobs-pay-low-wages-study-finds.html?hp (accessed February 12, 2013).

Raymo, J., M. Iwasawa, and L. Bumpass. 2008. *Cohabitation and Family Formation in Japan*. Osaka University, Graduate School of Economics, GCOE Discussion Paper no. 3.

Reardon, Sean F. 2011. "The Widening Achievement Gap between the Rich and the Poor: New Evidence and Possible Explanations." In *Whither Opportunity? Rising Inequality, Schools, and Children's Life Chances*, edited by Greg J. Duncan and Richard Murnane. New York: Russell Sage Foundation.

Reardon, Sean F., and Kendra Bischoff. 2011. *Growth in the Residential Segregation of Families by Income, 1970–2009*. Census Brief prepared for the Projection US2010. Available at www.s4.brown.edu/us2010/ (accessed June 3, 2013).

Rector, Robert. 1993. "Welfare Reform, Dependency Reduction, and Labor Market Entry." *Journal of Labor Research* 14 (3) (Summer): 283–97.

Reitz, Jeffrey G., Heather Zhang, and Naoko Hawkins. 2011. "Comparisons of the Success of Racial Minority Immigrant Offspring in the United States, Canada, and Australia." *Social Science Research* 40: 1051–66.

Ren, Ping. 2011. *Lifetime Mobility in the United States: 2010*. U.S. Census Bureau, American Community Survey Briefs, ACSBR/10–07, November.

Reskin, Barbara F., and Michelle L. Maroto. 2011. "What Trends? Whose Choices? Comment on England." *Gender & Society* 25 (1): 81–87.

Reskin, Barbara F., and Patricia A. Roos. 1990. *Job Queues, Gender Queues: Explaining Women's Inroads into Male Occupations*. Philadelphia: Temple University Press.

Richardson, Harry W., and Chang-Hee Christine Bae. 2004. *Urban Sprawl in Western Europe and the United States*. Aldershot, UK: Ashgate.

Richtel, Matt. 2005. "Outsourced All the Way." *New York Times*, June 21. Available at www.nytimes.com/2005/06/21/business/worldbusiness/21outsource .html?pagewanted = all (accessed February 11, 2013).

Riis, Jacob A. 1997. *How the Other Half Lives*. New York: Penguin Books. First published in 1890.

Riosmena, Fernando, Reanne Frank, Illana Redstone Akresh, and Rhiannon A. Kroeger. 2012. "U.S. Migration, Translocality, and the Acceleration of the Nutrition Transition in Mexico." *Annals of the Association of American Geographers* 102 (5): 1209–18.

Riosmena, Fernando, Rebeca Wong, and Alberto Palloni. 2013. "Migration Selection, Protection, and Acculturation in Health: A Binational Perspective on Older Adults." *Demography* 50 (3): 1039–64.

Rodriguez, Clara. 1989. *Puerto Ricans: Born in the U.S.A.* Boston: Unwin and Hyman.

Rosenblatt, Peter, and Stefanie DeLuca. 2012. "'We Don't Live Outside, We Live in Here': Neighborhood and Residential Mobility Decisions among Low-Income Families." *City and Community* 11 (3): 254–84.

Rosin, Hanna. 2012a. *The End of Men: And the Rise of Women.* New York: Riverhead Books.

———. 2012b. "I Ain't Sayin' He's a Gold Digger." *Slate* online, September 11. Available at www.slate.com/articles/double_x/doublex/2012/09/breadwinner_wives_when_the_women_make_more_money_who_holds_the_power_.single.html (accessed January 11, 2013).

Ross, Stephen L., and Margery Austin Turner. 2005. "Housing Discrimination in Metropolitan America: Explaining Changes between 1989 and 2000." *Social Problems* 52 (2): 152–80.

Roth, Louise Marie. 2006. *Selling Women Short: Gender Inequality on Wall Street.* Princeton, NJ: Princeton University Press.

Ruggles, Steven. 1997. "The Rise of Divorce and Separation in the United States, 1880–1990." *Demography* 34 (4): 455–66.

Rugh, Jacob S., and Douglas S. Massey. 2010. "Racial Segregation and the American Foreclosure Crisis." *American Sociological Review* 75: 629–51.

Ryan, Camille. 2012. *Field of Degree and Earnings by Selected Employment Characteristics: 2011.* U.S. Census Bureau American Community Survey Reports, ASCBR-11-10, October. Available at www.census.gov/prod/2012pubs/acsbr11-10.pdf (accessed January 21, 2013).

Sakamoto, Arthur, Huei-Hsia Wu, and Jessie M. Tzeng. 2000. "The Declining Significance of Race among American Men during the Latter Half of the Twentieth Century." *Demography* 37 (1): 41–51.

Salkever, Alex, and Vivek Wadhwa. 2012. "Why Entrepreneurship Needs Immigrants." *Inc.com*, October 15. Available at www.inc.com/alex-salkever/why-entrepreneurship-needs-immigrants.html (accessed March 12, 2013).

Sampson, Robert J. 2008. "Rethinking Crime and Immigration." *Contexts* 7 (1): 28–33.

Sanchez, Luis, John Iceland, Gregory Sharp, Matthew Hall, and Kris Marsh. 2010. *Racial and Ethnic Residential Segregation in the United States: Residential Patterns of Latinos/Hispanics, 1980–2009.* Changing American Neighborhoods and Communities Report Series, Population Research Institute, Penn State University, Report no. 5. Available at http://projects.pop.psu.edu/canc/segregation (accessed June 10, 2013).

Sandefur, Gary, and W.J. Scott. 1983. "Minority Group Status and the Wages of Indian and Black Males." *Social Science Research* 12: 44–68.

San Juan, E. 1995. *On Becoming Filipino: Selected Writings of Carlos Bulosan.* Philadelphia: Temple University Press.

Saulny, Susan. 2011. "Census Data Presents Rise in Multiracial Population of Youths." *New York Times,* March 24.

Schoen, C., R. Osborn, D. Squires, M. Doty, R. Pierson, and S. Applebaum. 2011. "New 2011 Survey of Patients with Complex Care Needs in Eleven Countries Finds That Care Is Often Poorly Coordinated." *Health Affairs* 30 (12): 2437–48.

Schoen, John W. 2012. "Great Recession Still Slamming the Middle Class." NBC News Economy Watch, September 13. Available at www.nbcnews.com/business /economywatch/great-recession-still-slamming-middle-class-994834 (accessed February 12, 2013).

Schoeni, Robert, Vicki Freedman, and Linda Martin. 2009. "Socioeconomic and Demographic Disparities in Trends in Old-Age Disability." In *Health at Older Ages: The Causes and Consequences of Declining Disability among the Elderly,* edited by David M. Cutler and David A. Wise. Chicago: University of Chicago Press.

Scholz, John Karl, Robert Moffitt, and Benjamin Cowan. 2009. "Trends in Income Support." In *Changing Poverty, Changing Policies,* edited by Maria Cancian and Sheldon Danziger. New York: Russell Sage Foundation.

Schuman, Howard, Charlotte Steeh, Lawrence Bobo, and Maria Krysan. 2001. *Racial Attitudes in America: Trends and Interpretations.* Rev. ed. Cambridge, MA: Harvard University Press.

Sharp, Gregory, John Iceland, Luis Sanchez, Matthew Hall, and Kris Marsh. 2010. *Racial and Ethnic Residential Segregation in the United States: Residential Patterns of Whites, 1970–2009.* Changing American Neighborhoods and Communities Report Series, Population Research Institute, Penn State University, Report no. 7. Available at http://projects.pop.psu.edu/canc /segregation (accessed June 10, 2013).

Sherman, Arloc. 2011. *Poverty and Financial Distress Would Have Been Substantially Worse in 2010 without Government Action, New Census Data Show.* Center on Budget and Policy Priorities Research Report, November 7.

Shoemaker, Nancy. 1999. *American Indian Population Recovery in the Twentieth Century.* Albuquerque: University of New Mexico Press.

Siebens, Julie, and Camille L. Ryan. 2012. *Field of Bachelor's Degree in the United States: 2009.* U.S. Census Bureau American Community Survey Reports, ASC-18, February. Available at www.census.gov/prod/2012pubs /acs-18.pdf (accessed January 18, 2013).

Simon, Patrick. 2012. *French National Identity and Integration: Who Belongs to the National Community?* Migration Policy Institute Report, May. Available at www.migrationpolicy.org/pubs/frenchidentity.pdf (accessed March 13, 2013).

Singer, Audrey. 2004. *The Rise of New Immigrant Gateways.* Living Cities Census Series. Washington, DC: Brookings Institution.

Singer, Audrey, Domenic Vitiello, Michael Katz, and David Park. 2008. *Recent Immigration to Philadelphia: Regional Change in a Re-emerging Gateway.* Brookings Institution Metropolitan Policy Program Report, November.

Singh, Gopal K., and Barry A. Miller. 2004. "Health, Life Expectancy, and Mortality Patterns among Immigrant Populations in the United States." *Canadian Journal of Public Health* 95 (3): 14–21.

Smeeding, Timothy M. 2008. "U.S. Income Inequality in a Cross-National Perspective: Why Are We So Different?" In *The Inequality Paradox: Growth of Income Disparity,* edited by James A. Auerbach and Rich S. Belous. Washington, DC: National Policy Association.

Smith, Adam. 2009. *An Inquiry into the Nature and Causes of the Wealth of Nations.* Reprint. Digireads.com Publishing. First published in 1776.

Smith, James P., and Barry Edmonston, eds. 1997. *The New Americans: Economic, Demographic, and Fiscal Effects of Immigration.* National Academy of Sciences, Committee on Population and Committee on National Statistics. Washington, DC: National Academy Press.

Smock, Pamela, and Fiona Rose Greenland. 2010. "Diversity in Pathways to Parenthood: Patterns, Implications, and Emerging Research Directions." *Journal of Marriage and Family* 72 (3): 576–93.

Stangler, Cole. 2012. "Obama Jobs Council Packed with Outsourcing Companies." *Huffington Post,* July 12. Available at www.huffingtonpost. com/2012/07/12/obama-jobs-council-outsourcing_n_1666443.html (accessed February 11, 2013).

Stevenson, Betsey, and Justin Wolfers. 2011. "Trends in Marital Stability." In *Research Handbook on the Economics of Family Law,* edited by Lloyd R. Cohen and Joshua D. Wright. Cheltenham, UK: Edward Elgar.

Stiglitz, Joseph E. 2012. *The Price of Inequality: How Today's Divided Society Endangers Our Future.* New York: W. W. Norton.

———. 2013. "Inequality Is Holding Back the Recovery." *New York Times,* January 19. Available at http://opinionator.blogs.nytimes.com/2013/01 /19/inequality-is-holding-back-the-recovery/ (accessed February 12, 2013).

Stone, Chad, Danilo Trisi, and Arloc Sherman. 2012. *A Guide to Statistics on Historical Trends in Income Inequality.* Center on Budget and Policy Priorities Research Report, October 23. Available at www.cbpp.org/files /11–28–11pov.pdf (accessed February 6, 2013).

Stone, Pamela. 2007. *Opting Out? Why Women Really Quit Careers and Head Home.* Berkeley: University of California Press.

Stowell, Jacob I., Steven F. Messner, Kelly F. McGeever, and Lawrence E. Raffalovich. 2009. "Immigration and the Recent Violent Crime Drop in the United States: A Pooled, Cross-Sectional Time-Series Analysis of Metropolitan Areas." *Criminology* 47 (3): 889–928.

Sugrue, Thomas J. 1993. "The Structure of Urban Poverty: The Reorganization of Space and Work in Three Periods of American History." In *The "Underclass" Debate: Views from History,* edited by Michael B. Katz. Princeton, NJ: Princeton University Press.

Sullivan, Kevin. 2012. "Other Countries Court Skilled Immigrants Frustrated by U.S. Visa Laws." *Washington Post,* February 18. Available at http://wapo .st/12ZVrZF (accessed March 14, 2013).

Taeuber, Karl E., and Alma F. Taeuber. 1965. *Negroes in Cities: Residential Segregation and Neighborhood Change.* Chicago: Aldine.

Takei, Isao, and Arthur Sakamoto. 2011. "Poverty among Asian Americans in the 21st Century." *Sociological Perspectives* 54 (2): 251–76.

Tavernise, Sabrina. 2013. "Health Toll of Immigration." *New York Times,* May 18.

Telles, Edward E., and Vilma Ortiz. 2008. *Generations of Exclusion: Mexican Americans, Assimilation, and Race.* New York: Russell Sage Foundation.

Thornton, Arland. 1989. "Changing Attitudes toward Family Issues in the United States." *Journal of Marriage and the Family* 51: 873–93.

Thorslund, Mats, Jonas W. Wastesson, Neda Agahi, Marten Lagergren, and Marti G. Parker. 2013. "The Rise and Fall of Women's Advantage: A Comparison of National Trends in Life Expectancy at Age 65 Years." *European Journal of Ageing* DOI 10.1007/s10433-013-0274-8.

Tolnay, Stewart E. 2003. "The African American 'Great Migration' and Beyond." *Annual Review of Sociology* 29: 209–32.

Turner, Margery, Michael Fix, and Raymond Struyk. 1991. *Opportunities Denied, Opportunities Diminished: Discrimination in Hiring.* Washington, DC: Urban Institute Press.

Turner, Margery Austin, Rob Santos, Diane K. Levy, Doug Wissoker, Claudia Aranda, and Rob Pitingolo. 2013. *Housing Discrimination against Racial and Ethnic Minorities 2012.* U.S. Department of Housing and Urban Development, Office of Policy Development and Research Report, June.

Turra, Cassio, and Irma Elo. 2008. "The Impact of Salmon Bias on the Hispanic Mortality Advantage: New Evidence from Social Security Data." *Population Research and Policy Review* 27 (5): 515–30.

United Nations. 2011. "World Urbanization Prospects, 2011 Revision." Population Division, Population Estimates and Projections Section online data. Available at esa.un.org/unup/Wallcharts/wall-chart.htm (accessed October 5, 2012).

———. 2012. "Table 2a. Life Expectancy." UN Social Indicators Data. Available at http://unstats.un.org/unsd/demographic/products/socind/ (accessed July 12, 2013).

U.S. Bureau of Labor Statistics. 2010a. "Labor Force Participation Rates among Mothers." TED: The Editor's Desk Internet release data. Available at www .bls.gov/opub/ted/2010/ted_20100507.htm (accessed July 30, 2012).

———. 2010b. "Sizing Up the 2007–09 Recession: Comparing Two Key Labor Market Indicators with Earlier Downturns." *Issues in Labor Statistics,* Summary 10–11 (December): 1–6.

———. 2011a. *Highlights of Women's Earnings.* U.S. BLS Report no. 1031, July.

———. 2011b. "Women at Work." BLS Spotlight on Statistics, March. Available at www.bls.gov/spotlight/2011/women/ (accessed January 24, 2013).

———. 2011c. *Women in the Labor Force: A Databook.* 2011 ed. U.S. BLS Report no. 1034, December. Available at www.bls.gov/cps/wlf-databook-2011.pdf (accessed January 23, 2013).

———. 2012a. "Labor Force Statistics from the Current Population Survey." Series Id LNS 14000000, accessed at http://data.bls.gov, retrieved February 28, 2012.

———. 2012b. "Wives Who Earn More Than Their Husbands, 1987–2011." Labor Force Statistics from the Current Population Survey. Available at www.bls .gov/cps/wives_earn_more.htm (accessed January 25, 2013).

———. 2012c. "Women as a Percent of Total Employed in Selected Occupations." TED: The Editor's Desk Internet release data. Available at www.bls.gov /opub/ted/2012/ted_20120501.htm (accessed January 23, 2013).

U.S. Census Bureau. 1993. "Table 4. Population: 1790 to 1990." Census 1990 Population and Housing Unit Counts, United States Summary. Available at www.census.gov/population/censusdata/table-4.pdf (accessed September 24, 2012).

———. 1998. *Population of the 100 Largest Cities and Other Urban Places in the United States: 1790 to 1990.* Population Division Working Paper no. 27. Available at www.census.gov/population/www/documentation/twps0027 /twps0027.html (accessed June 3, 2013).

———. 2009. "National Population Projections." U.S. Population Projections Program, Summary Tables.

———. 2010a. "Educational Attainment in the United States: 2010—Detailed Tables." Educational Attainment Current Population Survey Tables, table 2. Available at www.census.gov/hhes/socdemo/education/data/cps/2010/tables .html (accessed July 31, 2012).

———. 2010b. "A Half-Century of Learning: Historical Census Statistics on Educational Attainment in the United States, 1940 to 2000." Educational Attainment Research Report. Available at www.census.gov/hhes/socdemo /education/data/census/index.html (accessed July 31, 2012).

———. 2010c. "Selected Population Profile in the United States: 2010 American Survey 1-Year Estimates." Table S0201 for American Indian and Alaska Native Alone. Available at FactFinder2.census.gov (accessed March 5, 2014).

———. 2010d. "Urban, Urbanized Area, Urban Cluster, and Rural Population, 2010 and 2000: United States" from the 2010 Census Urban and Rural Classification and Urban Area Criteria webpage. Available at www.census

.gov/geo/www/ua/2010urbanruralclass.html#percent (accessed September 24, 2012).

———. 2011a. *American Housing Survey for the United States: 2009*. Current Housing Reports, Series H150/09. Washington, DC: U.S. Government Printing Office.

———. 2011b. "Centers of Population for the 2010 Census." Geography Division, March 2011. Available at www.census.gov/geo/www/2010census/center-pop2010/centerpop2010.html (accessed September 24, 2012).

———. 2011c. "Table DP02. Selected Social Characteristics in the United States: 2010 American Community Survey 1-Year Estimates." Available at FactFinder2.census.gov (accessed February 14, 2012).

———. 2011d. "Table F-5. Race and Hispanic Origin of Householder—Families by Median and Mean Income: 1947 to 2010." Current Population Survey Historical Tables. Available at www.census.gov/hhes/www/income/data/historical/families/ (accessed July 31, 2012).

———. 2011e. "Table FM-2. All Parent/Child Situations, by Type, Race, and Hispanic Origin of Householder or Reference Person: 1970 to Present." Current Population Survey Data, 2011. Available at www.census.gov/population/socdemo/hh-fam/fm2.xls (accessed February 17, 2012).

———. 2011f. "Table H-4. Gini Ratios for Households, by Race and Hispanic Origin of Householder: 1967 to 2010." Current Population Survey, Annual Social and Economic Supplements, Historical Income Inequality Tables. Available at www.census.gov/hhes/www/income/data/historical/inequality/ (accessed February 6, 2012).

———. 2011g. "Table MS-2. Estimated Median Age at First Marriage, by Sex: 1890 to the Present." Current Population Survey, Annual Social and Economic Supplement, Marital Status Historical Time Series Tables. Available at www.census.gov/hhes/families/data/marital.html (accessed March 6, 2014).

———. 2011h. "Table P-40. Women's Earning as a Percentage of Men's Earning by Race and Hispanic Origin: 1960 to 2010." Historical Income People Tables. Internet-released data. Available at www.census.gov/hhes/www/income/data/historical/people/2010/P40_2010.xls (accessed July 30, 2012).

———. 2011i. "Table 2. Poverty Status of People by Family Relationship, Race, and Hispanic Origin: 1959 to 2010." Historical Poverty People Tables. Internet-released data. Available at www.census.gov/hhes/www/poverty/data/historical/hstpov2.xls (accessed July 30, 2012).

———. 2012a. "Gaining and Losing Shares: Population Distribution by Region, 1790 to 2010." U.S. Census Bureau Data Visualization Figures, July 19. Available at www.census.gov/dataviz/visualizations/006/508.php (accessed June 4, 2013).

———. 2012b. "Gini Ratios of Families by Race and Hispanic Origin of Householder." Family Historical Income Tables, Table F-4. Available at www

.census.gov/hhes/www/income/data/historical/families/ (accessed February 6, 2013).

———. 2012c. "Income Limits for Each Fifth and Top 5 Percent of Families." Family Historical Income Tables, Table F-1. Available at www.census.gov /hhes/www/income/data/historical/families/ (accessed February 6, 2013).

———. 2012d. "Largest Urbanized Areas with Selected Cities and Metro Areas." Measuring America—People, Places, and Our Economy series, November 15. Available at www.census.gov/dataviz/visualizations/026/508.php (accessed June 3, 2013).

———. 2012e. *Statistical Abstract of the United States: 2012.* Washington, DC: U.S. Government Printing Office.

———. 2012f. "Table A-2. Percent of People 25 Years and Over Who Have Completed High School or College, by Race, Hispanic Origin and Sex: Selected Yeas 1940 to 2011." Educational Attainment data, CPS Historical Time Series Tables. Available at www.census.gov/hhes/socdemo/education /data/cps/historical/index.html (accessed January 18, 2013).

———. 2012g. "Table 2. Poverty Status of People by Family Relationship, Race, and Hispanic Origin: 1959 to 2011." Historical Poverty Tables, People. Available at www.census.gov/hhes/www/poverty/data/historical/people .html (accessed May 9, 2013).

———. 2012h. "Table 4. Poverty Status of Families, by Type of Family, Presence of Related Children, Race and Hispanic Origin: 1959 to 2011." Family Historical Poverty Tables. Available at www.census.gov/hhes/www/poverty /data/historical/families.html (accessed September 12, 2012).

———. 2012i. "Table 4. Projections of the Population by Sex, Race, and Hispanic Origin for the United States: 2015 to 2060." Population Division release NP2012-T4. Available at www.census.gov/population/projections/data /national/2012/summarytables.html (accessed February 15, 2013).

———. 2012j. "Table 8. Poverty of People by Residence: 1959 to 2011." People Historical Poverty Tables. Available at www.census.gov/hhes/www/poverty /data/historical/people.html (accessed June 7, 2013).

———. 2012k. "Table H-5. Race and Hispanic Origin of Household—Households by Median and Mean Income." Historical Income Household Tables. Available at www.census.gov/hhes/www/income/data/historical/household / (accessed February 1, 2013).

———. 2012l. "Table HH-1. Households, by Type: 1940 to Present." Families and Living Arrangements Historical Time Series. Available at www.census.gov /hhes/families/data/households.html (accessed July 1, 2013).

———. 2012m. "Women's Earning as a Percentage of Men's Earning by Race and Hispanic Origin: 1960–2010." Historical Income People Tables, Table P-40. Internet-released data. Available at www.census.gov/hhes/www/income /data/historical/people/2010/P40_2010.xls (accessed July 30, 2012).

———. 2013a. "CPH-T-5. Population Change for Metropolitan and Micropolitan Statistical Areas in the United States and Puerto Rico (February 2013 Delineations): 2000 to 2010." Census Population and Housing Tables (CPH-Ts). Available at www.census.gov/population/www/cen2010/cph-t /cph-t-5.html (accessed June 5, 2013).

———. 2013b. "Net Migration between California and Other States: 1955–1960 and 1995–2000." U.S. Census Bureau Data Visualization Figures, March 7. Available at http://www.census.gov/dataviz/visualizations/051/ (accessed June 5, 2013).

———. 2013c. "State and County QuickFacts: Austin (city), Texas." Data derived from Population Estimates, American Community Survey, Census of Population and Housing. Available at http://quickfacts.census.gov/qfd /states/48/4805000.html (accessed June 3, 2013).

———. 2013d. "Table A-2. Percent of People 25 Years and Over Who Have Completed High School or College, by Race, Hispanic Origin and Sex: Selected Yeas 1940 to 2012." Educational Attainment data, CPS Historical Time Series Tables. Available at www.census.gov/hhes/socdemo/education /data/cps/historical/index.html (accessed April 8, 2013).

U.S. Department of Homeland Security. 2012. "Table 2. Yearbook of Immigration Statistics: 2011." Data on Legal Permanent Residents. Available at www .dhs.gov/yearbook-immigration-statistics-2011-1 (accessed September 18, 2012).

U.S. Immigration and Naturalization Service. 2002. *Statistical Yearbook of the Immigration and Naturalization Service, 2000*. Washington, DC: U.S. Government Printing Office.

Valian, Virginia. 1999. *Why So Slow? The Advancement of Women*. Cambridge, MA: MIT Press.

Van Kempen, Ronald, and Alan Murie. 2009. "The New Divided City: Changing Patterns in European Cities." *Tijdschrift voor Economische en Sociale Geografie* 100 (4): 377–98.

Ventura, S.J., and C.A. Bachrach. 2000. "Nonmarital Childbearing in the United States, 1940–99." *National Vital Statistics Reports* 48 (16). Hyattsville, MD: National Center for Health Statistics.

Wadsworth, Tim. 2010. "Is Immigration Responsible for the Crime Drop? An Assessment of the Influence of Immigration on Changes in Violent Crime between 1990 and 2000." *Social Science Quarterly* 91 (2): 531–53.

Wakefield, Sara, and Christopher Uggen. 2010. "Incarceration and Stratification." *Annual Review of Sociology* 36: 387–406.

Wang, Wendy. 2012. *The Rise of Intermarriage: Rates, Characteristics Vary by Race and Gender*. Pew Research Center Social and Demographic Trends Research Report, February 16. Available at www.pewsocialtrends.org /files/2012/02/SDT-Intermarriage-II.pdf (accessed May 20, 2013).

Washington, Booker T. 1902. *The Future of the American Negro.* New York: Metro Books, 1969.

Waters, Mary C. 2009. "Optional Ethnicities: For Whites Only?" In *The Social Construction of Difference and Inequality: Race, Class, Gender, and Sexuality,* 4th ed., ed. Tracy E. Ore. Boston: McGraw-Hill.

Weber, Max. 1994. "Open and Closed Relationships." In *Social Stratification in Sociological Perspective,* edited by David B. Grusky. Boulder, CO: Westview Press.

Wenger, Michael R. 2013. "White Privilege." *Poverty & Race Research Action Council* 22 (4): 1–7.

Werner, Carrie A. 2011. "The Older Population: 2010." U.S. Census Bureau, 2010 Census Briefs, C2010BR-09, November.

Western, Bruce, and Christopher Wildeman. 2009. "The Black Family and Mass Incarceration." *Annals of the American Academy of Political and Social Science* 621 (1): 221–42

Westoff, Charles F. 1986. "Fertility in the United States." *Science* 234 (4776): 554–59.

White, Michael J., and Jennifer E. Glick. 2009. *Achieving Anew: How New Immigrants Do in American Schools, Jobs, and Neighborhoods.* New York: Russell Sage Foundation.

Wikipedia. 2012a. "John Snow." Wikipedia entry. Available at wikipedia.org (accessed September 1, 2012).

———. 2012b. "List of Tallest Buildings in the World." Wikipedia entry. Available at wikipedia.org (accessed October 5, 2012).

———. 2012c. "1918 Flu Pandemic." Wikipedia entry. Available at wikipedia.org (accessed September 1, 2012).

———. 2012d. "One World Trade Center." Wikipedia entry. Available at wikipedia.org (accessed October 5, 2012).

———. 2012e. "Skyscraper." Wikipedia entry. Available at wikipedia.org (accessed October 5, 2012).

Wildsmith, Elizabeth, Nicole R. Steward-Streng, and Jennifer Manlove. 2011. *Childbearing Outside of Marriage: Estimates and Trends in the United States.* Child Trends Research Brief, 2011–29, November.

Williams, Alex. 2012. "Just Wait until Your Mother Gets Home." *New York Times,* August 10.

Williams, Christine L. 1995. *Still a Man's World : Men Who Do "Women's Work."* Berkeley: University of California Press.

Williams, David R., and Selina A. Mohammed. 2008. "Poverty, Migration, and Health." In *The Color of Poverty: Why Racial and Ethnic Disparities Persist,* ed. Ann Chih Lin and David R. Harris. New York: Russell Sage Foundation.

Williams, David R., Selina A. Mohammed, Jacinta Leavell, and Chiquita Collins. 2010. "Race, Socioeconomic Status and Health: Complexities, Ongoing Challenges and Research Opportunities." *Annals of the New York Academy of Sciences* 1186: 69–101.

Williams, David R., and Michelle Sternthal. 2010. "Understanding Racial/ Ethnic Disparities in Health: Sociological Contributions." *Journal of Health and Social Behavior* 51: S15–S27.

Williams, Joan C. 2000. *Unbending Gender: Why Family and Work Conflict and What to Do about It.* New York: Oxford University Press.

———. 2013. "The Daddy Dilemma: Why Men Face a 'Flexibility Stigma' at Work." *Washington Post,* February 11. Available at www.washingtonpost. com/national/on-leadership/the-daddy-dilemma-why-men-face-a-flexibility-stigma-at-work/2013/02/11/58350f4e-7462-11e2-aa12-e6cf1d31106b_story. html?hpid = z6 (accessed February 11, 2013).

Williams, Joan C., and Nancy Segal. 2003. "Beyond the Maternal Wall: Relief for Family Caregivers Who Are Discriminated against on the Job." *Harvard Women's Law Journal* 26: 77–162.

Wilson, Jacque. 2013. "Your Thoughts: Americans Dying Earlier Than Their Peers." CNN iReport, January 14. Available at www.cnn.com/2013/01/14 /health/american-disadvantage-comments (accessed June 28, 2013).

Wilson, Jill H., and Audrey Singer. 2011. *Immigrants in 2010 Metropolitan America: A Decade of Change.* Brookings Institution, State of Metropolitan America Report, October.

Wilson, William Julius. 1978. *The Declining Significance of Race: Blacks and Changing American Institutions.* Chicago: University of Chicago Press.

———. 1987. *The Truly Disadvantaged: The Inner City, the Underclass, and Public Policy.* Chicago: University of Chicago Press.

———. 1996. *When Work Disappears: The World of the New Urban Poor.* New York: Alfred A. Knopf.

Wolff, Edward N. 2010. "Recent Trends in Household Wealth in the United States: Rising Debt and the Middle-Class Squeeze—and Update to 2007." Levy Economics Institute of Bard College, March. Available at www. levyinstitute.org/pubs/wp_589.pdf (accessed November 4, 2013).

———. 2013. "The Asset Price Melt-Down and the Wealth of the Middle Class." Census Brief prepared for the Projection US2010. Available at http://www .s4.brown.edu/us2010/Data/Report/report05012013.pdf (accessed May 8, 2013).

Wolff, Edward N., Lindsay A. Owens, and Esra Burak. 2011. "How Much Wealth Was Destroyed in the Great Recession?" In *The Great Recession,* edited by David B. Grusky, Bruce Western, and Christopher Wimer. New York: Russell Sage Foundation.

Wood, Gordon. 2011. *The Idea of America: Reflections on the Birth of the United States.* New York: Penguin Press.

Woodhouse, Leighton. 2012. "American Voters Are Getting All Mixed Up." *Huffington Post,* The Blog, November 20.

World Bank. 2012. "Mortality Rate, Infant (per 1,000 Live Births)." World Development Indicators data. Available at databank.worldbank.org/data / (accessed June 30, 2013).

Yen, Hope. 2009. "Multiracial People Become Fastest-Growing US Group." *Huffington Post,* May 28.

Zhang, Zhenmei, Mark Hayward, and Chuntain Lu. 2012. "Is There a Hispanic Epidemiological Paradox in Later Life? A Closer Look at Chronic Morbidity." *Research on Aging* 34 (5): 548–71.

Zhou, Min. 1999. "Segmented Assimilation: Issues, Controversies, and Recent Research on the New Second Generation." In *The Handbook of International Migration: The American Experience,* edited by Charles Hirschman, Philip Kasinitz, and Josh DeWind. New York: Russell Sage Foundation.

Index

Adams, John, 138

Adams, John Quincy, 138–39

African Americans: disadvantage and, 146–51; family instability and, 57–58; incarceration rates and, 150; income inequality and, 121–22, 121*fig.*, 144, 210; internal migration and, 11–12, 147; life expectancy and, 199–200; poverty rates among, 2–3, 144; residential segregation and, 12, 122, 123, 123*fig.*, 172–74, 173*fig.*, 181–83; single-parent households and, 46, 57–58. *See also* black-white line

agglomerations, 34

aging population. *See* elderly, the

Alba, Richard, 115, 130

Ambrose, Stephen, 139

"American apartheid," 11

American Community Survey, 225n66

American Dilemma, An (Myrdal), 147

American exceptionalism, 16, 208. *See also* individualism

American Express, 93

Angeles, Esther, 195, 196

Anglophone countries: immigrant integration in, 134; poverty rates in, 58–59; racial tolerance and, 161. *See also* Australia; Canada; United Kingdom

Apple Computer, 93

Asia: family patterns in, 19, 49; immigration from, 10, 11, 27, 28, 30, 36, 107, 111–14, 112*fig.*; outsourcing to, 93. *See also* China; Japan

Asian Americans: assimilation and, 116, 118*fig.*, 119, 120, 121, 122; education and, 11, 119, 154–55; experiences of, 146, 152–54, 156; family patterns and, 45; health outcomes for, 191; income levels and, 11, 120, 121, 143, 144, 155; national origins of, 154; post-1960s immigration and, 10, 11, 28, 30, 36, 107, 111–14, 112*fig.*; as proportion of immigrants, 113; segregation and, 12, 122, 123*fig.*, 173*fig.*, 174, 175*fig. See also* Chinese immigrants; Japanese immigrants; Korean immigrants

assimilation: concept of, 114–15; definitions of, 115–18; ethnic differences in, 154–55; evidence on, 118–24; international comparisons and, 133–34, 186; trends in, 10, 141. *See also* educational attainment; immigration; income inequality; residential segregation

Associated Press, 85

Austin, Texas, 165, 167, 178, 181, 226n2

Australia, 134, 161

automobiles, 34, 86, 170, 175, 204

Text:	10/14 Miller Text
Display:	Miller Text
Compositor:	IDS Infotech Ltd.
Printer and binder:	Maple Press